NEW
Edition

The Ultimate Sourcebook for Storage Ideas and Materials

NEW Edition

Joseph R. Provey

1001 Ideas for Kitchen Organization, New Edition
Editor: Colleen Dorsey
Technical Editor: David Schiff
Designer: John Hoch

ISBN 978-1-58011-844-6

Library of Congress Control Number:2019948120

We are always looking for talented authors. To submit an idea, please send a brief inquiry to acquisitions@foxchapelpublishing.com.

Printed in Singapore

Current Printing (last digit)
10 9 8 7 6 5 4 3 2 1

Creative Homeowner®, *www.creativehomeowner.com*, is an imprint of New Design Originals Corporation and distributed exclusively in North America by Fox Chapel Publishing Company, Inc., 800-457-9112, 903 Square Street, Mount Joy, PA 17552, and in the United Kingdom by Grantham Book Service, Trent Road, Grantham, Lincolnshire, NG31 7XQ.

Acknowledgments

Thank you to the many kitchen designers, photographers, and kitchen-storage product manufacturers that made this book possible. Special thanks to Mary Jane Pappas, CID, ASID, of Pappas Inc., Minneapolis, Minnesota, for sharing her kitchen storage and organization wisdom. Thanks, also, to Kathie Robitz, the editor of *1001 Ideas for Kitchen Organization,* for her input and encouragement and for being a pleasure to work with, as always.

Contents

Introduction

When most of you think of good kitchen design, you probably think of fabulous appliances, gorgeous cabinetry, and beautiful floors and countertops. But they're not the half of it—though they will collectively claim the lion's share of your budget. Good kitchen design is about two far-less-glamorous ingredients: organization and storage.

Just consider the benefits: smart storage and organization can save you enormous amounts of time and effort every week. Whether you're making a school lunch or preparing a dinner party, having what you need where you need it will speed up the task. Imagine: no more digging around in a jam-packed drawer for a knife to cut the sandwich or sorting through a pile of clippings for a favorite recipe.

A well-ordered kitchen, in which working is a pleasure, is also one where you're more likely to spend time working. In wan era when many parents rely on fast food to feed their families, more meals at home can mean more nutritious, healthier diets—not to mention saving thousands of dollars a year on eating out.

Left Whether you're planning a complete kitchen remodeling or reorganizing the kitchen you already have, improving your storage and organization can save time, effort, and money every time you use it.

Your Storage Style

No, the issue is not whether you prefer country to contemporary. Storage styles have to do with more fundamental preferences. Do you want a kitchen where, at day's end, everything is stowed away in drawers or behind cabinet doors? Or do you find that functional items are a pleasure to look at and prefer to have everything in the open where you can admire them? Or perhaps you are somewhere in between?

Sometimes such preferences are personal. Other times there are simple reasons. If, for example, you have an open floor plan and don't want to see pots and pans while relaxing in the family room, an out-of-sight approach to storage may be your choice. On the other hand, if your hobby is cooking and you like your tools within easy reach, without having to open a door or drawer, open storage may be the answer. Julia Child famously kept her pots and pans hanging in the open on pegboard. Most homeowners prefer a bit of both, hiding some items in cabinets and putting others on open shelves, hooks, or racks. Nevertheless, think about the storage style that best suits you. The approach you choose will affect many of the design decisions that you'll have to make during the course of your kitchen remodeling or reorganization.

Top Today's open-plan kitchens feature islands that increase storage and counter space. But they rely on traditional elements, too, including cabinets, shelves, and baskets.

Bottom This kitchen, inspired by country kitchens of the past, makes good use of hooks, pegs, baskets, and narrow shelves.

Opposite Contemporary design subscribes to the belief that everyday objects should be beautiful—and visible. Glass cabinet door-and-drawer fronts, as well as backsplash rail-and-hook systems, do the trick.

Kitchen Evolution

Before the Industrial Revolution, the kitchen was a very different place. Centered on an open hearth, kitchenware was homemade or handcrafted by the town blacksmith and other local craftsmen. Families had relatively few kitchen implements. Storage was less of an issue than it is today—a few shelves could handle much of the typical kitchen's contents. Many foods were stored outside the kitchen in larders, smokehouses, and root cellars. In the early nineteenth century, however, technological advances and mass production changed things. The iron range displaced the hearth. Cooking tools became less expensive and multiplied in number. The kitchen also had greater demands placed upon it. Iceboxes displaced root cellars and brought food storage into the house. Mass-produced jars and tins allowed for new methods of food preservation—and new demands for storage in the kitchen. The advent of modern cooking fuels (gas in 1860 and electricity by the end of the century) ushered in a new era in kitchen appliances. The evolution of the kitchen continues today. The average homeowner has hundreds of items that need a home. Cabinet systems have evolved to hold this trove and to keep it manageable. In addition, manufacturers have devised hundreds of ways to store the overflow on walls and ceilings, under cabinets, and in every empty corner imaginable. Appliance manufacturers, for example, offer their wares in every size and configuration, allowing you to put only what you use most where you need it most. Split fridges and freezers, for example, allow you to put the fridge where it's handy, without gobbling up prime real estate with a less-used freezer. Many appliances can now perform multiple tricks, another space-conserving opportunity.

Left **In this book, you'll find out how to use every cubic inch of space for storage, from up near the ceiling to behind the toe kick panel—and everywhere in between.**

What This Book Will Deliver

1001 Ideas for Kitchen Organization has been created to help you design a kitchen that's right for you. Part 1, "The Essentials," covers the two things that are fundamental to optimal storage: organizational wisdom and cabinets. In Chapter 1, "Finding Efficiency," you'll learn how to make decisions about how to increase your available storage. You'll also learn how to go about deciding where to put things for maximum efficiency. Chapter 2, "Cabinets and Accessories," will explain the many choices you have when buying cabinets. It will also show you how to outfit new or existing cabinets to suit your needs.

Part 2, "Beyond the Cabinet," discusses the storage options that are "outside the box." Chapter 3, "Countertop and Under-Cabinet Storage," for example, is loaded with ideas for how to use the valuable kitchen real estate that lies between your countertop and wall cabinets. In Chapter 4, "Overhead and Vertical Spaces," you are encouraged to look around for useful storage opportunities that are often neglected. They include walls, windows, doors, ceilings, and even appliance fronts. Chapter 5,

Top left Want to get serious about organization? Find a spot for a kitchen command center for the business of everyday life. You'll discover how.

Top right Buying kitchen cabinets ranks high in remodeling expenses. See Chapter 2, "Cabinets and Accessories," for guidance on getting the most for your dollar.

"Getting Creative with Leftovers," suggests ways to use leftover nooks and crannies for useful storage just when you thought you'd run out of space. The chapter deals with all those necessities that need a home but are often simply stashed in a corner. What's the best place for cleaning supplies, step stools, pet food, tool kits, and the fire extinguisher? You'll find the answers.

Part 3, "Specialized Storage," covers everything from where to store food so it lasts to where to keep the pen for writing your shopping list. In Chapter 6, "Cool and Cold Storage," this book fills you in on how to use your refrigerator and freezer more effectively, as well as what new and exciting units to consider when you remodel. It also lets you know the proper way to store your finest wines. Chapter 7, "Trash and Recyclables," gets down and dirty, describing the best ways to stow garbage, recyclables, and compost. Chapter 8, "Kitchen Offices and Message Centers," offers ideas for incorporating a desk, files, electronics, and a message center into your kitchen plan—and tips on how to keep them orderly.

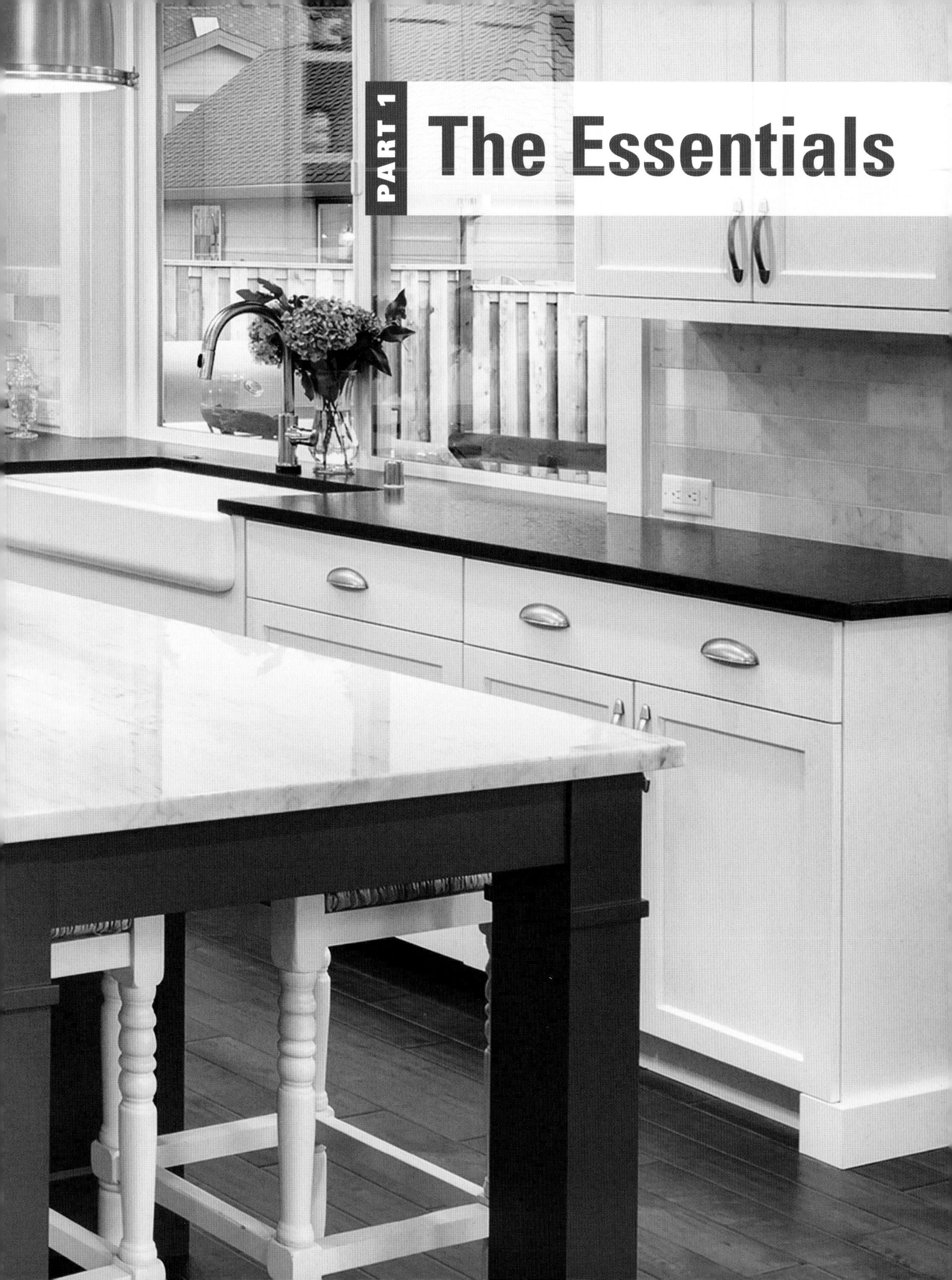

PART 1 The Essentials

Campbell's

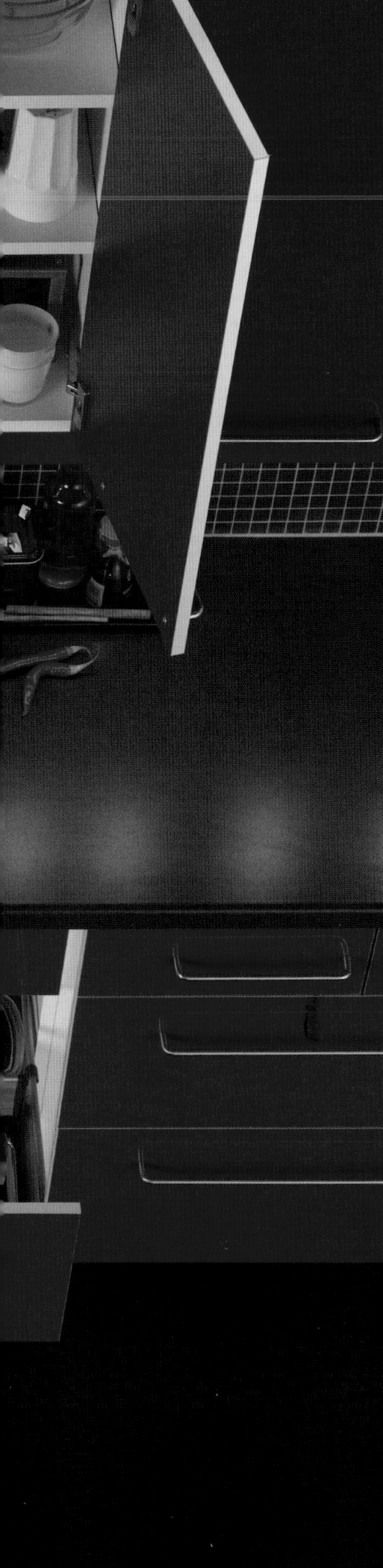

CHAPTER 1

Finding Efficiency

Before delving into the guidelines for creating a well-organized kitchen with lots of sensible storage solutions, it's important to be clear about the difference between storage and organization. The former has to do with better use of space, accessibility, and clever hardware. The latter has more to do with how to group items and where to put them.

You may design a kitchen so that every single utensil, pot, or box of cereal is stored without wasting a single cubic inch. But that doesn't necessarily mean your kitchen will be well organized or an efficient place to work. To perform all of the daily tasks that take place there, quickly and easily, everything will need to be optimally *stored* in places that result in optimal *organization*. A bag of flour may be optimally stored in a clear, airtight container on a shelf that's clearly lit and within easy reach, but if that shelf is on the other side of the kitchen from where you do your baking, it's not optimally organized. Now move the flour container to a shelf over the counter where you bake. It may still be in a less than optimal place if you bake infrequently or if some other item that you use every day would be better stored there.

There is often no right answer for everyone. Too much depends on the size of your kitchen, the people it serves, and your cooking habits. Notice, however, we didn't say that optimal organization depends on your budget. A low-budget kitchen remodeling can be a dream in terms of efficiency. Conversely, there are many high-end kitchens that are a nightmare to work in. In this chapter, we spell out the rules of optimal storage and organization.

Left **An efficient kitchen has storage for everything and locates that storage where you'll need it when engaged in kitchen activities.**

Make the Most of Your Space

What do the catch phrases "maximize your space," "avoid wasting space," and "saving space" really mean? They all boil down to getting more from the storage space you have (or plan to have in the case of remodeling or new construction). To do this, you may need to use all of the available space in your kitchen, whether it's up by the ceiling, on the floor of a closet, or buried deep in a corner cabinet. The soffits above your wall cabinets, for example, can be fitted with small cabinets or shelves for less-used items, such as a collection of flower vases or a fondue pot. Put rolling tubs on the floor under shelves in a closet or walk-in pantry and store paper goods and cleaning supplies inside. Use clever hardware to pivot and pull your way to the deepest recesses of any cabinet.

Sometimes the "wasted" space is right before your eyes. Open any kitchen cabinet and observe how much of it is actually used for storage and how much is empty. In other words, is there a big void above your collection of soup cans? Often, you'll find you can add 30 to 50 percent more storage to a cabinet simply by optimizing the placement of shelves. Get into the habit of thinking in terms of cubic inches/volume when planning storage. Otherwise, you're likely to waste much of your prime storage space.

Above When buying cabinets for a remodeling or when upgrading existing cabinets, make full use of today's improved hardware and smart organizational features.

Right Specialty storage solutions make the most of your cabinet space, allowing access to high shelves and providing room for everything from recyclables to root vegetables.

SMARTtip

Pare Down

Get rid of what you don't use. Do the lobster pot or second waffle iron you got as a wedding present need to be stored in the kitchen? Do you ever plan on using that big pressure cooker? In many kitchens, as much as half the available space is gobbled up by dishware and cookware that is used rarely or not at all. Unnecessary duplication can also cause kitchen crowding. You may need two or even three saucepans, but you don't need five. And do you really need to have three dozen mugs? Keep only the ones you prefer to use, and donate the rest to Goodwill or the Salvation Army.

Top **A corner space is one that is typically difficult to use because of limited access. This angled shelves-and-drawer detail is just one solution offered by cabinet manufacturers.**

Bottom **Pullout bins and shelves, along with improved lazy Susans, bring stored items into view—and make them more accessible, too.**

Think Size Before You Buy

Don't buy bigger than you need. Careful selection of coffee makers, toasters, and wine racks can make the difference between ample and inadequate counter space. Similarly, bulky food packaging— especially when it comes to snack foods—can contribute to an overcrowded cabinet or refrigerator. When possible, avoid buying individual-size packages because the packaging-to-contents ratio is high.

Downsizing large appliances can make an even bigger difference when it comes to getting the most from the space you have. Many manufacturers, inspired by trends in Europe, offer compact ranges, fridges, freezers, ovens, and dishwashers. Multipurpose appliances offer space-conserving opportunities as well. Smart refrigerators are available with touch screens that help keep you organized and entertained. (See "Smart Fridges," page 200.) A convection microwave oven cooks in either mode, making a dedicated microwave redundant in many cases. An over-the-range microwave, combined with a range hood, is another space-conserving combo. There are even under-counter combination washer/dryers.

Above Split refrigeration allows you to use prime kitchen space more efficiently. Put the fridge near all the action and put the less-frequented freezer on the outskirts. Use the free space you've created for items you need for meal preparation.

Left Compact and multipurpose countertop appliances, such as this combination processor-blender-mixer, can save space, too.

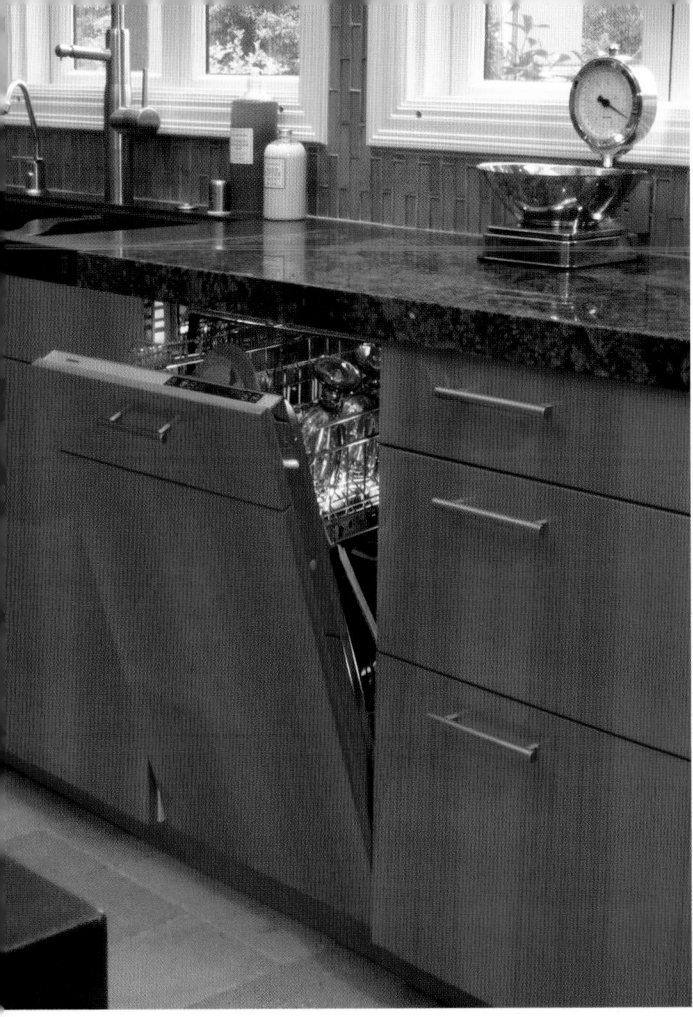

SMARTtip

Save Money and Space

Buy nonperishable items and paper goods in bulk, but store only enough for a week or two in the kitchen. Put the rest on utility shelves in a basement, garage, or storage room. When you run low in the kitchen, replenish.

Top Dishwashers come in many sizes, including this compact 18-inch (45cm) unit. Buy the size that fits your needs, and you'll conserve space and energy.

Bottom Cooktops, such as this compact five-burner unit, offer another way to put storage where you need it. Think how nice it would be to have your pots and pans organized in deep drawers right where you need them.

Appliances that Store

Refrigerators, walk-in pantries, and refrigerated wine cellars were made for storage. It may not be as evident, however, that other appliances present storage opportunities. Your range probably has a storage drawer at the bottom or along the side. It's usually big enough for keeping broiling and roasting pans. Look above the range, too. Some range hoods include built-in warming shelves and racks that keep needed utensils close at hand. Having two dishwashers has also gained favor in one- or two-person households. Put the plates, bowls, glasses, and flatware you use daily in one of the dishwashers; run a load; take the items out as you need them; and put them in the other dishwasher when they're dirty again. The dual dishwashers do double-duty: washing and storing.

Opposite The range shown here includes pullouts and drawers to keep cookware handy. Some range hoods, washers, dryers, and barbecue grills also offer storage.

Bottom An appliance's main function is to do its job, but some have built-in storage, too. This coffeemaker has a warming drawer that keeps cups where you need them.

SMARTtip

Space-Saving Containers

When space is tight, use stackable square or rectangular containers on counters and shelves and in the fridge because they take up less space than round ones and are easier to keep organized than plastic bags. Seek out containers that nest or collapse when not in use. Use rectangular baskets and other containers to store small items on shelves. They store compactly, and you can quickly pull them down to the countertop, where it's a lot easier to find what you're looking for.

Collapsible silicone colanders can help you conserve storage space—and are a colorful change from stainless steel. Where space is tight, consider similar space-saving products, including collapsible measuring cups.

SMARTtip

Jettison Bulky Packaging

Upon buying space-gobbling items, such as family-size bags of chips, repackage them in appropriate containers or bags. They'll consume less space and stay fresher. In the case of frozen meats, you'll be able to defrost just what you need and no more. Caution: observe strict sanitary practices when repacking meats and poultry to keep from introducing bacteria as you handle them.

FAGOR

Accessibility Is Key

Just as important as using all available space is making sure that what you store is easily accessible. Your storage solutions may be sized correctly and located exactly in the work area where you'll need them, but if they're hard to get to, they will not qualify as optimal. There are several simple rules for avoiding such problems.

Always put items back in their proper place. Otherwise, you'll spend half your time searching for the right tool or ingredient. This is especially important when two or more cooks will be sharing the same kitchen.

Avoid piles. If your serving dishes are under your dinner plates, which are in turn under your dessert plates, you're going to have a problem. Ditto for your cutting board collection. Either you must perform the precarious feat of pulling out the plate you want from under the others, or you have to lift half the stack and lay it aside while you grab the one you want. Instead, add shelves or use racks so that each grouping of dishes or boards is separate and easy to access. Vertical racks can work, too, but they will generally take up a bit more space because you need dividers to keep the items upright.

Heavy items, if not stored on the countertop, are best stored between waist and eye level. Avoid storing heavy pots or fragile items where you have to stretch to reach them. Drop a cast-iron cooking pot, and your kitchen floor could be damaged. Or, worse, you could drop something on yourself.

Below Horizontal cabinet doors that open upward allow you to access or reload contents without the doors getting in your way—and with little danger you'll ever bump your head on them!

Above Utensils that fit drawer organizers like pieces in a puzzle leave no excuses for putting the pizza cutter in the wrong drawer.

Above Vertical storage beats piles, especially overhead. You only have to be able to reach the bottom corner of a cookie sheet to pull it down.

SMARTtip

Storage Strategies

Tiers allow you to see what's in store behind the first row. You can buy tiered shelf inserts at many home-goods stores, or you can build them for little or no cost. (See page 59.)

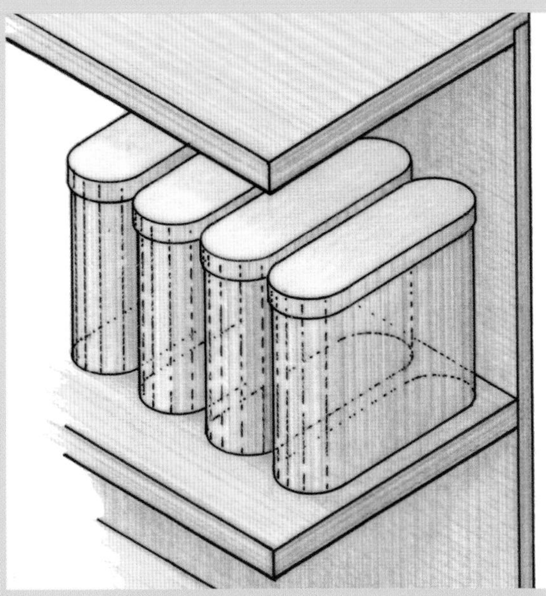

Elongated, clear containers like these make good use of cabinet space and allow you to see what you have. Always choose food containers that have airtight lids.

Helper shelves make it easy to reach the dinner plates without having to remove the dessert plates first. Many models are available, or you can build your own. (See page 57.)

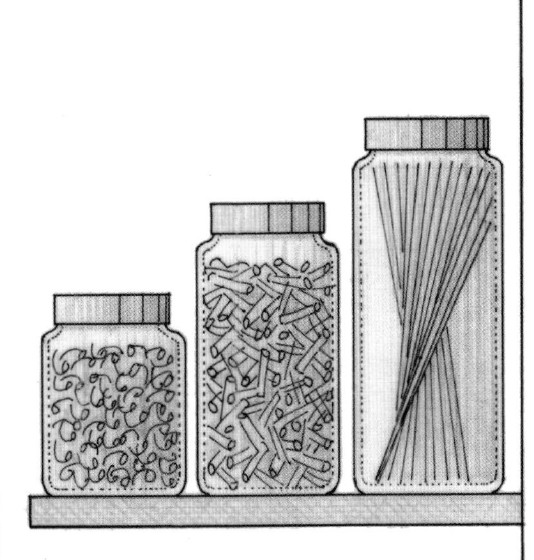

When loading a cabinet, put the tallest items toward the back, as shown in this section view. That way, you can see smaller items up front, but the taller items remain visible.

Visibility Counts

Try not to store items where you can't see them, such as behind rows of canned, boxed, or bagged goods. Putting larger items toward the back of a shelf and smaller items up front will help. Tiered inserts are sometimes a good solution, too. They allow you to view all of the contents on a shelf or in a cabinet. Because the tiers raise each successive row of goods from front to back, there's no need to pull out every soup can to grab the one you want. (See the illustration on page 25.) Another solution is to store dry goods, such as flour, beans, and rice, in long, deep, clear containers. (See the illustration on page 25.) The contents will be visible, and you can minimize or eliminate having to put some items where they can't be seen. If clear containers are not available, use labels so you know the contents without having to pull it off the shelf. Remember, visibility is a great memory prompter. If you can't see it, you may forget you have it.

Good lighting also makes it easier to see what you need. To do so with a cabinet, illumination must be able to reach inside the cabinet. Ideally, it should come from several angles so that items are not in shadow. Nor should your body cast a shadow in the area where you're searching. (See the illustrations on this page for optimal placement of lights along a run of cabinets.) For countertops, consider under-cabinet lighting. Then, whether you're using the under-cabinet space for chopping vegetables or reading a recipe, you'll have good visibility. Lighting base cabinets with shelves is more difficult. One solution is to build in lighting. Connect it to a door switch so it automatically comes on when you open the cabinet door. Another is to install pullout shelves or to install base cabinets with deep drawers. With either approach, your ceiling lighting should be adequate.

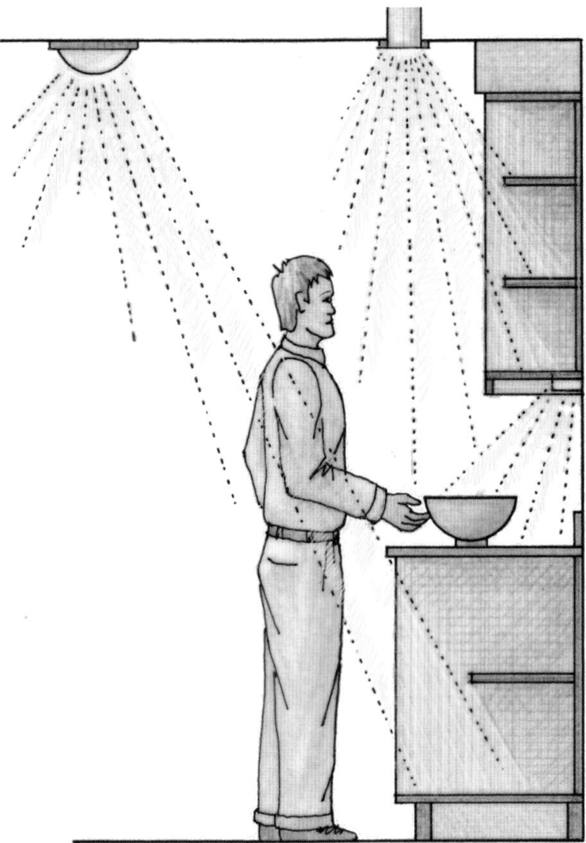

Above Lighting counters and cabinets takes some thought. This illustration shows one way to do it. Lights inside cabinets are another solution.

SMARTtip

Lighten Up

It's fine to go with dark cabinet exteriors if that's your preferred look, but you may want to use light colors for cabinet interiors and for shelves. As light from ceiling fixtures strikes the light-colored surfaces, it will reflect onto the items you store there, making them easier to see—and find. Alternately, use pullouts, which enable you to move stored items into the light.

Top This well-lit kitchen includes downlights in the ceiling, uplighting over cabinets, fixtures over cabinet openings, lighting inside and under cabinets, and even a light strip along the floor beneath the pantry cabinets.

Bottom Here's the same kitchen with many of the lights turned off.

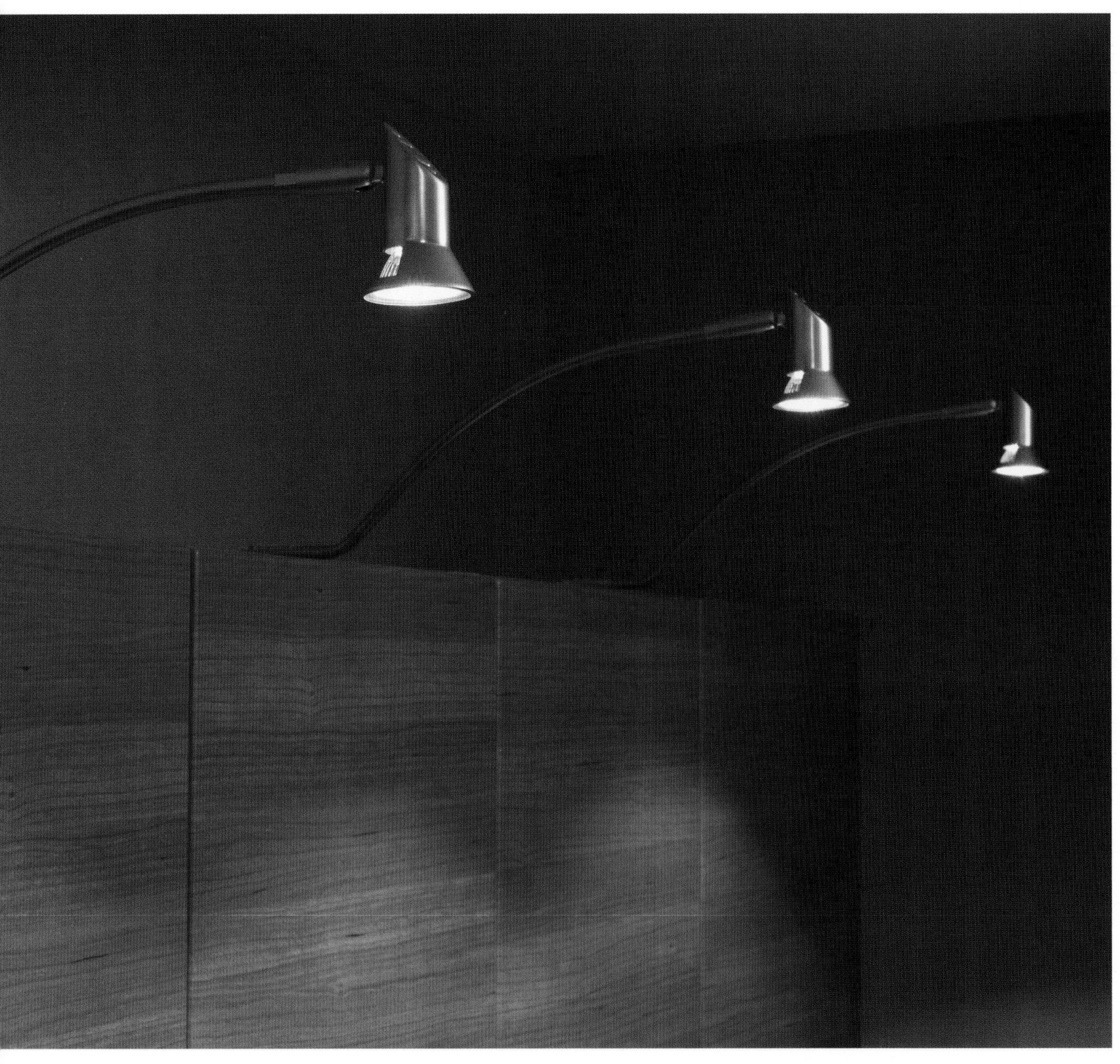

Above These fixtures, which are mounted to the cabinet tops, throw light inside when the doors are open, without interfering with the door swing.

Opposite These fixtures cast plenty of light along the countertop—an area that would otherwise be partially shaded by the cabinets or the cook.

Above In-cabinet lighting is meant to display contents stored behind glass doors. Glass shelves enhance the visual effect.

Opposite Under-cabinet lighting is also available with energy-saving fluorescent fixtures. LED lights have also become very popular for this purpose.

To See or Not to See

Deciding whether you want be able to see your stored items or not is often a compromise between aesthetics and functionality. Some people like to showcase items, but that's not important to everyone. Others prefer a less-cluttered look and allow the cabinetry to be the dominant element. If you want to have your cake and eat it, too, check out these solutions.

Roll-down shutters, when open, provide complete access to serving bowls, pitchers, and other stored items whenever they're needed.

When the shutters are closed, the contents are hidden and protected from dust and grease. These stainless-steel shutters are easy to wipe clean using a mild detergent.

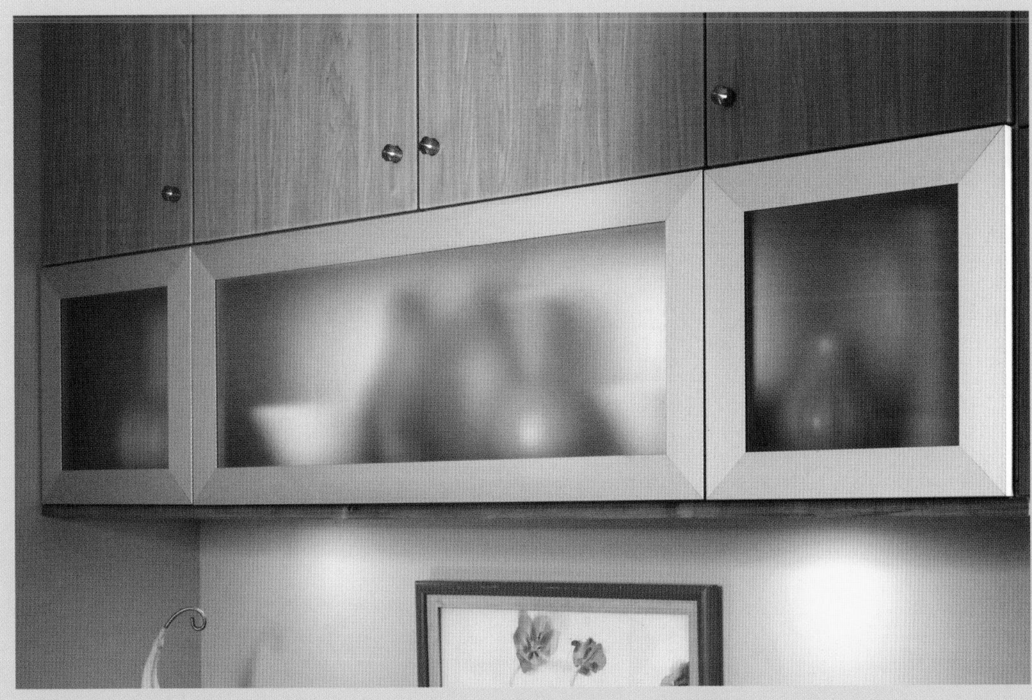

Translucent doors offer an interesting alternative to clear glass when you're not sure you're willing to keep contents in full view.

The textured glass camouflages the cabinet's contents, but still allows you to see what's inside.

Cabinet Construction

Differences in cabinet construction and hinges affect storage convenience as well. Framed cabinets have rails and stiles that reduce the cabinet opening by about 1 inch (2.5cm) in width and height. This slightly reduces access and can limit the size of storage baskets and bins that you may want to use to organize small items. Frames also obstruct your vision, especially of items at the back of a shelf. Besides being more accessible, frameless cabinets have a sleeker look with doors that completely cover the cabinet front. Sliding doors are another sleek option.

Today, cabinets of all types most often have cup hinges, which are sometimes called European-style hinges. The cup of these hinges fits into a shallow round recess drilled into the door and the inside of the cabinet. These are easier to install than traditional mortised leaf hinges and have adjustment screws so doors can be aligned after installation or realigned if they sag. The best cup hinges allow the door to open 180 degrees, but some stop at 120 degrees or even 90 degrees.

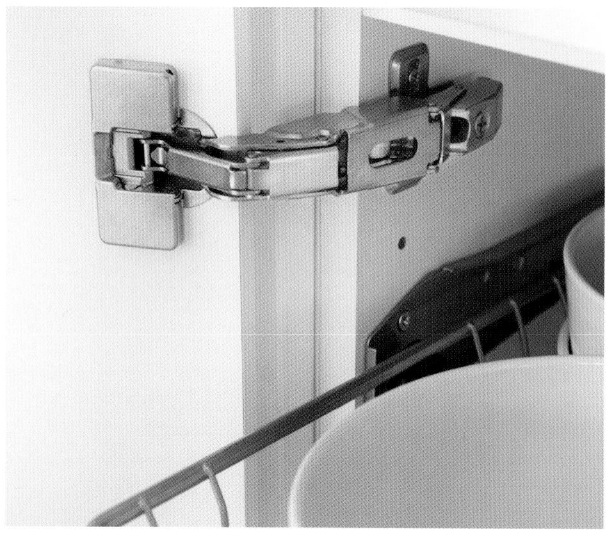

Above The best cup hinges allow doors to swing open 180 degrees. This provides full access to contents without interference from doors.

Right (all) Framed cabinets have rails and stiles that stiffen construction but slightly reduce the cabinet opening. Frameless cabinets rely on simple box construction, sometimes with knockdown (KD) joint fasteners. With stiles eliminated, access to contents is easier. Sliding-door cabinets eliminate the nuisance of swinging doors, but only one side of the cabinet can be open at a time.

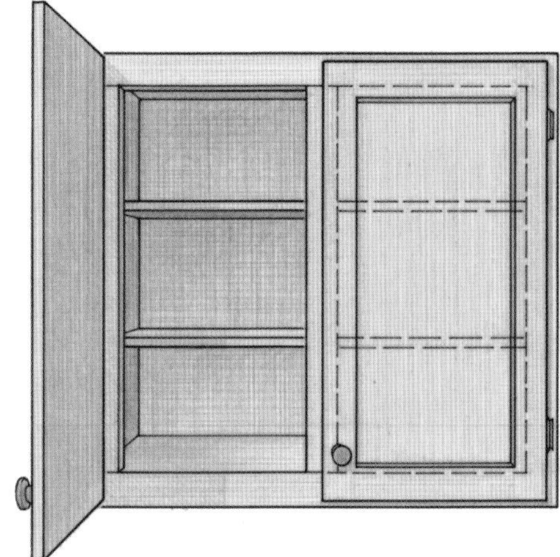

Framed Cabinet

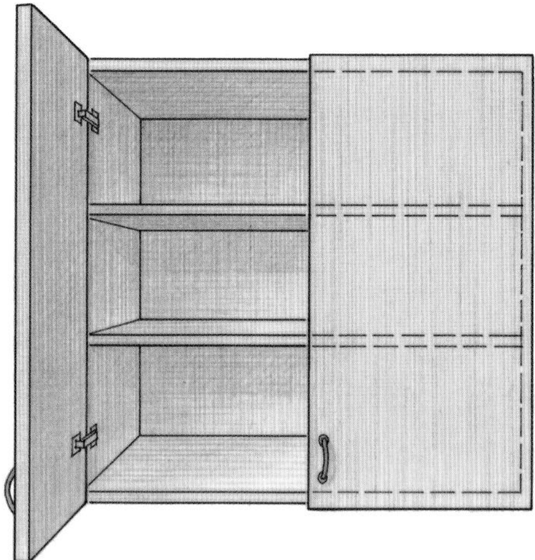

Frameless Cabinet

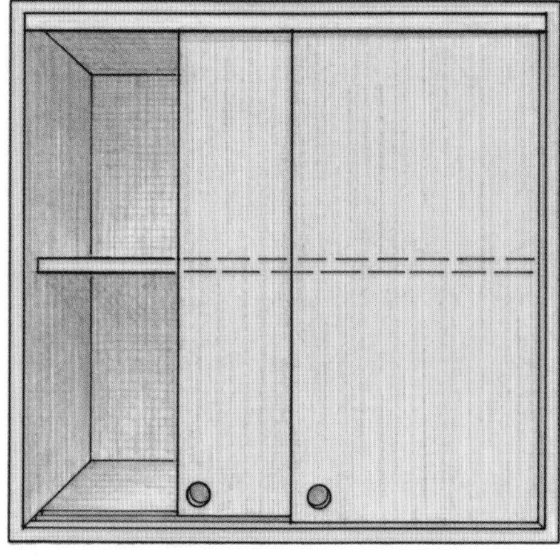

Sliding-Door Cabinet

Framed versus Frameless

Framed cabinets typically reveal rails and stiles, even with doors and drawers closed, as shown here.

Frameless cabinets present far fewer lines to the viewer because doors and drawers reveal little, if anything, when closed.

Framed cabinets are typically used for country kitchen decor. Their construction harkens back to the days before plywood.

Frameless cabinets most often have flat doors and drawer fronts, but they are also available with more traditional raised panels.

Most framed cabinets have a stile behind where the doors meet, avoiding an unsightly gap.

Frameless cabinets tend to complement today's popular stainless-steel appliances better than framed cabinets do.

Method to Organization Madness

There are many ways to organize. This is one that works well. First, think about how you use your kitchen and make a list of the activities you perform there. There's no standard list, but yours will probably include basic activities such as unpacking groceries, preparing meals, cleaning up after meals, and collecting recyclables. It may also include more specialized activities such as making school lunches, baking, canning, and feeding the cat. Check out the list on page 45 for additional possibilities, and tailor it to best describe your activities. Or keep a journal for a few days, jotting down each activity after you engage in it. Be specific. Don't write "cleaning up" if you mean "cleaning the countertops" rather than "washing the floor." For most people, these count as distinct activities. Be sure to include nonculinary activities as well, including watching TV and checking e-mail, if you do them in the kitchen.

Next, prioritize the activities according to how frequently you engage in them. A good way to do this is to assign a number from 1 to 10 to each activity, with 10 being several times a day and 1 being rarely or seldom. In many homes, for example, "preparing breakfast" might garner a 7 rating, while "setting the table" or "cleaning the counter" might be scored a 9 or 10. On the other end of the scale, "setting the dining room table" might only get a 2 or 3. If any of the activities on your list is typically done under time pressure, such as making coffee or making school lunches, add a point or two.

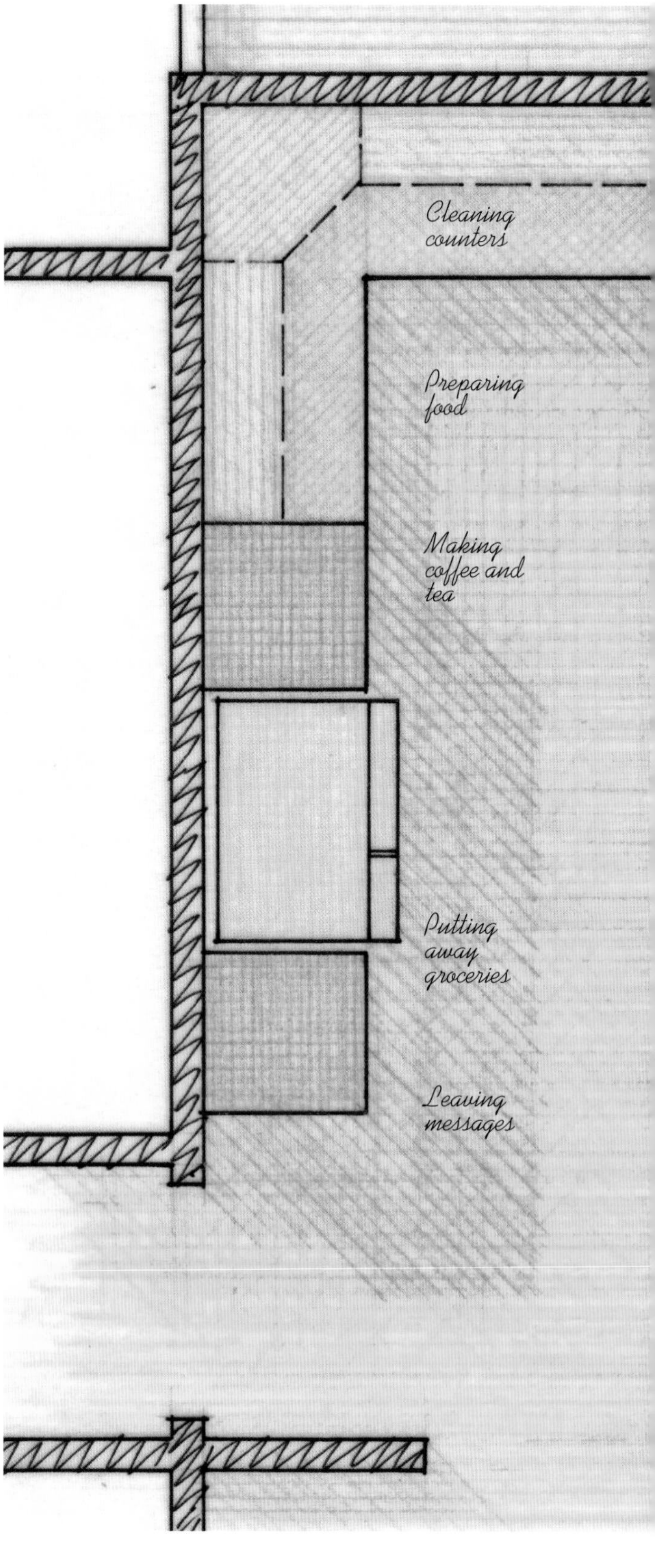

Right **Create an activities map of your kitchen. It should include the general locations of typical daily activities, such as those listed on page 45. Once you have activities located, list the items needed to perform each one, and then prioritize the activities and begin to pinpoint what will go where.**

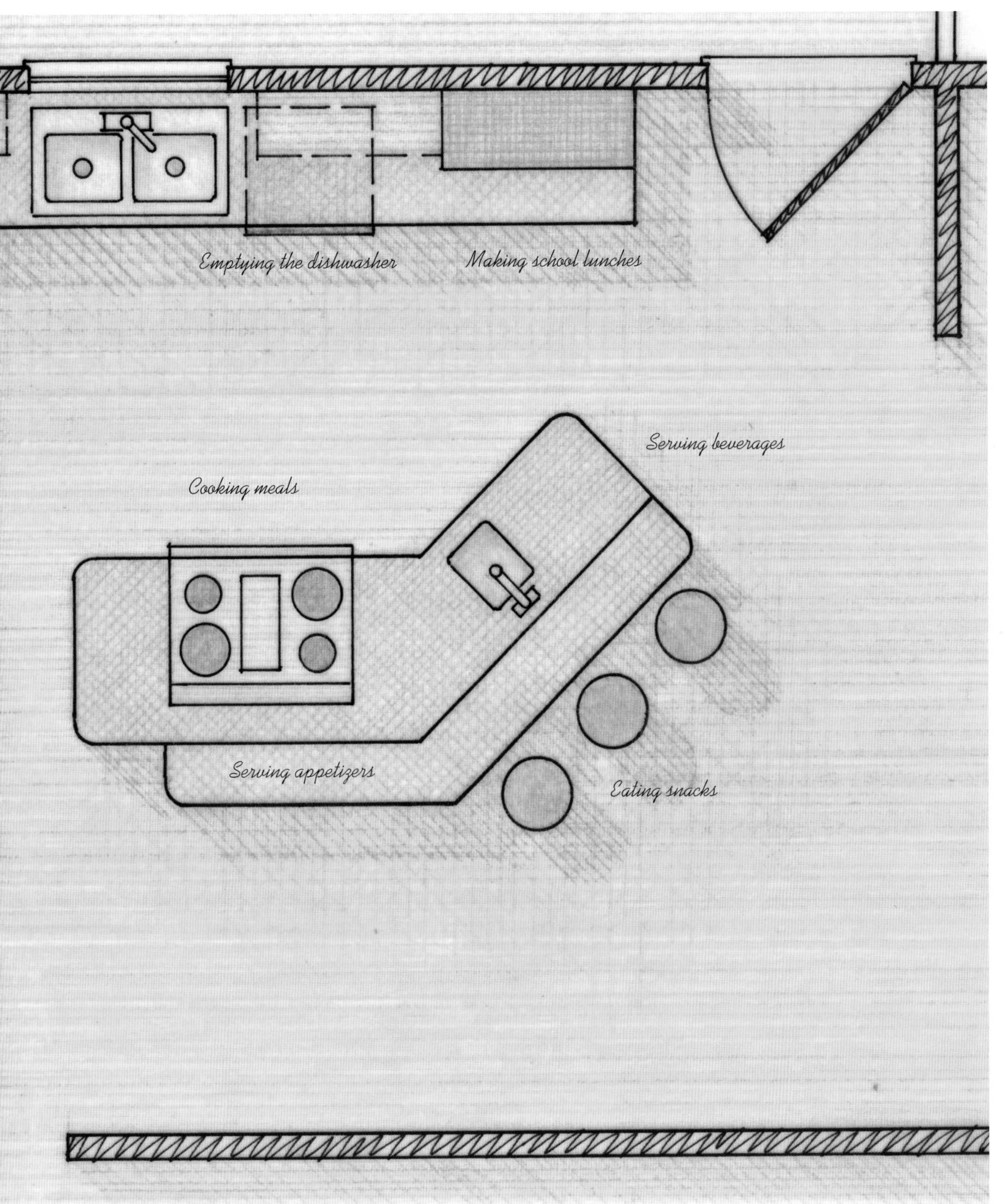

Emptying the dishwasher
Making school lunches
Serving beverages
Cooking meals
Serving appetizers
Eating snacks

Connect Items to Activities

Once you've completed the list of activities suggested on page 36, start a second list of the items you need to perform each activity. Under "baking," for example, list measuring cups and spoons, cookie sheets, rolling pins, and the like. Under "watching TV," you may list eyeglasses, notepad and pencil, and TV remote. Under "making school lunches," your list may include sandwich wrap, napkins, plastic containers, and paper lunch bags. Under "serving meals," be sure to include trays, serving spoons and forks, trivets, potholders, and so on. Once again, tailor the lists to your habits and preferences. If you cook Asian-style meals, your "prepping dinner" list will probably include a wok, cooking oils, sauces, herbs, cutlery, a cutting board, and wok utensils. If your breakfast routine includes coffee or tea, juice, vitamins, and a baguette with butter, be sure your list includes sweeteners, mugs, juice glasses, pills, a cutting board, and a bread knife. If you drink tea, your list may allow for a dozen blends, along with preferred sweeteners and tea-making equipment.

You can probably guess where all of this is headed. Armed with your lists and priority ratings, you'll be better prepared to make all sorts of storage and organization decisions that would otherwise be wildly confusing. The final step is to assign activities, and the items associated with them, to specific locations within your kitchen. The best way to do this is to pencil them onto your kitchen floor plan. (See the illustration on pages 36–37.) Begin with your highest-priority activities. If you scored "making coffee" a 9, indicate your preferred location before deciding on where to put a 3-rated "serving wine." Follow your instincts. Put "preparing dinners" near a counter that is close to the range. Some activities may go in two places. "Unpacking groceries" may be listed near the fridge and the pantry. If two or more activities are vying for the same prime location and there's not room for both, the one with the higher-use priority should get the nod.

Right A beverage center is a nice luxury for a kitchen. Include storage for wine and other beverages, glasses, a decanter, and trays—and don't forget a bottle opener and a corkscrew.

Top This informal kitchen, with its three sinks, can easily accommodate two cooks. Don't hesitate to store duplicates of inexpensive cooking aids, such as measuring cups and spoons, if your kitchen has two work stations and you have the space.

Bottom Make table-setting easier by storing everything you need near your kitchen table. This table-setting center includes shelves and a rack for tableware as well as drawers for flatware and napkins.

Be Ready to Compromise

Of course, none of this is an exact science. You will need to compromise on the assignment of activities and placement of items based on many variables, including the availability of suitable storage, weight of the item, and indoor "climate" conditions. Spices, for example, are a bit tricky to place. Optimal storage as far as freshness is concerned is a cool, dark place away from light, heat, and humidity. But the farther away from your prep and cooking areas they are, the more time you waste retrieving them. You may want to keep small containers of your most-used spices a few feet (about a meter) from the stove and store the rest in a cabinet or drawer that isn't too close to any heat or moisture sources. Rarely-used spices can be kept in the freezer.

The best location for an activity or item will not always be clear. Take glasses and mugs, for instance. Where do you put them? Near the dishwasher is often a good choice. Another option is near your dining table. You may want to store glasses near the fridge or sink and mugs near your coffeemaker.

If you're reorganizing an existing kitchen, you'll be somewhat limited in where you can put things. Scarce cabinetry around the range, for example, may force you to put some meal-prep items in less-than-ideal spots. But if you're planning a remodeling, you have an opportunity to better match activities with the appropriate items, and items with ideal storage design. Show the lists to your designer or architect so he or she can accommodate your wishes.

Above Many cooks like to have flatware near the range for stirring and tasting, so don't hesitate to store some in a nearby drawer.

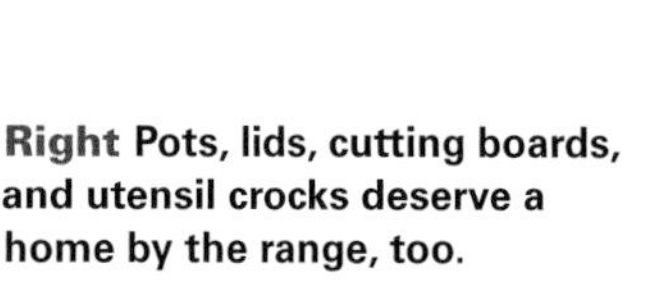

Right Pots, lids, cutting boards, and utensil crocks deserve a home by the range, too.

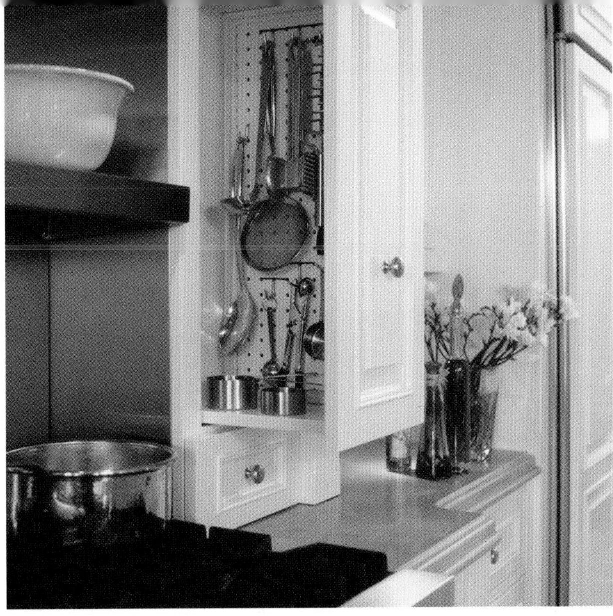

Top left A pullout pegboard on the side of a range is another great way to store necessary cooking implements at arm's reach.

Top right Open shelves above and below a cooktop, along with a backsplash rack, will help make cooking a pleasure.

Bottom left Deep base-cabinet drawers—properly organized, of course—are the stuff of dream kitchens.

Bottom right Even a narrow shelf under the range hood can make the difference between a good cooking experience and a stressful one.

Above Install your chopping block next to the base cabinet that houses your pullout trash can or compost pail to make handling kitchen scraps a snap.

Left Build a snack center around your microwave with a pullout shelf and drawer combo.

Bottom left Put dish towels where you need them—right beside the sink. This pullout "filler" rack utilizes what might otherwise be wasted space.

Bottom right A wet bar is a great place for stowing beverage-related supplies.

Exceptions to the Rule

Sometimes putting items in multiple locations makes sense, assuming the items are used frequently and won't hog too much space. Put one set of measuring tools in your dinner-prep area and another in a baking center. Keep napkins with everything you'll need for setting the table, but also keep some in a dispenser or basket near the microwave or out on the porch if you eat meals there.

In other cases, you may prefer an entirely different organizational logic just because it's easier for you to remember. For example, some cooks prefer to keep all large utensils together in a big crock, regardless of their various uses. In a small kitchen it simply may not matter all that much whether you have to walk a few extra steps to grab the implement you need.

A few cleaning activities may also be excluded from the above logic. Cleansers and detergents are typically grouped under the sink or in a broom closet regardless of where they're used. A cooktop cleaner, for example, needn't be stored near the cooktop. In general, cleaning supplies are stored together, separate from food items.

Below The relationship between activity areas is key. It's easy to dry items in the cleanup area and put them on the shelves—and just as easy to take them down and set them on the snack bar when needed.

Subfolders for the Kitchen

Whether you're getting ready to reorganize an existing kitchen or preparing to move into a brand-new one, it's essential to refine your organization by grouping related items together as much as is feasible. Think of it as making "subfolders," as you would on your computer. In your beverage-prep area, put your favorite teas together in one basket and sweeteners in another. In the food-prep area, separate your baking spices from seasonings for entrées. In your snack storage area, group the snacks for kids apart from those for adults. You may even choose to divide supplements, medicines, and vitamins according to family member. Such secondary storage groupings are critical to ease of use.

For the week or two leading up to your organization day, collect small baskets, jars, tins, canisters, racks, hooks, bins, and drawer organizers that you think will help you fine-tune your kitchen organization. Measure your cabinets and drawers beforehand so you don't end up with containers that are too big for your shelves and cabinet openings. If you're not sure what sizes or how many to buy, collect an assortment of temporary containers. Food containers from the supermarket, candy boxes, corrugated shipping boxes, and the like can serve as stand-ins until you have a better idea of what to purchase. If you're reorganizing an existing kitchen, gather some larger boxes and packing materials. You'll want them to stow items you rarely use and to move them to the attic or basement for storage.

If organizing your kitchen in a day seems daunting, tackle only a few areas at a time. Once everything is neatly tucked away, take your kitchen for a test run. Do you like the new order? You're bound to want to make some changes for aesthetics or to improve work flow.

Above Subdivided drawers are a great way to refine your kitchen organization. Here, spices, utensils, and liquid seasonings each have their own section.

Opposite top Your cookbooks may have a nice spot on a shelf, but what about all those treasured recipe clippings? Create a recipe nook and mount a cookbook holder beneath it.

Opposite bottom left As mentioned earlier, having your daily tableware all in one place makes sense. Fine-tune the organization by putting cups in the cupboard and dishes in a deep drawer.

Opposite bottom right When space is tight, one storage space may need to support several activities. Use dividers and organizers to keep items from mingling.

SMARTtip

Coffee, Anyone?

If you're an avid coffee drinker, it may be nice to have all your supplies in one spot. Establish a place in your kitchen (or near where you eat breakfast) where you can put your coffeemaker or espresso machine, coffee beans, coffee grinder, coffee filters, sugar, mugs, and spoons. It will make those early mornings just a little bit easier.

Common Kitchen Activities

- Baking
- Canning and freezing
- Checking e-mail
- Cleaning counters
- Collecting compost
- Collecting recyclables
- Collecting trash
- Eating snacks or meals
- Emptying the dishwasher
- Feeding a dog or cat
- Handling school-related paperwork
- Leaving messages for the family
- Making coffee and tea
- Making or answering phone calls
- Making school lunches
- Ordering take-out food
- Paying bills
- Preparing bottles or meals for a baby
- Preparing meals
- Preparing snacks
- Processing mail
- Putting away groceries
- Reading the newspaper
- Searching for recipes
- Serving beverages
- Serving meals
- Serving meals on the porch, deck, or patio (or anywhere else that's not the kitchen)
- Setting the dining room table
- Setting the kitchen table or counter
- Socializing
- Sweeping the floor
- Taking vitamins and medicines
- Washing the floor
- Watching TV
- Watering plants

Storage Safety Guidelines

The kitchen is full of hazardous items, from harsh chemicals to sharp knives. Careful storage can prevent accidents from happening and help take care of them quickly when they do.

- **Lock up hazardous chemicals** if children live in or frequent the house. Consider replacing your regular cleaning supplies with ones that are more environmentally friendly and nontoxic—and often cheaper! Research uses for baking soda, washing soda, white vinegar, and lemon juice.
- **Label (with a date)** repackaged freezer items. Label other food items that don't come with their own use-by dates. Discard refrigerated leftovers after three days.
- **Bacteria can contaminate food** through careless food handling and storage. Keep everything clean, including hands, shelves, and storage containers.
- **Store sharp cutlery and carving forks in holders,** not loose in drawers where you are likely to cut yourself while fishing out the right knife. Avoid storing sharp objects in a utensil crock. If you must, train every kitchen user to store sharp items sharp end down.

An unorganized knife drawer can be hazardous to reach into. Use a knife holder to keep your fingers safe.

- **Close cabinet doors** immediately after getting what you need. Leave a door open, and you're likely to hit your head. If you like the convenience of open doors, consider frameless cabinets with sliding doors, or dispense with doors altogether and go with open shelves.

Special hardware like this can do the heavy lifting for you, which is especially nice if your back is suspect.

- **Avoid storing heavy items** on high shelves from which they may accidentally fall while you're reaching for them. Avoid storing heavy items on low shelves as well, especially if you're prone to back problems.
- **Do not overstuff cabinets,** especially with heavy, fragile items that may fall to the floor and send shards flying.
- **Never store items** in ways that would encourage young children to climb on counters.
- **For the elderly** or physically challenged, consider countertop storage that's wheelchair accessible. Use base-cabinet drawers instead of shelving behind doors to store items they may need.
- **Keep a basic first-aid kit** within easy reach. Fill it with bandages, adhesive tape, and a disinfecting ointment. Keep a first-aid manual with emergency instructions on hand, too.
- **Post the number** of the Poison Control Center near your phone. Speak to them before administering ipecac syrup or activated charcoal.
- **Keep a fire extinguisher** on hand. The best kind for kitchens is labeled "ABC," meaning it can handle all types of fires, including grease fires. Baking soda (never water!) can also be used for grease fires.

Improved Child-Proof Door Lock

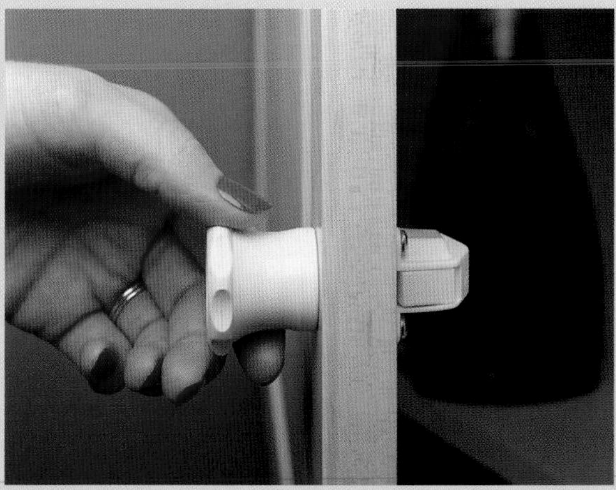

A magnetic knob must be used to disengage this lock. Store the knob where a child cannot get to it.

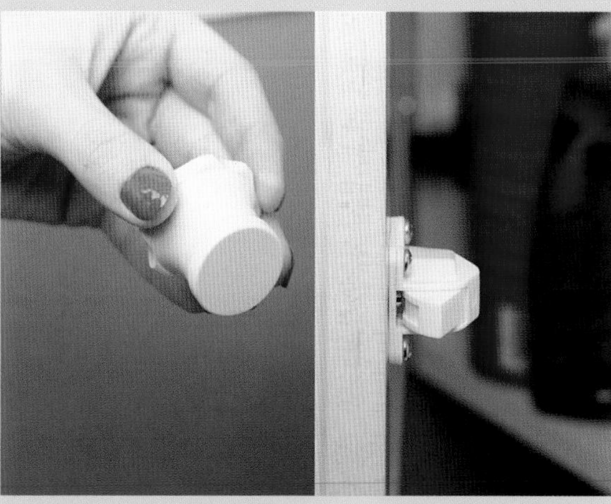

This photo shows how the latch engages as the magnetic knob is removed.

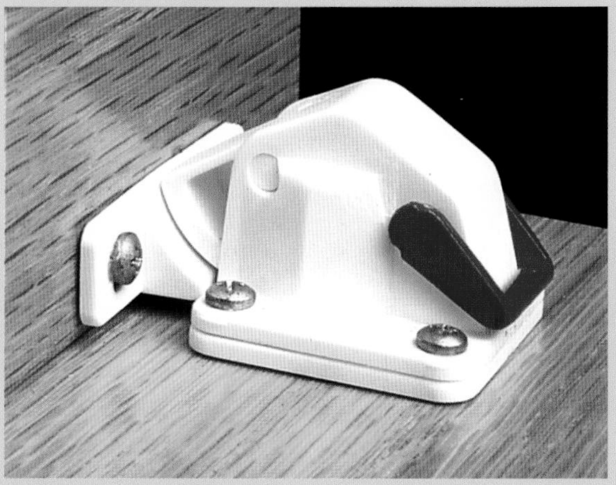

When the lock is engaged, even the most determined toddler will be unable to open the cabinet door.

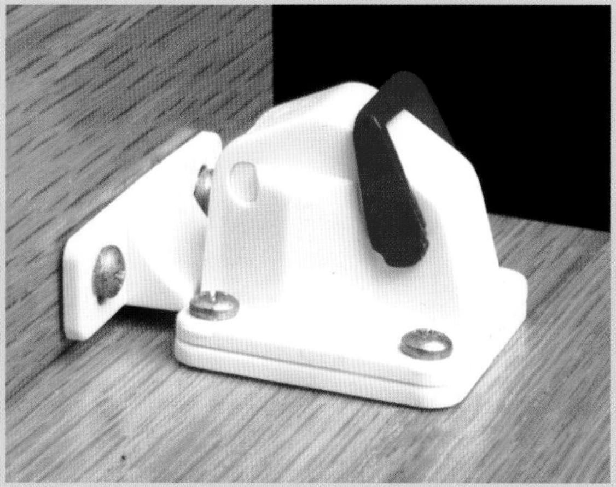

Here, the lock is disengaged and the door opens normally.

SMARTtip

Keep Up to Date

To ensure top quality of the foods you eat, use the oldest products first and the newer ones later. It helps to store the newer items behind the older ones. For products without printed open dates (sell-by, use-by, expiration, and pack dates), you may want to apply labels and write in your own purchase date. Use airtight containers when appropriate. Store breads and cakes at room temperature and use within three to seven days or freeze. Storing them in the refrigerator will cause them to become stale faster. (See "How Long to Store It," pages 48–49.)

How Long to Store It

Type of Food	Time	Handling
STAPLES		
Barley	2 years	Cool, dry place; airtight container
Bread crumbs	4 months	Cool, dry place; airtight container
Brown rice	6 months	Cool, dry place; airtight container
Brown sugar	18 months	Cool, dry place; airtight container
Bulgur	5–6 months	Cool, dry place; airtight container
Cornmeal and hominy grits	1 year	Cool, dry place; airtight container
Dry milk (nonfat)	1 year	Cool, dry place; airtight container
Honey and syrups	1 year	Refrigerate after opening
Olive oil	6 months	Cool, dry place
Pasta	1–2 years	Cool, dry place; airtight container
Rice	1 year	Cool, dry place; airtight container
Sugar, granulated	Indefinitely	Cool, dry place; airtight container
Sugar, powdered	18 months	Cool, dry place; airtight container
Vegetable oil	1 year	Cool, dry place
Wheat germ (unopened)	8–12 months	After opening, refrigerate or freeze in airtight container for 5–6 months
White flour	10–15 months	Cool, dry place; airtight container
Whole wheat flour	3 months	Cool, dry place or refrigerator or freezer; airtight container
Wild rice	6 months	Cool, dry place; airtight container
VEGETABLES		
Onions	1–3 months	Cool (room temperature or below), dry place
Potatoes	1–3 months	Cool (45°–50°F [7°–10°C]), dry, dark place
Squash, hard-rind	1–3 months	Cool (60°F [15°C]), dry place; one week only at room temperature
Sweet potatoes	1–3 months	Cool (60°F [15°C]), dry place; one week only at room temperature
CANNED FOODS (metal cans or glass jars)		
Cheese spread and foods (unopened)	2–5 years	Cool, dry place
High-acid canned foods: juices (apple, orange, tomato, etc.), tomatoes, grapefruit, apple products, mixed fruit, berries, pickles, sauerkraut, and vinegar-based products	12–18 months	Cool, dry place
Home-canned products: all types	1 year	Cool, dry place
Low-acid canned foods: meat and poultry products, vegetable soups (except tomato), spaghetti products, potatoes, corn, carrots, beans, beets, peas, pumpkin, etc.	2–5 years	Cool, dry place
Shortening	2 years	Cool, dry place

Type of Food	Time	Handling
DRY PACKAGED FOODS		
Biscuit/baking mix	6 months	Cool, dry place
Cake mix	6 months	Cool, dry place
Cereals	1 year	Cool, dry place; tightly sealed or airtight container
Soup mix	1 year	Cool, dry place
DRIED FOODS		
Dried apricots	3 months	Cool, dry place; refrigerate in airtight container after opening or freeze for longer storage
Dried peas and beans	1 year	Cool, dry place; airtight container
Dried prunes and raisins	9 months	Cool, dry place; refrigerate in airtight container after opening or freeze for longer storage
HERBS, SPICES, AND CONDIMENTS		
Cream of tartar	Indefinitely	Cool, dry place
Ground spices and herbs	2–3 years	Cool, dry, dark place; replace when aroma fades
Salt	Indefinitely	Cool, dry place
Seasoning mixes in foil packets	2 years	Cool, dry, dark place; replace when aroma fades
Tabasco	30 months	Cool, dry place
Vinegar	30 months	Cool, dry place
Whole spices	4–5 years	Cool, dry, dark place; replace when aroma fades
Worcestershire	30 months	Cool, dry place
BEVERAGES		
Bottled water	2–5 years	Unopened, in glass or plastic containers with foil seal; cool, dry, dark place
Coffee (canned)	1 year	Cool, dry place
Juices	12–18 months	Cool, dry place; refrigerate after opening
Soft drinks (soda)	8 months	Cool, dry place
Tea	18 months	Cool, dry place; airtight container

Courtesy of Rutgers NJAES Cooperative Extension

KOK I SVERIGE

CHAPTER 2

Cabinets and Accessories

Cabinetry has been at the heart of kitchen storage for centuries. As a result, there are hundreds of products out there from which to choose. As you examine styles and features, keep in mind that new technology and design priorities are changing the ways that cabinets are used.

For instance, fewer wall cabinets are being used. Advances in hardware for drawers and pullout trays have allowed base-cabinet space to be maximized, so there is less need for upper storage. In addition, kitchens in newer homes built with an open floor plan have less wall space and more windows. Also, the accessibility of base cabinets fits nicely with the movement toward "universal design" (designing homes for maximum usability by people of all ages and abilities). However, wall cabinets still play a major role in many kitchens, and if you have a small kitchen they are certainly essential. They also can be an important design element, such as when used with glass doors to show off your prettiest dishes.

Another change is an increase in the use of large drawers in base cabinets. Drawers have the edge in a lot of ways. They can handle heavy items, open and close with the touch of a finger, and take advantage of all usable space inside the cabinet. They also bring stored items into the light, where you can see them. Cabinets with doors, however, have a traditional look that many people like. They are ideal for storing large items and are well suited to pantry storage. No matter what cabinet configuration you choose, you'll find ways to maximize every inch of your kitchen on the following pages.

Left It's hard to allocate funds to the unglamorous interiors of your cabinets, but it may well be the best money you spend.

Maximizing Cabinet Storage

To get the most out of your cabinets, consider adding the following accessories:

- **Pullouts, also called rollout trays,** allow you to see and reach all items—no more forgetting about the ones stuck in the back. Some are made specifically for certain items, such as pots and lids, or food.
- **Two- or three-tier "stepped" organizers** can help keep small cans and jars in sight.
- Prevent gravy packets and other small items from getting lost by putting them in a **basket or plastic container**.
- Hang racks on the **inside of your doors** for easy access to small items.
- Take advantage of the vertical space in your cabinets by adding **helper shelves** that give you a second shelf above your existing one. These shelves help you avoid tall stacks of things—it's much easier to get to that serving bowl if you don't have six bowls stacked on top of it.
- For hard-to-reach spots (like over the fridge), there are **pull-down shelves** that bring contents down to your level and then fold back up again.

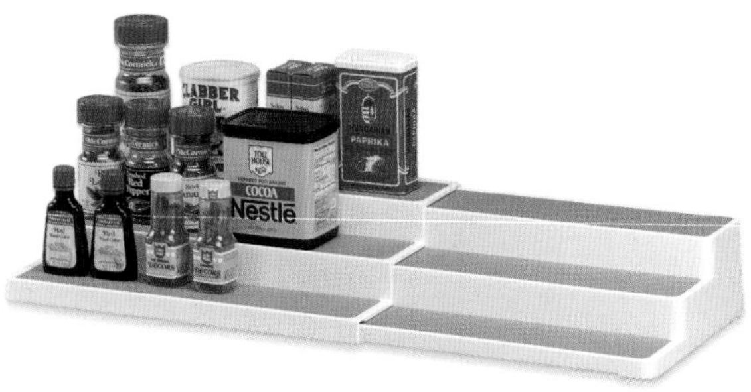

Opposite far left Tiered shelves for spices and other small containers may be used on a shelf or countertop. They are available at many home stores. This one expands to suit your needs.

Opposite top Pullout trays make the most of cabinet space because there is no need to allow clearance above stored items for access.

Opposite bottom Shallow racks mounted on the back of a cabinet door will improve access to stored items. Use such racks for small items to avoid putting too much weight on cabinet door hinges.

Top When storing related items, such as pots and their lids, it's easier to roll out a single tray-and-shelf unit than it is to open and close several pullouts.

Bottom These hinged shelves pivot open to allow access from two sides, which is ideal for organizing small items. With shelves that move or rotate, opt for guards to keep containers from getting knocked down if jarred.

Above Items on pull-down shelves are easy to reach when the shelf is in its down position. Guard rails help keep items from shifting.

Top right With a retracted pull-down shelf, there is a trade-off between easier access and loss of space for storage.

Bottom right Whenever possible, look to maximize your storage space. If you mount the pull-down shelf hardware higher in the wall cabinet, you may be able to use the cabinet's bottom shelf to store measuring cups, salt and pepper shakers, and other small items.

SMARTtip

Step Up to Storage

Upper shelves are often underutilized because they can't be easily reached. Investing in a quality step stool will help solve this problem. Many fold compactly and can be stored in narrow spaces. They can even be built into the toe kick under a base cabinet. Others roll on wheels, so you can slide them into a closet when they aren't needed. If you've got a small kitchen with high ceilings, you could even install a second row of wall cabinets above the first and use a rolling library ladder to reach them.

Top Helper shelves, which increase cabinet storage capacity, are available in many styles and materials. You can also make your own for almost no cost. (See page 58.)

Bottom Put your morning cereal at your fingertips with a slide-out bin. Slide-out bins are a great way to store paper goods, bags of pet food, and other bulky items, too.

More Wall-Cabinet Options

Top left Pullout racks put stored items at eye level and arm's reach. With this unit, access requires only a single pull. There's no need to swing open a door first.

Top right With this unit, you must open the door first. Once you have, though, the shelves rotate and pull out for complete, unobstructed visibility and easy access.

Bottom When planning a new kitchen, carefully consider how you will use the cabinetry. This unit combines shelves, door racks, drawers, and cubbies.

Opposite top left Cabinet doors that swing up are less likely to get in the way. Locking hinge hardware allows you to leave them open until your task is complete.

Opposite top right This built-in wine rack is just one of the many special features offered by cabinet manufacturers.

Opposite bottom left This lazy Susan pullout combo is similar to the unit shown top right, but the side panels may hinder visibility and access.

Opposite middle right Swing-out shelves are another way to improve access. Store backup supplies or items you don't use often on the rear shelves.

Opposite bottom right In situations where countertops aren't needed, tall wall cabinets with glass doors are a great way to store all sorts of cookware and dinnerware. They allow you to see and reach contents easily.

Maxwell House

Building a Helper Shelf

A helper shelf, also known as a half shelf, can increase both the capacity and accessibility of cabinets by providing two shelves in the place of one. Helper shelves can be made to any width but typically are used on one side of the cabinet only, keeping the other side free for taller items. This project uses a ½ x 8 x 12-inch (1.3 x 20.3 x 30.5cm) plywood shelf on two ¾ x 5½ x 8-inch (1.9 x 14 x 20.3cm) supports, but you can vary dimensions to suit your cabinet. If you use plywood for your project, use iron-on edging to conceal the edges.

1. To attach edging, apply heat with an iron and immediately apply pressure with a block of wood. Although not shown here, it's a good idea to put aluminum foil between the iron and edging to prevent scorching. Clamp in place for support.

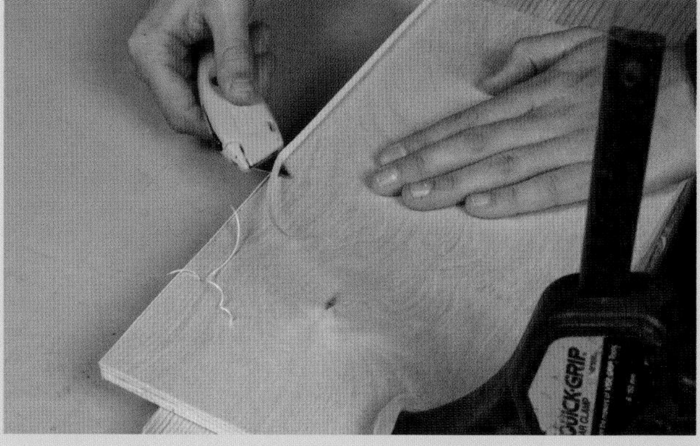

2. Trim excess veneer with a utility knife and finish the edge with a sanding block for an invisible joint. Once again, it's wise to clamp your workpiece to a table or workbench.

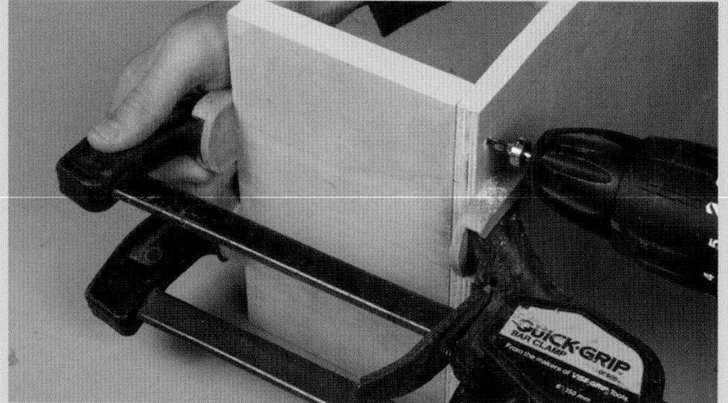

3. With the shelf clamped to the sides, drill pilot holes for screws using a countersink bit.

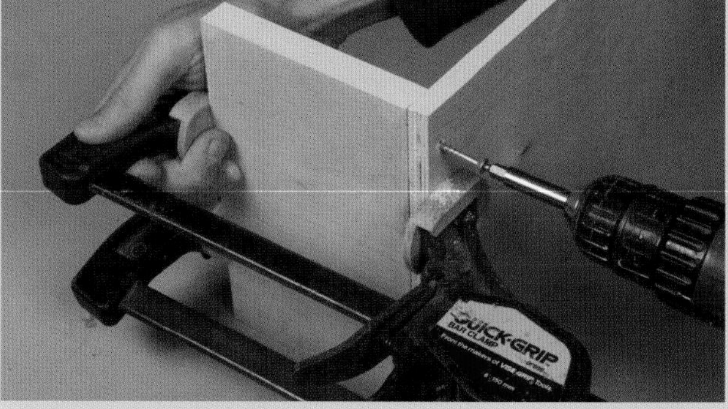

4. Attach the pieces with 1½-in. (40mm) flathead screws. For an extra-strong joint, apply carpenter's glue prior to driving the screws.

Building a Tiered Shelf

Tiered shelves don't increase the storage capacity of cabinets, but they will make it easier to see and access the canned goods you have. The shelf heights in the version shown are 1¾ and 4¼ inches (4.5 and 10.8cm) tall. When cutting to length, each shelf should be ⅛ inch (0.3cm) less than the cabinet width or you may not be able to maneuver the assembly into position.

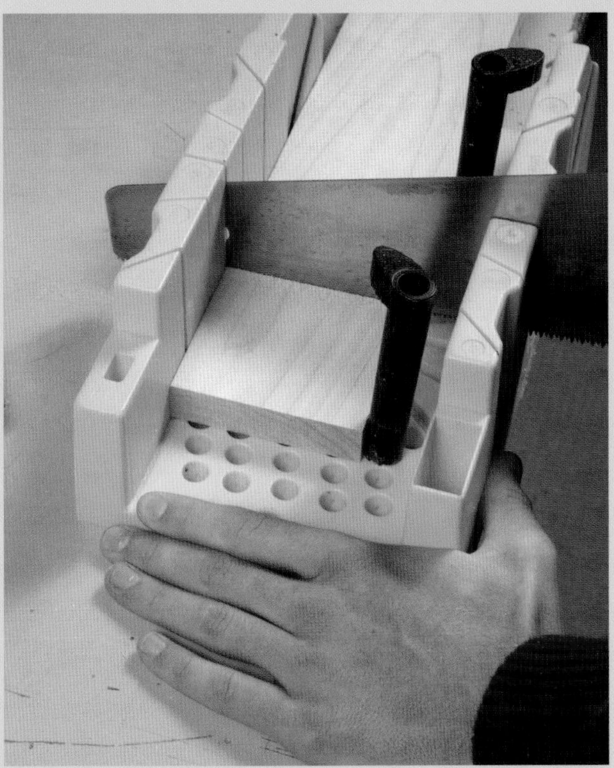

1. After measuring the width of the cabinet and determining the height you want for the shelf, cut the pieces to length. The miter box ensures square cuts.

2. Using a pneumatic nailer or hammer, nail the shelves to the supports. Applying glue will ensure a long-lasting joint but is not necessary because the shelves won't be subject to lateral stress.

Base Cabinets

Base cabinets have come a long way in the past 10 years or so. The growing availability of heavy-duty full-extension drawer slides, pullout pantries, and corner-cabinet solutions means that even budget-minded remodelers can have cabinets that maximize every inch of space. Another great thing about base cabinets is that all members of the family, from children to the elderly, can reach what's inside.

Base cabinets are getting bigger, too. There's no rule about needing to stick with standard 24-inch-deep (60cm-deep) units. Some homeowners and designers are opting for deeper, 30-inch (75cm) base cabinets. In return for 6 inches (15cm) of floor space, you get significantly bigger base-cabinet drawers and shelves. Your countertops get deeper, too—with more than enough space for canisters, countertop appliances, large carving boards, and more.

If you're buying new cabinets, take full advantage of base-cabinet options—even if it means cutting your budget in other areas. Buy fewer upper cabinets or select a less-expensive countertop material. Fancy granite countertops won't do you much good if you spend frustrating minutes each day trying to find things that are buried in the back of dark cabinets. If you are reorganizing an existing kitchen, there are plenty of after-market kits available to add pullouts, lazy Susans, and other organizers to your cabinets.

Right **In new kitchens, maximizing base-cabinet space and focusing less on above-countertop space is the trend.**

Right In this kitchen, oven-side drawers are ideal for storing oils.

Opposite top Drawers have even staked claim to new territories. These angle-fronted units use most of the space that's buried in the corner. Closed, the drawers look like any others.

Opposite bottom Drawers have their advantages, but opt for some open shelves, too, especially ones combined with vertical storage, as shown under the cooktop in this kitchen.

SMARTtip

Wood Sizes

When shopping for lumber, know that that actual thickness and width dimensions are smaller than nominal sizes, whether in imperial measurements or metric measurements. Boards described as 1 inch thick are actually ¾ inch thick, while lumber described as 2 inches thick measures 1½ inches thick. Nominal widths up to 6 inches are actually ½ inch narrower, while nominal widths of 8 inches or more are ¾ inch narrower. For example, a nominal 1x4 (25x100mm) measures ¾ inches by 3½ inches (19 x 89mm), while a 2x10 (50x250mm) measures 1½ inches by 9¼ inches (38 x 235mm).

Drawer Options

When selecting drawers for your kitchen, consider what you want to store in them. Wide, shallow drawers are good for utensils and other kitchen gadgets. Avoid deep drawers for these items because they will just end up piled on top of one another. On the other hand, deep drawers are perfect for pots and pans, dishes, or small appliances. Make extensive use of adjustable drawer dividers or dish caddies to keep items separated. Drawer inserts can help you establish one specific spot for each knife, ladle, or spice jar. (Select inserts that are dishwasher safe for easy cleaning.) Adjustable pegs and pegboard inserts work well for storing dishes. If you have old drawers that don't pull out all the way, look into replacing the drawer boxes with new ones that will accommodate full-extension slides. You should be able to reuse your old drawer fronts.

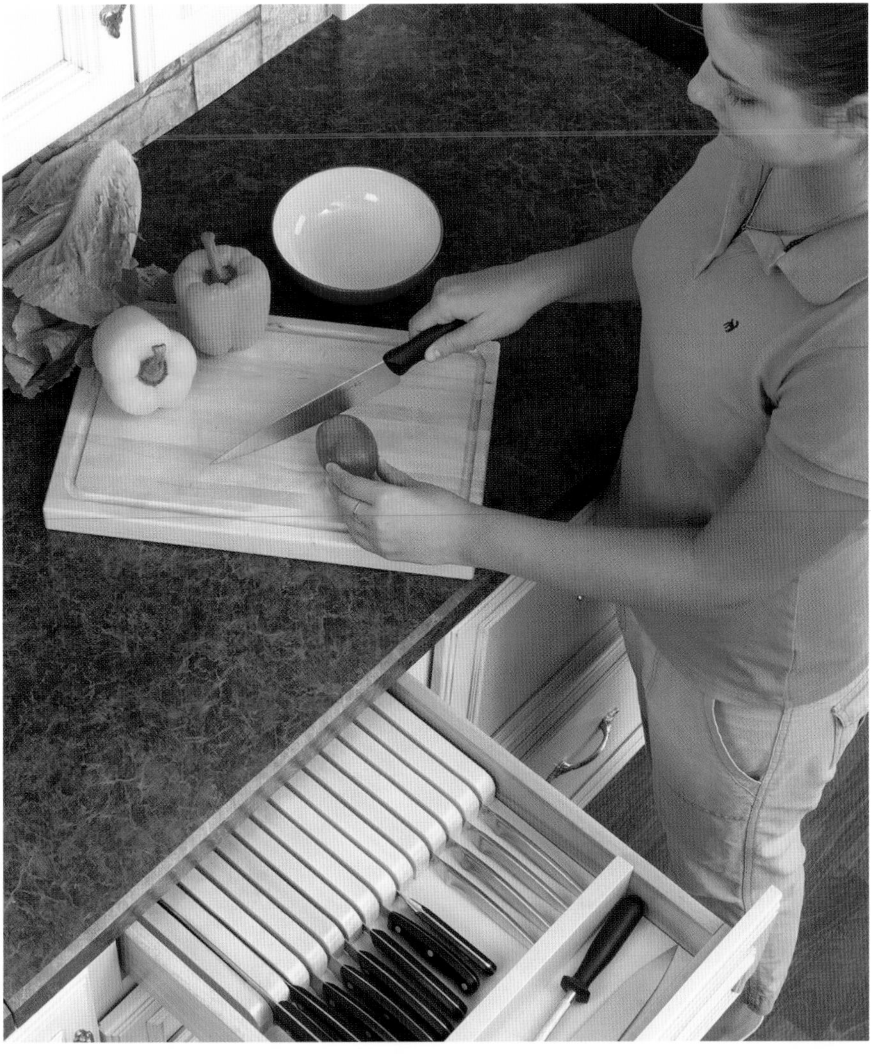

Opposite Plastic organizer inserts are the easiest to keep clean. Simply remove the insert and wash it in the sink.

Top Shallow drawers are ideal for knives and carving tools. Some come with just enough space to store a cutting board, too.

Bottom Many designers recommend solid drawer sides and fronts. For the dividers and drawer bottom, however, you may opt for medium-density fiberboard (MDF) covered on all sides with melamine (a tough resin laminate). It will ease cleanup in case of a spill.

SMARTtip

Adding the Soft Touch

When you push a soft-closing drawer, it slows just before closing completely, preventing the drawer from noisily slamming shut and adding a touch of luxury to your kitchen. You can order soft-closing drawers if you are installing new cabinets. There is also soft-closing hardware that can be easily and inexpensively retrofitted to existing drawers.

Top-Drawer Drawers

Above Aftermarket drawer inserts are available in many materials and sizes, including expandable units.

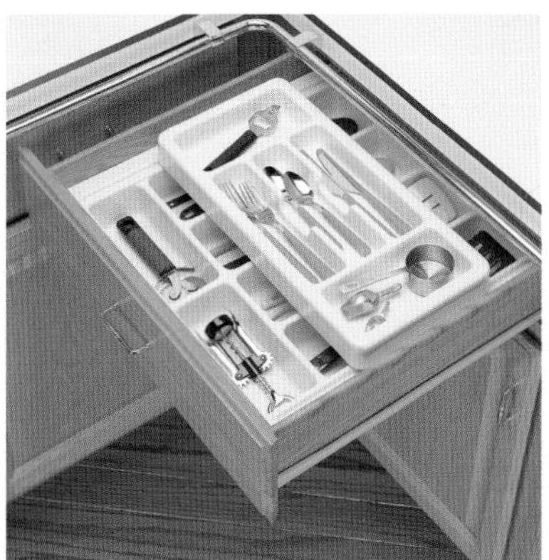

Top A two-tier knife rack stores more knives in the same space than a conventional knife holder.

Middle left Many cooks prefer a spice drawer to keep seasonings at their fingertips. Keep the labels visible to reduce the amount of time spent searching for the thyme!

Middle right Drawers with built-in wire organizers allow good visibility of stored items. They also weigh less than wood or fiberboard drawers, making them easier to open.

Bottom left Scallop-shaped cutouts in dividers make it easier to grasp flatware.

Bottom right Two-tier drawer organizers allow you to store more in a drawer *and* to keep it organized.

Building a Drawer Organizer

Some designers recommend waiting until you've moved into your kitchen to decide how to organize your drawers. If you heed their suggestions and don't buy drawer organizers already built in, adding them later is easy—and less costly if you make them yourself. You can make organizers to suit your exact needs using ½ x 2-inch (1.3 x 5cm) pine strips. As a bonus, the dividers will solve a common problem with many inexpensive drawers: sagging drawer bottoms. The insert acts as a stiffener once it's installed with screws.

1. Cut stock ½ x 2-in. (1.3 x 5cm) pine, sold at most home centers, to length using a miter box and handsaw (shown), or with a miter saw.

2. Assemble the pieces with glue and 1-in (2.5cm) brads. Wipe off excess glue immediately using a damp cloth. Apply a coat of water-based (acrylic) varnish before installation.

3. Place the assembly in the drawer, and mark its location as shown. Remove the insert, and drill three holes for the mounting screws between your marks.

4. Attach the organizer using three 1-in. (2.5cm) flathead screws driven through predrilled holes in the drawer bottom. Use a block of scrap wood to hold the insert tight against the bottom while installing the screws.

FLORIDA GRAPEFRUIT

Big Base Drawers

Top The dish holders in this drawer keep dishes from sliding. They also make it easy to lift the stack out of the drawer and onto a counter when it's time to set the table.

Bottom The narrow dividers at the front of this drawer hold lids for the corresponding cookware stowed behind them.

Top left Simple drawer dividers can also be used to keep dishes and small appliances corralled.

Bottom left This two-for-one configuration includes a pullout and a deep drawer.

Top right Deep, wide base-cabinet drawers are great, but don't forget the dividers. They'll keep contents from becoming a jumble.

Bottom right Put a deep drawer fitted with stainless-steel wire dish racks next to your dishwasher to speed the chore of unloading dishes.

Opposite top left The pegs in this drawer can be rearranged to accommodate the various sizes and shapes of your dishes. They prevent plates and bowls from shifting and being damaged when you open and close the drawer.

Opposite top right The sliding Plexiglas top on this bread drawer lets you see what you have on hand without sliding the top back.

Opposite bottom Don't need a lot of bread storage? Opt for an insert like this one. It's shallow enough to store other items beneath it.

Top left The plastic top on this bread drawer has a sliding lid for access.

Top right This bread drawer is lined with stainless steel on all sides, making it easy to clean.

Bottom right Two tiers turn this base drawer into a wine cabinet.

Pullout Trays

Top Large pullout trays are especially suited to storing large pots, pans, and their lids.

Bottom Base cabinets do much more than they used to in the past. This one is fitted out as a pantry, with door racks, adjustable shelves, and pullout trays.

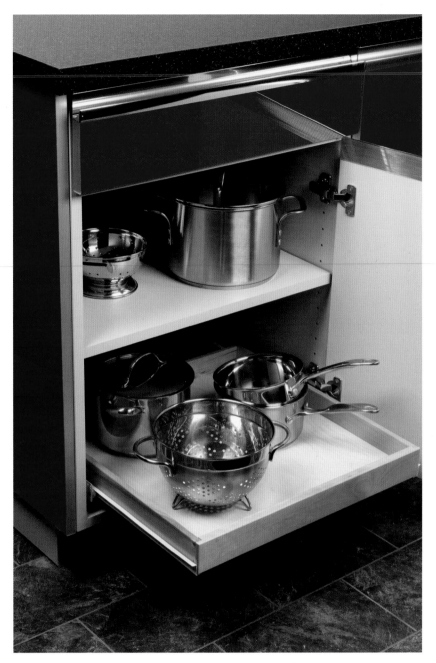

Top left Opening this unit is a one-step operation, as opposed to standard pullouts, which require you to fully open the cabinet door before you can draw them out.

Bottom left Guardrails are a must on pullouts. They keep stored items from slipping off the edge and crashing to the floor.

Right Opt for adjustability when installing pullout trays. If your storage needs change, it will be easy to change tray heights.

Top In wide cabinets, divide trays in halves or thirds (as shown) so you don't have to open two doors to gain access.

Bottom Wire trays are sturdy and can be customized for storing everything from large mixing bowls and colanders to soda cans and spice containers.

Top Some stainless-steel wire units come with vertical dividers for storing trays, cookie sheets, and pot lids.

Bottom left Guardrails can be decorative, as shown on these pullout trays.

Bottom right Pullout trays are ideal for storing plastic food containers. Include an organizer to store the lids.

Retrofitting a Pullout Tray

Adding two pullout trays—sometimes referred to as simply pullouts or rollout trays—vastly improves the capacity and accessibility of any base cabinet. It's a simple project that even a novice do-it-yourselfer can tackle with success. Order trays exactly 1 inch (2.5cm) narrower and about an inch (2.5cm) shorter than the cabinet opening, or build your own. Note that some cabinet doors, when open, project slightly into the opening. If that is the case, order a tray width that will clear the doors, and then use shims (visible in photo 2 below) as necessary.

1. With the mounting bracket on the slide and resting on the cabinet shelf, level the bracket and mark the front edge. Note: for a pullout tray at the bottom of the cabinet, the rear bracket will rest on the cabinet floor.

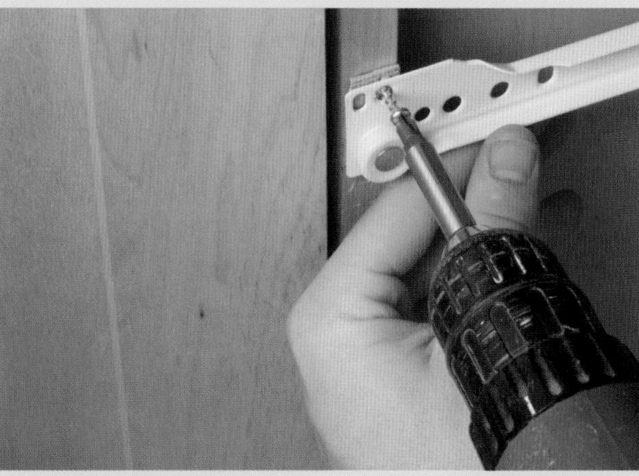

2. To attach the slide to the stile, drill pilot holes and drive two mounting screws. In this case, a shim was required to allow the tray to clear the cabinet door. The shim was tacked on with a brad before the slide was attached.

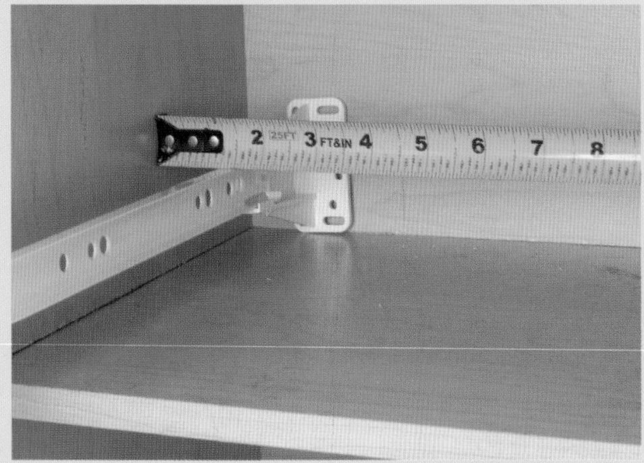

3. Measure the distance from the side of the cabinet to the slide at the front, and then adjust the position of the rear bracket so it is the same distance from the side before securing it to the cabinet back with screws.

4. Attach the other halves of the slide to the bottom edges of the tray, with the front (the nonroller end) of the slide flush with the front of the tray.

Pantry Cabinets

Almost all kitchens end up with narrow cabinets in some spots, and these used to be hard to use for storage of anything other than cookie sheets. Pullout pantries are a wonderful way to put these narrow spaces to work. A pullout pantry is basically a tall, narrow drawer (usually 9 to 15 inches [23 to 38cm] wide) with long, narrow shelves inside, ideal for storing dry goods. A more traditional pantry cabinet with doors usually consists of shelves on the inside of the doors, plus either pullout wire shelves or foldout wooden shelves inside. The key is that each shelf is narrow so all items can be seen and food doesn't get lost in the back. Both types of pantries are usually available as base cabinets or tall cabinets meant to match the height of your refrigerator or upper cabinets. Full-height lazy-Susan systems are also available for corners.

Above Tall, deep pantry cabinets with lots of shelves are perfect for storing canned goods, dry goods, and bottles of all sizes.

Top left A pullout pantry, sometimes called a pullout spine, has several advantages: one-pull opening, excellent use of available space, and good visibility of stored items. You may, however, have to walk from one side of the pantry to the other to find what you need.

Top right This high-performance pantry cabinet has adjustable shelves and pullouts.

Bottom Strive for a balance of shelves, pullouts, and drawers in your kitchen plan.

Opposite top right Pantry cabinets can be used for storing cookware, too. This unit has two sets of door shelves and two sets of foldout shelves.

Opposite bottom right Looking for the ice bucket? Pivot either hinged shelf to gain access to the fixed shelves at the rear of the pantry cabinet.

Above A pantry cabinet that is used for storing large items, especially in significant quantities, doesn't require expensive pullout hardware. Deep shelves work just fine.

Top right Wire pantry shelves make it easy to see what you have on hand.

Middle right A wire "ladder" fastened to the cabinet door accepts wire shelves for small items. To prevent cabinet doors from sagging, do not overload them.

Bottom right Tall pantry pullouts can become very heavy. Divide the spine into two—top and bottom—to avoid problems created by excessive weight.

Top left Full-height pantry pullouts are possible, but make sure the hardware is going to meet your load demands—and fit your budget.

Top right This pantry cabinet setup offers more storage options. Keep smaller items in the wire baskets where you can see them, and put heavy items in the wooden bins.

Bottom left Pantry cabinets can fit under the counter, too. This one boasts both pullout shelves and trays.

Corner Cabinets

Corner cabinets are spaces that are notoriously difficult to use, but there are some decent options to help you maximize them. Lazy Susans are a good solution if your corner-cabinet footprint is fairly square (as opposed to rectangular) and the cabinet door is in the corner (not off to one side). Corners that are set at a 45-degree angle can take best advantage of the space with a full-circle, pie-cut, or D-shaped lazy Susan. One drawback to lazy Susans is that they make it difficult to clean the cabinet or to reach things that fall off in the back. (Opt for one with shelf sides at least an inch [2.5cm] high to help prevent that.) They are also best suited for smaller items such as food or spices because the post in the middle prevents larger items from fitting. Lazy Susans get a lot of wear and tear, so choose a heavy-duty one that is built to last.

If you don't like the idea of a lazy Susan, another option for cabinets with a corner door is an "easy reach" cabinet. Its large door opening and two fixed L-shaped shelves make it easier to see and reach items in the back. It is ideal if you wish to store oversized items such as large bowls or pots. Drawers are also possible in the corner. They work best in 45-degree corners, but some cabinet manufacturers offer 90-degree corner drawers. You lose some of the space in the back, but if you need more drawers in that particular area of the kitchen, they may be your best choice.

The other type of corner cabinet is a rectangular "blind" cabinet (where the cabinet door is on one side of the corner or the other). A good, though pricey, solution is a blind cabinet pullout system. This usually involves two upper baskets and two lower baskets that pull out and then slide over so that you can reach the contents of each one. Because the baskets are rectangular, they make excellent use of space in a blind cabinet. However, you are depending on a rather complex mechanism, so be sure you have a good warranty. A less-expensive option (though it doesn't maximize space as efficiently) is a half-circle (also called a "half moon") lazy Susan.

Above (all) It used to be difficult to make good use of space in a corner, but no longer. Innovative corner-cabinet hardware brings stored items into the light with a few pulls and tugs. Open the door, and slide out the first pair of shelves. Push that unit to the left, and then pull out the second pair of shelves.

Top left Want to keep it simple? Use angled, open shelves instead of a corner wall cabinet.

Bottom left Another approach is to angle the corner base and wall cabinets, as shown here. It sacrifices some cabinet space but gives you a bit more counter space—and everything is easily accessible.

Top right Half-circle lazy Susans are one of the more elegant solutions for utilizing buried corner space. They don't use every inch of available space but are far less costly than the expensive pullout shown opposite. (See pages 86–87 for more lazy Susan options.)

Bottom right Pull and pivot the first shelf unit to where you can reach stored items, and then slide the shelves buried in the corner into view.

Lazy Susan Options

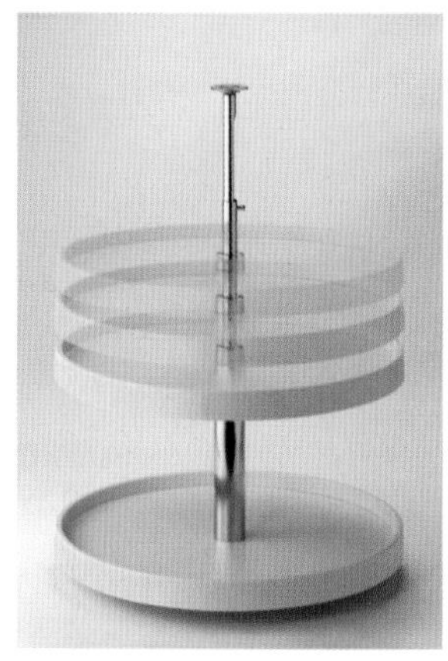

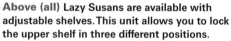

Above (all) Lazy Susans are available with adjustable shelves. This unit allows you to lock the upper shelf in three different positions.

Top right When this lazy Susan rotates, the cabinet door, which is affixed to the shelves, rotates as well.

Bottom right Bin-style lazy Susans hold contents securely. The bins are mounted on the shelves—there's no center post to get in your way.

Left D-shaped lazy Susan shelves are designed to maximize 45-degree corner-cabinet situations.

Below The D-shaped lazy Susan shelves look like this.

Above Pie-cut lazy Susans optimize the space in a 90-degree corner. Detents stop the rotation in the position shown, allowing the bifold door to close.

Above Half-circle lazy Susans are also available with vinyl-coated wire shelves.

Sink Cabinets

Storing items under the sink is often challenging because of the plumbing there, the possibility of leaks, and the need for access to make the occasional but inevitable repair. Quarter-round shelving in the rear corners is helpful but not so easy to reach. A U-shaped pullout tray that fits below or around the pipes is better. If necessary, be sure that it's easy to remove for access to valves. A low-tech solution is a pair of cleaner caddies. You can devote one to supplies for cleaning windows, counters, and appliance surfaces and the other to tougher jobs such as floors and ovens. Of all the storage spaces in a kitchen, sink cabinets typically contain the most hazardous substances. If there are young children in your life, buy safety locks for the doors. There are several varieties, most of which are inexpensive and effective.

Above A drawer at the bottom of an under-sink cabinet is a good way to deal with a difficult-to-utilize space.

Above Bring cleaners and detergents into the open with a U-shaped pullout.

Below This full-extension unit can be installed in less than an hour with minimal skills and basic tools. The cutout portion of the tray accommodates the plumbing.

Top Quarter-round shelves and adjustable racks on the door make the most of the space under this sink.

Bottom left Simple plastic bins offer a low-cost solution for storing cleaning products.

Bottom right A bottom-mounted tray lets you pull cleaning supplies to within easy reach. Dish towels slide forward, too.

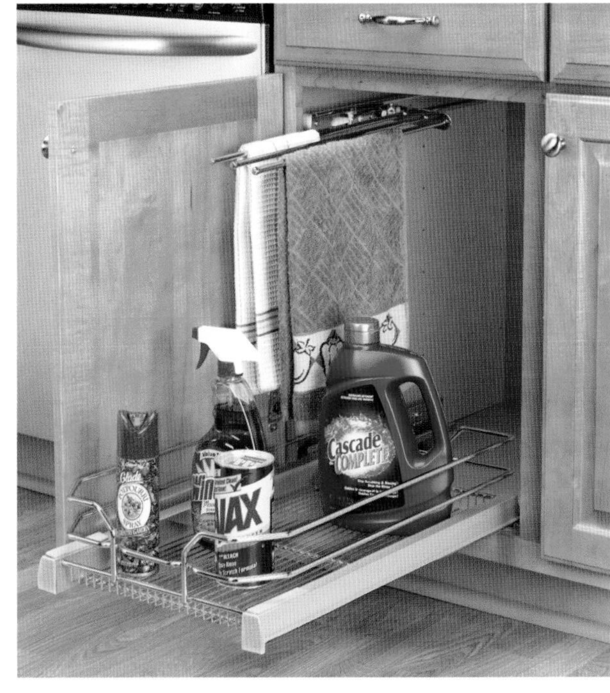

Kitchen Islands

Kitchen islands are, at their simplest, a grouping of base cabinets or shelving units with a countertop. Their design, however, can be much more elaborate. Islands can incorporate snack bars, kitchen offices, sinks, and any number of appliances. When considering an island for your kitchen, think about how your decisions can improve storage and organization. Moving a cooktop to an island, for example, will free counter space and wall space (previously devoted to the exhaust hood) near the range. Installing a sink or an under-counter microwave will also mean relief for perimeter counter space. Placement of the island is important, too. You'll want island storage close to the kitchen activity areas it supports.

Many islands can be made deep enough or long enough so you can have cabinets or drawers on one side and shelves on the other—an ideal place to store your cookbooks or to build in a kitchen office. In a small kitchen, consider an island on wheels to add storage and counter space where you need it. Park it out of the way when it's not in use. Whatever design you settle on, be sure to include towel bars and hooks for dish towels and potholders. Also include outlets so you can run your waffle iron and other countertop appliances without resorting to an extension cord.

Opposite top Islands are a great place to snack, but don't underestimate their storage potential. This island includes cabinets, drawers, and a cart garage.

Opposite bottom Six large drawers on each side of this island provide an enormous amount of storage in this contemporary kitchen.

Top Shaped to accommodate traffic flow, this island houses the microwave, provides plenty of storage, and serves as a snack bar.

Bottom Clever under-counter shelves, drawers, and cabinets make this island versatile enough to store a wide variety of items, including mugs, cups, and dishware.

Islands that Store

Left Islands and peninsulas, such as the one seen here, can also house wine cellars and other under-counter appliances.

Top The side of an island that faces away from the kitchen's work area can be used to house your culinary library.

Bottom Kitchen islands range from simple units to far more elaborate designs. This unit with a single shelf and a couple of drawers is a good example of a simple yet functional island.

Above This island, which includes storage at both ends, is a perfect spot for informal meals. The built-in wine rack, liquor cabinet, and bar sink make it a beverage center when entertaining.

Top This slightly more complex island includes two large cabinets installed back to back, end shelves, and a countertop overhang large enough for two people to sit comfortably.

Bottom The open shelves of this two-level island display decorative cookware, while the raised countertop keeps the sink area out of sight.

Island Details for a Custom Look

Above Built from ten cabinets, this large island can house a majority of your cookware and dishware.

Top Kitchen cabinet manufacturers allow you to customize your kitchen island with stock or semi-custom components, ranging from the simple shelving shown here to more elaborate components.

Bottom This kitchen island add-on provides an off-the-countertop home for a microwave.

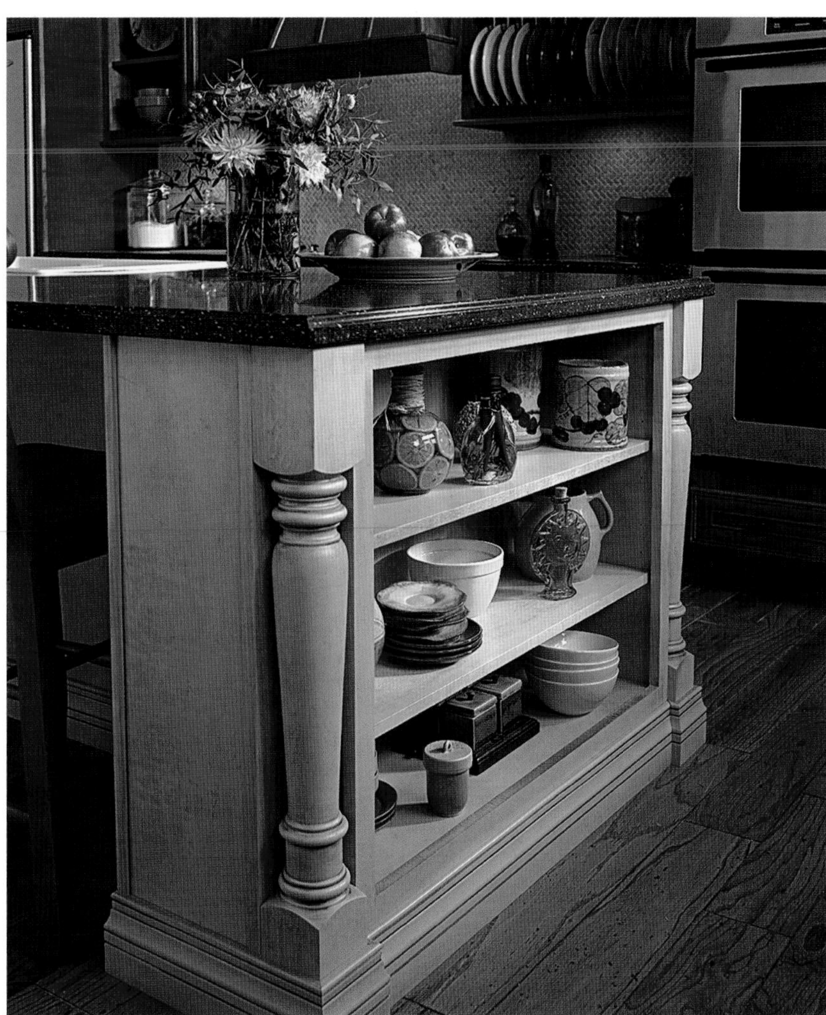

Opposite Drawers are a natural for kitchens—but only if opening them doesn't create a traffic jam.

Top Islands, which have become the focal point of many kitchens, are the obvious choice for displaying pottery or serving pieces.

Bottom left Even a shallow space can offer useful storage, as the end of this island proves.

Bottom right Pullout baskets and a tier of countertop cubbies are other ways to improve your island's storage.

Buying Cabinets

You can buy cabinets in four ways.

Knockdown cabinets are packed flat and unassembled, so you can drive them home. Styles, materials, and finishes are limited, but cost is low.

Stock cabinets are manufactured in standard sizes. (See the chart at right.) They are usually available for shipment within days of placing your order. They can also be purchased at home centers if you have a truck to get them home. Styles and finishes are limited, but costs are usually less than semi-custom or custom cabinets. Many accessories can be retrofitted to improve performance.

Semi-custom cabinets are built in standard sizes but come in a variety of styles, materials, and finishes. Some modifications to size may be possible. Many also come with built-in accessories, such as rollouts and tilt-out trays. Semi-custom cabinets must be ordered well ahead of time.

Custom cabinets are typically built in local cabinet shops. You can specify nonstandard sizes and choose materials and accessories. Such cabinets offer the greatest design flexibility, but the custom approach is typically the most expensive option.

Standard Cabinet Dimensions (in inches)

Cabinet	Width	Height	Depth
Base unit	9–48 (in 3-in. increments)	34 ½	24
Drawer base	12–30, 36 (in 3-in. increments)	34 ½	24
Sink base	18–48 (in 3-in. increments)	34 ½	24
Blind corner base	27–48 (in 3-in. increments)	34 ½	24
Corner base	36–48 (in 3-in. increments)	34 ½	24
Drop-in range base	18–48 (in 3-in. increments)	34 ½	24
Wall unit	9–48 (in 3-in. increments)	12–18, 24, 30	12, 13
Tall cabinet (oven, pantry, broom)	18–36 (in 3-in. increments)	84, 90, 96	12–24

Standard cabinet dimensions may vary in your country and/or be measured in metric units.

Common Cabinet Types

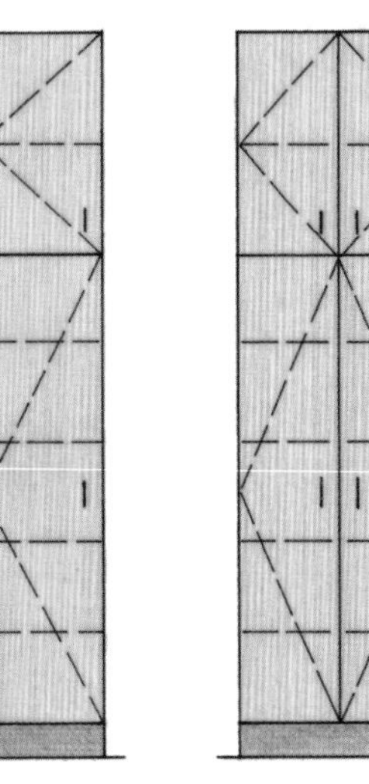

Utility

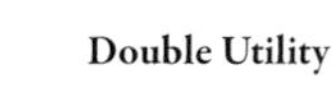

Double Utility

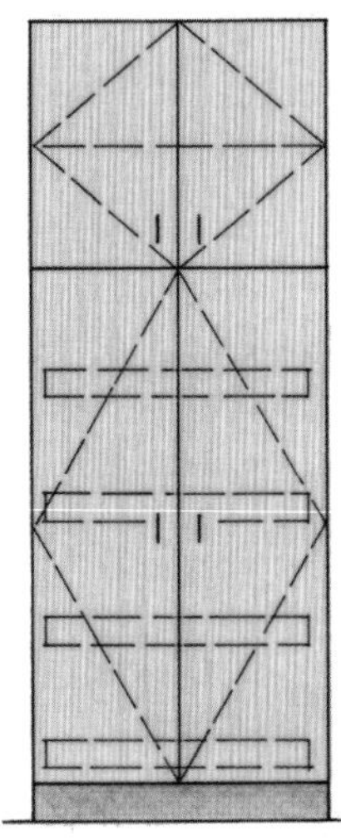

Pantry with Rollouts

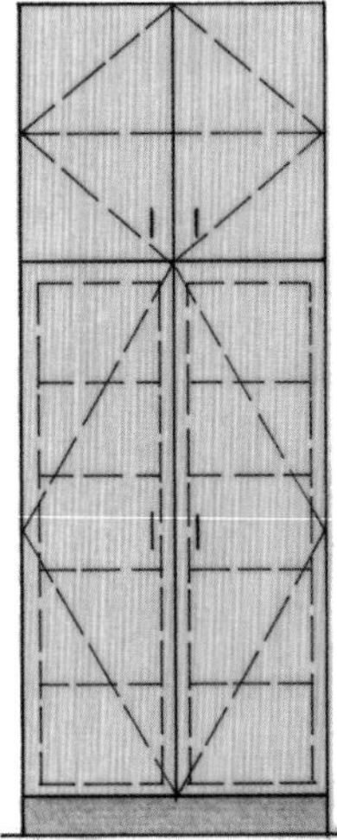

Pantry

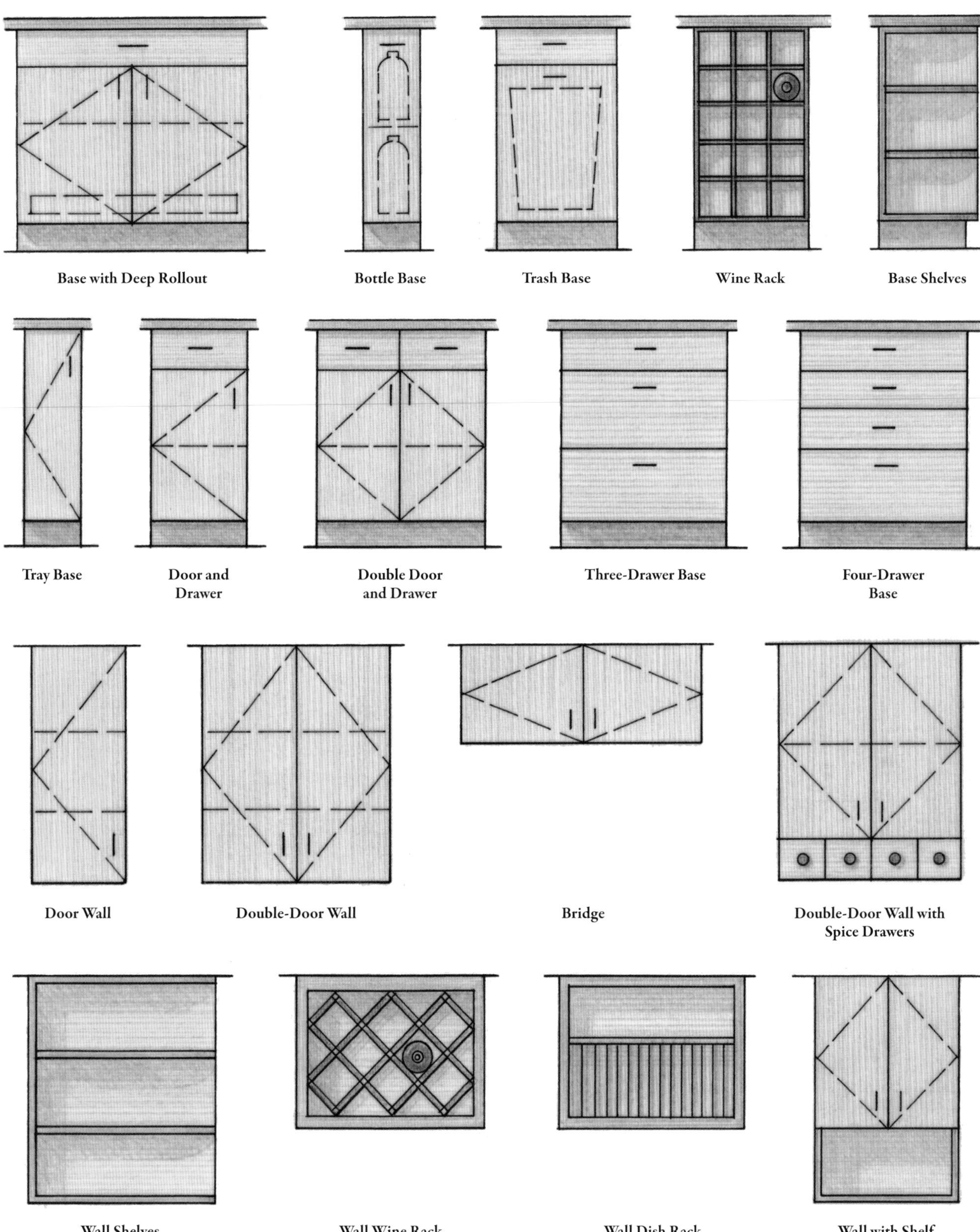
Base with Deep Rollout
Bottle Base
Trash Base
Wine Rack
Base Shelves
Tray Base
Door and Drawer
Double Door and Drawer
Three-Drawer Base
Four-Drawer Base
Door Wall
Double-Door Wall
Bridge
Double-Door Wall with Spice Drawers
Wall Shelves
Wall Wine Rack
Wall Dish Rack
Wall with Shelf

Left Raised-panel doors and drawer fronts are typically used in traditional-style kitchens with framed cabinets. The doors are made of wood, and the hinges may be exposed or concealed.

Right Flush door panels and drawer fronts are typically used with frameless cabinets. They may be made of plywood or composition board (also called fiberboard) covered on all sides with a laminate. The hinges are concealed.

SMARTtip

Cure Shelf Sag

Even ¾-inch-thick (2cm-thick) composition board shelves may eventually sag in a wide cabinet. To fix the problem, measure the distance between the shelf and the shelf bracket and cut two strips of ¼ x 1-inch (0.6 x 2.5cm) wood to that length. Attach one to the cabinet back and the other to the inside of the center stile. Together, they will prevent the shelf from sagging. Use double-sided tape to attach the wood strips so they can be easily removed if you change the shelf height.

Wide shelves made of composition board are likely to deflect under heavy loads. Make these simple shelf supports to solve the problem.

Assessing Cabinet Quality

Quality cabinets are made with durable, long-lasting materials, such as solid wood, plywood (covered with hardwood veneer or plastic laminate), better grades of composition board (also called fiberboard), and stainless steel. In general, the more solid wood or high-grade plywood, the better. High-density polymers and medium-density fiberboard (MDF) can also produce a good cabinet, but only if used properly. Avoid cabinets with face frames (rails and stiles), shelving, backs, or drawer bottoms made with particleboard. Instead, choose solid wood for the face frames and plywood or MDF for the rest.

Joints are crucial to cabinet durability. The best drawers have dovetailed drawer fronts and bottoms set into grooves in solid wood sides. With MDF, look for recessed mechanical fasteners that securely lock the joints together when they're tightened with a wrench or screwdriver. Composition boards joined with screws and staples are susceptible to failure.

Whenever possible, opt for adjustable shelves, adjustable pullout trays, and adjustable lazy-Susan shelves. You will be able to customize heights to suit your storage needs. Also, choose full-extension drawer slides over the standard-extension slides that only allow you to see and get access to 75 percent of your drawer space.

Obviously, few homeowners are qualified to assess cabinet quality while examining cabinets in a showroom. That's where the Kitchen Cabinet Manufacturers Association (KCMA) steps in. It tests cabinets for compliance with standards developed by the American National Standards Institute. The KCMA certification seal ensures that the cabinet you're purchasing meets construction and materials criteria and has passed performance tests for loading, joint tightness, impact resistance, finish wearability, hinge and drawer operation, and the like.

Above It's worth spending a bit extra for full-extension, heavy-duty drawer hardware, especially when using drawers for heavy loads.

Above Dovetail drawer joints give cabinetry the look of fine furniture and are strong and durable.

Places for Pots and Pans

Pots and pans are big and bulky and tend to take up a lot of space. In addition, it seems like the lid you need is always the one that is hiding in the back under all the rest. If you're short on cabinet space, hanging pots and pans from a pot rack may be your best bet. But if you want to store them in your cabinets, there are ways to help keep them better organized:

- Some **pullout trays** are specifically made for pots and pans. They usually have a large shelf or two for the pots and smaller spaces designed to hold the lids.
- If you like the idea of hanging pots but don't want them out for all to see, consider **hanging them inside a large cabinet**. You can run a towel bar across the top and hang pans and lids from S-hooks.
- **Wire cookware organizers** can be added to drawers or shelves. They are designed to hold saucepans and lids.
- Small pans can hang from hooks on the **inside of cabinet doors**.
- **Lids can also hang** on the inside of cabinet doors in a lid rack.
- **Keep only your frequently used items** in the prime cabinet space near the stove.
- **Find alternative locations** (such as a closet) for storing extra-large pots that can eat up a lot of cabinet room.

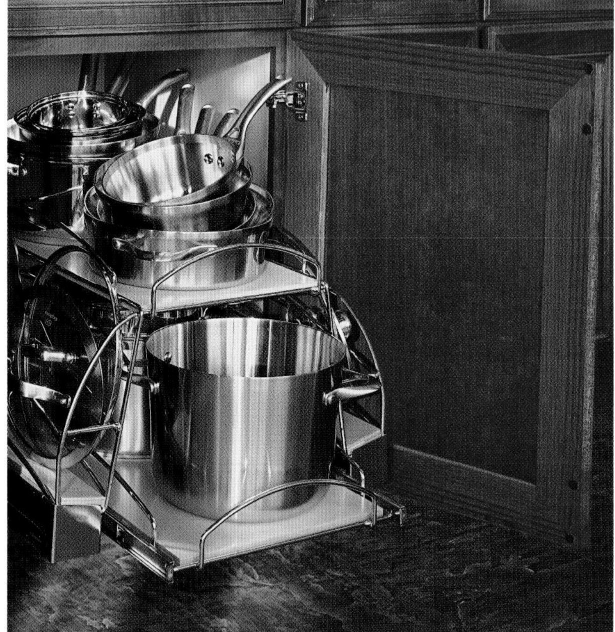

Above A pair of rollouts spaced as shown can store an entire collection of pots and pans. This is fine for a kitchen short on space, but if you can, use larger rollouts so you won't ever have to hassle with getting a pan from the bottom of a pile.

Bottom left Several manufacturers offer racks specifically made for pots, pans, and lids.

Bottom right Opt for high guardrails to keep pots from spilling over the edge.

SMARTtip

Space-Saving Containers

If you stack nonstick pots or pans, place a paper towel or paper plate between them so they don't scratch each other. Throw out any nonstick pans where the coating is scratched or peeling.

Top This drawer puts cookware close to the countertop, where it's easier to reach than when stored in a cabinet or hanging overhead from a pot rack.

Middle You can purchase pan and lid racks as aftermarket accessories from home-improvement stores.

Bottom left This pullout for lids slides out from under the cabinet shelving (removed for photo clarity).

Bottom right Two large rollouts are ideal for storing all of the pots, pans, and lids used in most kitchens. Locate them near where you use them or near where they get washed and dried.

Bakeware and Serving Pieces

Cookie sheets, muffin tins, cutting boards, and serving platters aren't much easier to store than pots and pans. Try the following to help keep them from overwhelming your cabinet space:

- Focus on the **items you use frequently**. Many items are only used in the five weeks between Thanksgiving and New Year's Day—they should not be taking up prime cabinet space all year long.
- **Tray dividers** allow you to store trays and platters on their side, which takes up a lot less horizontal space and lets you grab one without having to move the others.
- **Narrow cabinets**, as well as pullout drawers designed for "filler" spaces where cabinets meet walls and appliances, are also good spots to store trays.
- **Toe kick drawers**, though not ideal, can be used to store trays lying flat.
- Large serving bowls and platters are often pretty enough that they can be **stored in view**, such as on top of upper cabinets (though they will collect grease and dust).
- **An "easy reach" corner cabinet** is another good spot for oversized items.

Left Rollouts with tapered sides make it easy to see and remove cutting boards and cookie sheets but prevent these items from toppling.

Opposite left Inexpensive vinyl-coated wire dividers can be screwed to the base of any cabinet, preferably a narrow one with little other practical use.

Opposite middle Some rollouts will allow you to adjust divider widths to suit your vertical storage needs.

Opposite right Holders for large, flat items can be fastened to the inside of a cabinet door.

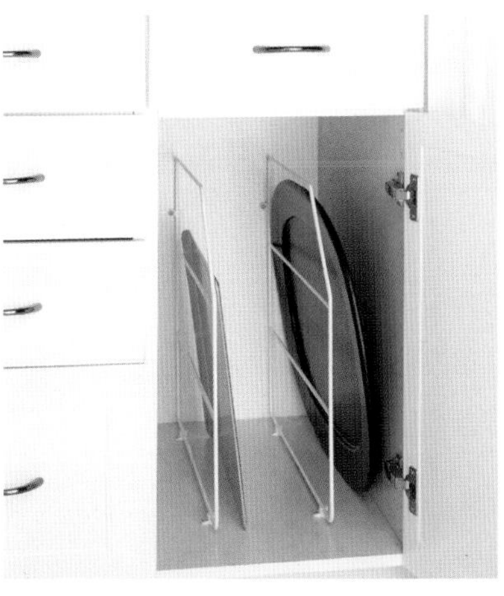

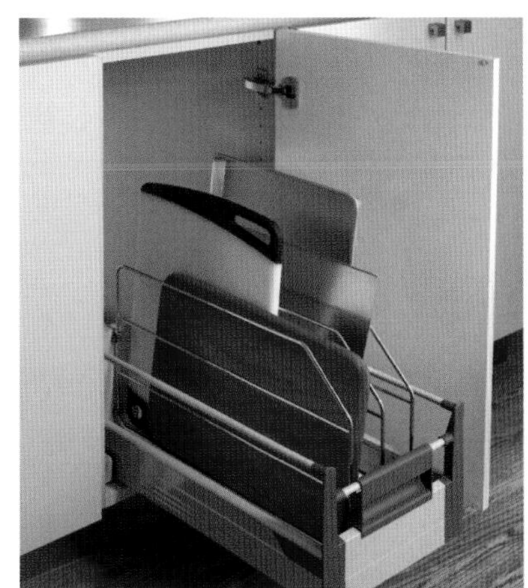

Making Tray or Lid Holders

An easy-to-build dowel rack makes it simple to access items that are best stored vertically. The base is made from ¾ x 1-inch (2 x 2.5cm) pieces of wood, cut to desired length, and ½-inch (1.3cm) dowels. The vertical dowels are spaced 1½ inches (3.8cm) apart, which is good for platters and cutting boards. For muffin tins and cake pans, use wider spacing. The rack can sit on a counter, atop a fridge, or in a cabinet.

1. A doweling jig ensures that holes for the dowels are straight, and a stop on the bit ensures that each hole is the same depth.

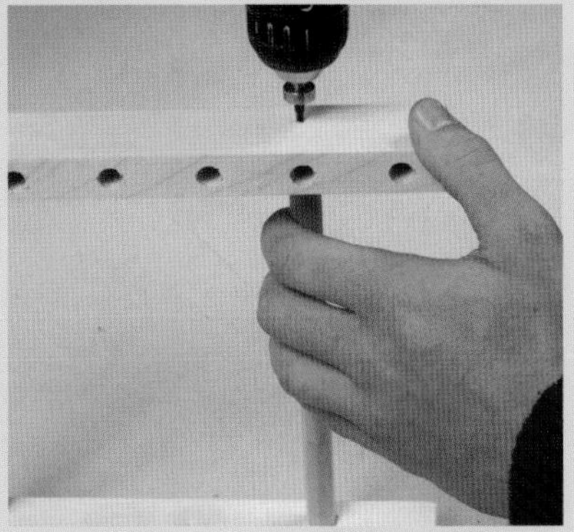

2. Use a countersink bit to prepare the hole for screws that join the sides to the dowels, and then join the sides to the dowels with 1¼-in. (30mm) flathead screws.

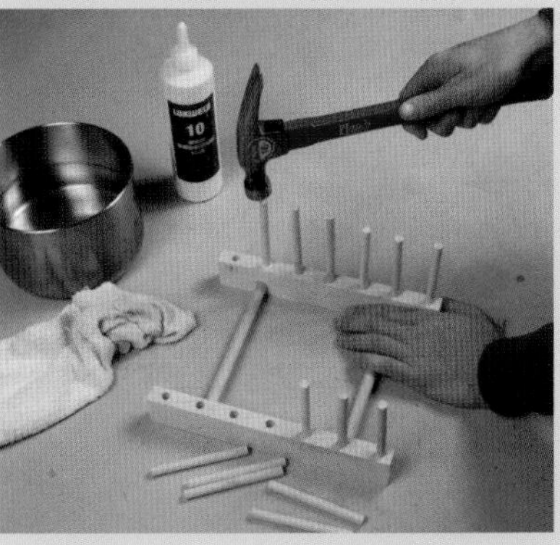

3. Tap ½-inch (1.3cm) dowels into place after applying glue. Wipe excess glue away immediately with a damp cloth.

Utensils, Tools, and Gadgets

Your most-used cooking tools (spoons, spatulas, tongs, and so forth) should probably be out in view near your stove, either hanging from the backsplash or in a utensil crock. But that leaves a lot of other items that need storage:

- Make liberal use of **drawer dividers and inserts**. Use dividers to separate larger items such as ladles and hand mixers. Use inserts to separate smaller items like measuring spoons and meat thermometers.
- If you want to store small items in deeper drawers, **use stacking trays** that slide over one another.
- **Group items by type**—keep all spoons together, all knives together, and so on.
- Also **group by use**—keep prep tools, such as peelers and garlic presses, near your food-prep area and serving tools, such as corkscrews and pizza cutters, near your dishes.
- **Knife-drawer inserts** are a good way to store knives without having a big knife block that takes up space on your counter.
- Hang utensils on hooks from the **back of cabinet doors** (though the door will be noisy to open and close).
- Tall, narrow "filler" drawers can also be used with a **vertical pegboard system** for hanging utensils.
- Don't forget that organizers designed for drawers can also be used on **pullout trays**.

Opposite bottom left Put spatulas, tongs, and other serving utensils near where you put prepared food onto platters or plates.

Opposite top right A pegboard organizer allows you to arrange your utensils as you like—and easily rearrange them as you see fit.

Opposite middle right Don't put more than a few implements in each compartment, or it will be difficult to spot the item you need.

Opposite bottom right Many cooks like to keep a set of flatware near where they cook, for testing, tasting, and stirring. This drawer does double duty, storing the flatware set and various food wraps.

Top Without the between-drawer rails you'll find on faced cabinets, faceless cabinets allow for deeper drawers or two drawers behind a single front as shown here.

Bottom This two-tier drawer houses cookware in the deeper drawer below and flatware in the shallower top tier.

Tableware Storage

Dishes, glasses, and flatware are among the kitchen's most-used items, so it's important for them to be easily accessible. Some suggestions:

- Store your tableware **outside the main work triangle** so that family members can get to it without getting in the chef's way.
- **New-style deep drawers** are designed to handle heavier weights, which means you can even store dishes in them. This makes it easier for kids to help themselves. Use a plate rack or adjustable pegboard system to keep dishes from sliding around.
- **Tall pantry cabinets** make a good place to store glasses and plates at a convenient height.
- **Under-cabinet racks** can also be used inside of cabinets to hang stemware or mugs from the bottom of an upper shelf. This will free up space on the shelf below for dishes.
- **A three-tier plate rack** in the cabinet or on the counter will help you take advantage of vertical space and still keep dinner plates separate from salad plates and soup bowls.
- **Don't let your flatware overflow** from one section to another in your drawer organizer. Either buy an extra-deep organizer or use two separate ones.
- An alternative to storing flatware in drawers is to **store it in small containers** on a shelf. Use one container for forks, one for spoons, and so on. Make sure the containers have a broad, heavy bottom so they don't tip over easily.

SMARTtip

Learn to Adjust

Use cabinets with adjustable shelving to fit specific items. Storing those 3-inch (7.6cm-high)-high mugs in a shelf space that is 8 inches (20.3cm) high is a waste of space. Adjustable shelves can be spaced as necessary.

Serving platters, typically tough to store, may be stored flat or displayed vertically if you opt for adjustable shelving.

Opposite top Pullout trays pack more tableware per cubic inch than any other cabinet accessory.

Opposite bottom This double-decker drawer's top tier is for napkins, making it the perfect companion to a drawer for dinner plates.

Top Dish caddies allow you to safely bring a full stack of plates to the countertop when it's table-setting time. They can also assist in transferring dishes from the dishwasher back to the drawer.

Bottom The transfer from dishwasher to dish storage doesn't get easier than having a dish drawer rack, such as this one, parked next to the dishwasher.

Food Where You Can Find It

One of the biggest problems with food storage is "out of sight, out of mind." If you can't see it, you forget to eat it. If you're tired of having foods quietly outlive their expiration dates in the back of your cupboard, try the following:

- Store all of your food in **one section of the kitchen** to make it easier for you (and guests) to quickly find all the items you need.
- Keep food on **shallow or narrow shelves** so that you don't get more than a few cans deep. Pullout pantries and specially designed pantry cabinets make good use of this rule.
- **Pullout trays and slide-out bins** are essential when storing food in base cabinets. Two narrow side-by-side trays are better than one wide tray.
- Store the **same kinds of food together**—snack foods on one shelf, baking essentials on another. Imitate the way your grocery store organizes its shelves.
- Put your **newest food in the back of the shelf** and bring older foods to the front after you grocery shop.
- Use **helper shelves and "stepped" organizers** to keep jars and cans in sight and take advantage of vertical space.
- Special racks for the **inside of cabinet doors** are available to hold spices and other foods packed in small containers.
- Place your **heaviest items on the bottom shelf** because it is the sturdiest.

Opposite top A well-stocked pantry cabinet means you won't to have to ask a neighbor for a can of tomato paste in the midst of making your special sauce. Put items with the latest use-by dates at the back of your shelves.

Opposite bottom Rollouts make it easy to check your food and beverage inventory.

Top Microwave popcorn is even more convenient when you store it in the same cabinet as the microwave itself.

Bottom left A door-mounted spice rack doesn't add storage space, but it saves you from digging through deeper shelves to find the spices you need. (To build your own spice rack, see page 114.)

Bottom right When storing food in cabinets, keep like items together. Airtight, transparent containers make it easy to see what you have.

Building a Door-Mounted Spice Rack

Door-mounted spice racks with acrylic fronts provide good visibility and accessibility for your herbs and spices. This project requires the use of a table saw or router, so it's not for beginners. You'll also need a plastic-cutting blade for cutting the acrylic fronts to size. We recommend the feathered wooden jig shown in step 3 for safety. It's clamped to the table saw tabletop and holds the workpiece snug against the fence while making the cut. Be sure to use a push stick for safety, too. Note: the saw guard was removed for photo clarity. It should be used to prevent accidents whenever possible.

1. Cut the grooves for the ¼-in. (0.6cm) acrylic fronts using a table saw. Set the blade height to 5⁄16 in. (0.8cm), and set the fence ¼ in. (0.6cm) from the blade for the first pass and ⅜ in. (0.9cm) for the second pass. (If you are using acrylic fronts of a different thickness than stated, adjust the blade distances accordingly.)

2. Cut the long pieces to length using a miter saw (or miter box and handsaw), but don't cut the sides to length yet.

3. To make a recess for the keyhole hangers, use a ½-in. (1.3cm) diameter bit in a table-mounted router to cut a channel in the grooved material you'll be using for the sides.

4. Cut the sides to length, once again using a miter saw or miter box and handsaw. Always cut so that the blade width is to the waste side of your cut mark.

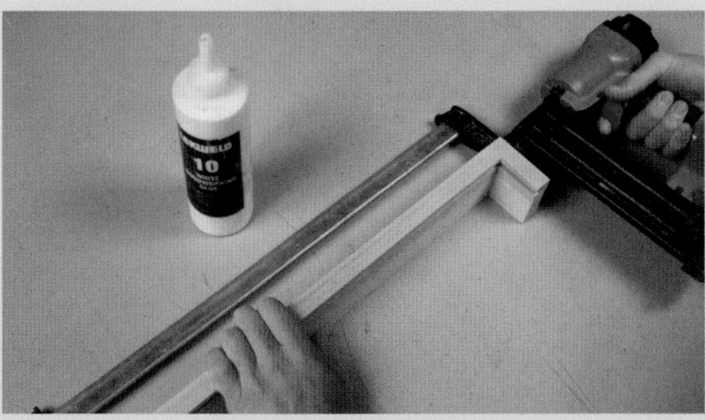

5. Apply glue, clamp the side to the bottom, and secure it using a brad nailer and 1½-in (3.8cm) fasteners. If you're using a hammer and finish nails, predrill the nailhole to ease the operation and to avoid splits.

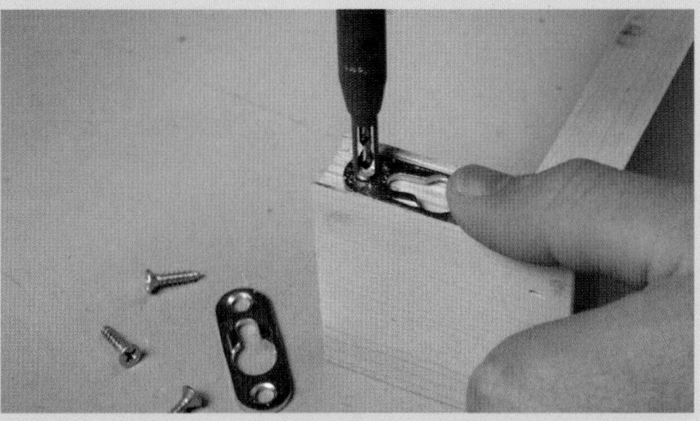

6. Use a self-centering bit (if you have one) to drill pilot holes for the keyhole hangers. They should fit in the channels you cut with the table saw. Next, trace the keyhole hanger opening.

7. The hangers will slip over the heads of the screws in the cabinet door. To make room for these screws, remove the hanger and drill two overlapping shallow recesses. A Forstner bit works best, or you can use a ¼-inch (0.6cm) chisel.

8. Attach the keyhole hangers using the screws provided. Now you are ready to install screws in the cabinet doors, leaving heads protruding so you can slip the hangers over the screws.

Small-Appliance Options

Appliances are problematic to store for two main reasons: cords and attachments. Cords get tangled or stuck underneath other items in the cabinet. Attachments get mixed up and are easily misplaced.

- Use **cord clips or rubber bands** to secure cords when an appliance is not in use.
- Store larger appliances on **pullout trays** so that you can take one appliance out without moving all the others.
- Store your smallest appliances (like hand blenders and mini choppers), along with their attachments, in **plastic containers.** Put lids on each container, and stack them if space is tight. Be sure to put a label on the side where you can see it.
- **Designate a storage spot** for attachments, and keep each group of attachments in a labeled bag, container, or basket.
- Special **appliance lifts** are shelves that lift up out of a cabinet and bring a mixer or other heavy appliance up to counter height. These keep large appliances off your counter and save your back the strain of lifting them.
- Store smaller appliances in a deep drawer, and **use dividers to create a spot** for each one.

Right To save counter space—and your back—use lifts for heavy appliances. Keep in mind, however, that using a mixer on a lift will often result in some of the ingredients ending up on the floor.

Opposite top Rollouts are the ideal way to store your collection of toasters, blenders, mixers, and the like.

Opposite bottom Store appliance accessories in baskets (together with the appliance when feasible) so you can find the attachment you need the moment your recipe suggests you use it.

PART 2 Beyond the Cabinet

CHAPTER 3

Countertop and Under-Cabinet Storage

Counter space is like prime real estate: there just isn't enough to go around. Almost all kitchen activities require some counter space, whether it's to chop an onion, pile dirty dishes, or set down a bag of groceries.

Therefore, one of the keys to efficiency is to maximize your counter space. An uncluttered countertop makes it easy to lay out your ingredients and cook with minimum fuss. And it makes cleanup a breeze—the last thing you want to do is lift ten things out of the way just to wipe up some crumbs.

Nevertheless, there is a vast array of items that can be stored on the counter. In this chapter you will learn about everything from small appliances, dish racks, and cutting boards to paper towel holders, spoon rests, and sponges. The fact that so many items can sit on the counter doesn't mean that they should. In fact, a general rule of thumb to follow is that if you can hang it or put it in a convenient drawer or cabinet, do so.

The countertop area should be reserved for high-use items: the kinds of things that you use so often that constantly getting them out of a drawer or cabinet would be tedious. This is also an area of kitchen storage where you can show your personal style. When selecting items for your counter, remember that they will always be in view, so choose items that are visually pleasing as well as functional.

Left Your countertops are an opportunity to show off your style.

Know Your Options

Countertop items can be stored in several ways. Consider your options, as well as the issues that apply to each, before making your decision.

On the countertop: As mentioned earlier, this is normally where you don't want to put things. Items set on the countertop have to be cleaned around, and they reduce areas you need for food preparation and cleanup. That said, there are some things you may want to store on the counter. A big mixer or flour canister, for example, may be too heavy for you to lug out of a cabinet every time you want to use it. In addition, there are some things, such as cutting boards and cooking utensils, you use too often to put away all the time. The counter is good for items you want to remember, too, such as that apple a day you promised yourself. Pile fruit in a tiered stand, and it won't take up much space on the surface.

Hung from an upper cabinet: There are many ways to hang things under a cabinet, from simple cup hooks to special holders designed for specific items. You can hang everything from wine glasses to coffeemakers. This is a good way to keep items in view and accessible. Before you buy, be sure the item will fit your cabinet and that it won't get in the way of any under-cabinet lighting.

Mounted on the backsplash: The backsplash is the perfect place to store those small items that you use every day. There are neat "rail systems" you can buy that consist of a metal rail that runs along the backsplash with various baskets, racks, and hooks that hang from it. It provides a way to store spices, paper towels, utensils, and more. You can move, add, or remove storage options as necessary. Not everyone needs a fancy rail system, though, and you can hang things by themselves on the backsplash just as easily. For example, attaching your spice rack to the wall might free up just the amount of space you need. Even if your backsplash is stone or tile, there are ways of mounting items—all you need is the proper drill bit and fastener. Inquire at your local hardware store or home center for the solution that's best for your situation.

In a counter-level drawer or cabinet: While the above options are usually better for items that see frequent use, don't forget about drawers and cabinets that sit on the counter. Many cabinetry manufacturers are now offering this type of storage. The insides of cabinet doors are a particularly good place to hang things, and drawers can be a great way to keep small items handy. One major plus to this type of storage is that the items stay a lot cleaner.

Right A cookbook holder, hung from under a cabinet, conserves valuable counter space and keeps cookbook pages from becoming stained.

Top Countertops are like magnets—lots of things, from keys to house plants, are drawn to them. Use rail systems, shelves, and even window ledges to keep counters ready for action.

Bottom You may want to give items you use every day—a coffee maker or toaster, for example—a permanent place on your counter.

More Counter Options

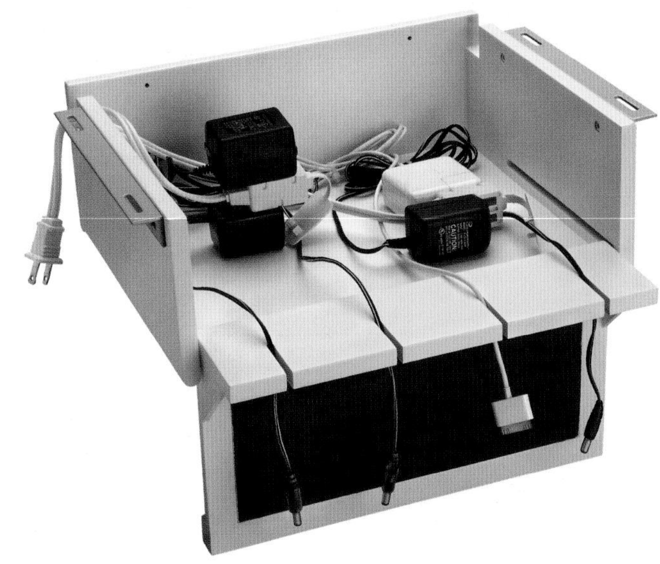

Opposite top Rail systems tend to look best in contemporary-style kitchens.

Opposite bottom Shown prior to mounting to the underside of a wall cabinet, this unit accommodates four chargers and has only one line to plug into an outlet. The slotted panel pivots up and slides into the closed position, and the front panel lifts up to become the shelf.

Top Cubbies, apothecary drawers, and open shelves are better suited to traditional-style kitchens.

Middle The trade-off to bringing cabinetry to the countertop is that you lose valuable surface space for meal preparation.

Bottom Rail systems come with myriad storage components, but don't overdo it. They can make a kitchen feel cluttered if you're not careful.

Build It In

If you're building new or doing a major remodeling, you may want to consider some built-in storage options at countertop level. This gives you storage at the most convenient height—you don't have to reach or stoop. It also helps combat clutter by hiding items that would normally be left out on the counter. Common options include appliance garages, drawers, backsplash nooks, and shelves.

Keep in mind, though, that built-in options will limit how you will be able to use the space. With open counter space you can always clear things to make room for a large project or move things around as your needs change. With a built-in, such as a wine rack, you can't. If your existing counter space is scarce, skip the built-ins. But if you have space to spare, this is a nice way to keep things looking neat.

Opposite top A shallow shelf adds storage without taking up too much counter space.

Opposite middle In the same kitchen, a similar countertop shelf unit has a second, slightly deeper top shelf. Again, it's done in a way that leaves adequate counter space for kitchen tasks.

Opposite bottom This kitchen's open shelves keep cookbooks and the microwave off the counter.

Top By building storage at the same level as the countertop, pulling out heavy appliances is a lot easier. Note: there are two ways to access the appliances stored in this cabinet.

Bottom When the mixer is placed back in its cabinet, the countertop is easy to clean and ready to serve other purposes.

Betty Crocker's COOKBOOK
American Cookbook
Mario Batali Simple Italian Food
The World's 100 Best Recipes
ITALIAN COOKING
FROM VINES TO WINES
FAMILY COOKBOOK
NATURAL HEALING COOKBOOK

SMARTtip

Multipurpose Backsplash

A simple way to add some storage is to install a shallow shelf on your backsplash. A 4-inch-wide (10cm-wide) shelf can hold spices, cooking oils, canisters, glasses, and such. If you tend to leave things out where you can reach them easily, this is a good way to confine the clutter and keep it off your main work surface. The shelf can run the entire length of your backsplash or just in a specific area, such as near the sink or stove.

Opposite top **Glass and wine racks convert this counter space into a wine-serving center. Keep your decanter in a nearby cabinet.**

Opposite bottom **Apothecary drawers and open shelves installed above the countertop are a good way to store recipes and cookbooks.**

Left **Drawers at countertop level can also harbor recipes or the basics for a micro kitchen office, but you'll have to clear the counter before you can pull them open.**

Below **Countertop drawers work best at the end of a counter, where they're less likely to disrupt food-prep tasks.**

Garage the Appliances

An appliance garage is a special type of cabinet that sits on your countertop and usually has a roll-up or flip-up door. Your small appliances can be stored inside, and you can just shut the door when they're not in use. This helps hide all the messy cords and means your appliances can be worn-looking or mismatched without being eyesores. However, be aware that if you put your most-used appliances in an appliance garage, you may end up never closing the door.

Where should you put an appliance garage? Near your food-prep area is probably your best bet because that's where you use most small appliances. A corner is often a good choice because it makes use of "dead" space that isn't very convenient to use as a work surface anyway. Consider electrical outlet locations as well—you'll want to be sure you have an unused outlet inside the garage for plugging in appliances when you use them.

Top Putting everything you need to make a pot of coffee in or near an appliance garage will speed up and streamline your morning routine.

Bottom A corner is often a good place for an appliance garage because the space is difficult to use for food preparation.

Opposite bottom Flip-up garage doors, such as the one on this garage-cabinet combo, are generally easier to open than tambour-style doors (shown in photo at bottom of this page).

SMARTtip

Move the Microwave

The microwave can take up a huge amount of counter space. To make matters worse, you can't set anything in front of it because it will get knocked off the counter when you open the door. Consider building the microwave into your upper or lower cabinets, putting it above the stove, or setting it on an open shelf above the counter. Or get rid of the microwave completely and install a combination microwave-convection oven. If you have small children or anyone in your family uses a wheelchair, keep the microwave low so that everyone can reach it. Do not put it where a child would have to reach over a hot stove to use it. If you're worried about a child playing with the controls, install a kill switch so you can cut off power when the microwave is not in use.

Setting Your Sink Straight

Your sink area sees a lot of use—rinsing dishes, washing your hands, getting a drink of water, filling pots, draining pasta, and cleaning vegetables are just some of the activities it serves. And with all the food and soap in the area, it tends to get messy fast, so easy cleanup is a top priority.

Items that you will want to keep within reach of the sink include dish soap, hand soap, hand lotion, sponges, dishcloths, scrub brushes, dish rack, cloth towel, and paper towels. You may also want to keep glasses or paper cups nearby if you drink tap water. And storing a cutting board near the sink makes it easy to wash and chop vegetables.

Two options that can help organize your sink area are the sink tilt-out and the over-the-sink shelf. The sink tilt-out is a small drawer in front of the sink that tilts out from the bottom on hinges. It's often an option you can choose when buying your cabinetry, or you can add one to existing cabinetry by purchasing a kit at your local home center. The drawer is usually pretty shallow, but it's a handy place to store sponges and brushes. The over-the-sink shelf is exactly what is sounds like: a shelf that runs behind the sink. It's usually raised about 6 inches (15cm) off the countertop, stands on legs, and has a notch to accommodate the faucet. This is a great example of converting wasted space to usable space. Before you buy, be sure it will fit around your faucet and spray nozzle.

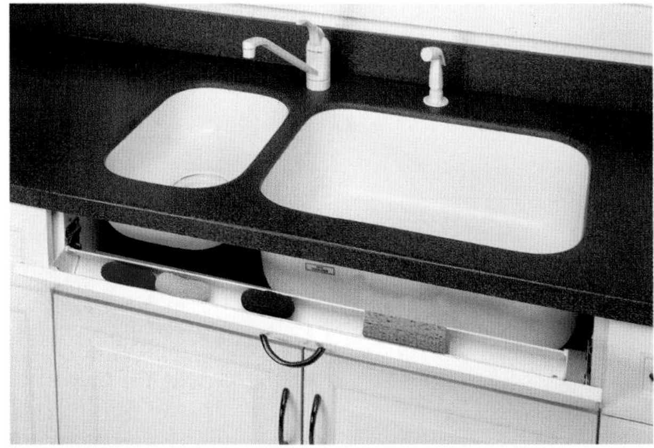

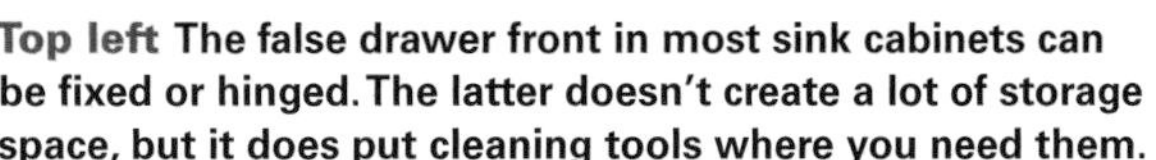

Top left The false drawer front in most sink cabinets can be fixed or hinged. The latter doesn't create a lot of storage space, but it does put cleaning tools where you need them.

Top right Sink tilt-outs, available for all sizes of sink cabinets, make a perfect home for sponges, scouring pads, and bars of soap. Opt for a tilt-out that you can remove easily for cleaning.

Bottom Most tilt-outs, which eliminate the clutter around the sink, close with a magnetic catch. Spring-loaded hinges, such as the one shown here, are also available.

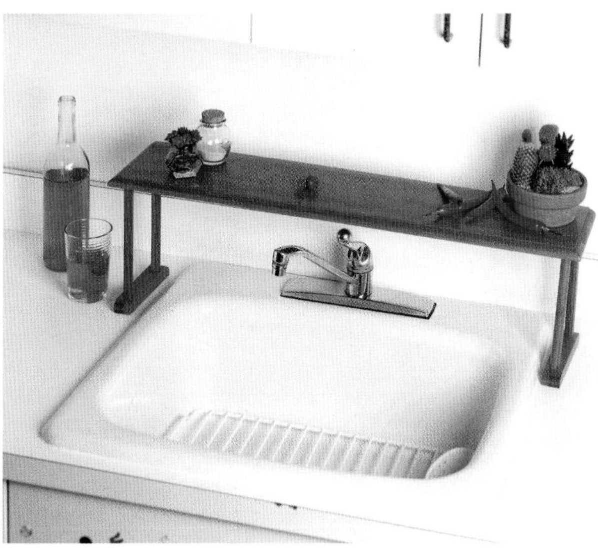

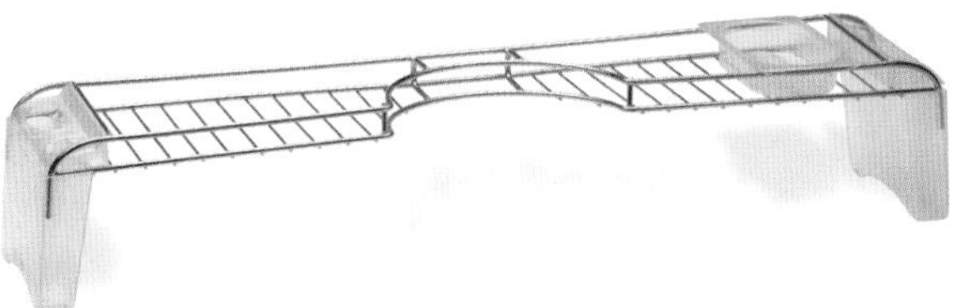

Top This shelf sits at the back of your sink and effectively doubles the counter space there. The notch in the middle allows the unit to fit around the faucet.

Middle Wooden over-the-sink shelves provide a perfect place for a small potted plant. Be sure to measure how much clearance you'll need above the faucet before you buy a shelf.

Bottom Over-the-sink shelves are typically made of stainless steel or vinyl-coated wire (shown here). They are an inexpensive way to add space in a kitchen locale that is often cramped.

More Sink Storage Ideas

Top left A paper towel holder that sits on the counter doesn't save space but is easily carried to where you need it. It also prevents the bottom of the roll from soaking up countertop puddles. The clamp on this model keeps the roll from unraveling.

Bottom left A common—and effective—solution is the paper towel rack that mounts under a wall cabinet.

Right A narrow shelf mounted to your backsplash is another good way to gain valuable storage space around the sink area.

Sink Cleanup Tools

It's important to have a dedicated spot for even the smallest items. Little baskets are available for sponges—some stick to the side of the sink with suction cups, while others hang over the divider between double sinks. Other items, such as scrub brushes and steel wool, can be stored in a sink tilt-out, on the dish rack, or in a container under the sink.

If you use a dishcloth, hanging it over your faucet is not your best option. Install a small towel bar or hook instead so it isn't constantly in your way. A towel bar can be hung on the backsplash, under an upper cabinet, or inside the cabinet door under the sink. This goes for towels you use to dry your hands as well. And don't forget paper towels. Hang them up if at all possible, at a height all family members can reach. A good place is behind a base-cabinet door.

Bottles of dish soap tend to get gummy and become an eyesore (and their packaging isn't that pretty either). Two alternatives are to store them in the cabinet under the sink or to purchase a pump soap dispenser that matches your kitchen decor. Pump dispensers can also be used for hand soap and hand lotion. Built-in countertop dispensers are also available. They fit inside a hole bored through your countertop and connect directly to a small, under-counter reservoir or to a large reservoir on the floor of the base cabinet via a tube.

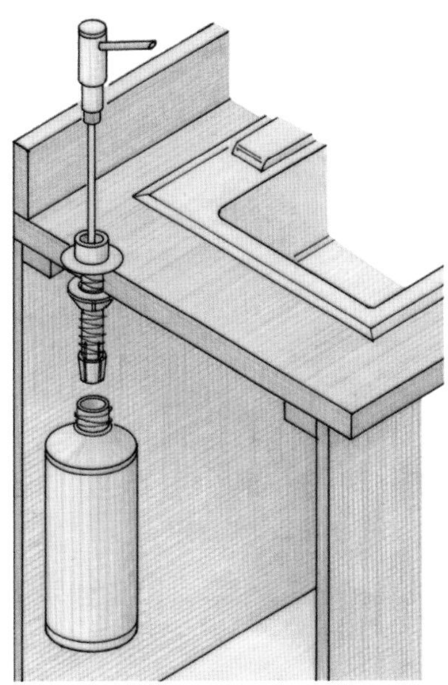

Dispenser Detail

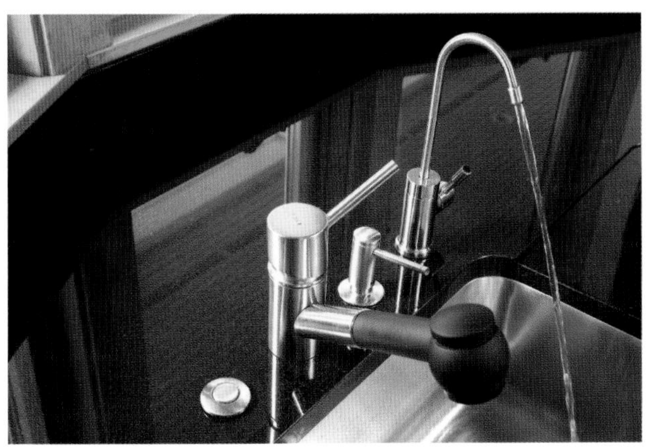

Top To maximize counter space around a sink, choose a pullout faucet and install a built-in soap dispenser. The former eliminates the need for a separate pullout sprayer. The latter puts the dish soap reservoir under the countertop (see illustration above) and eliminates messy bottles and countertop pumps.

Bottom Save space on the countertop by installing a hot-water dispenser at your sink.

Drying Dishes

A dish rack is by far the biggest item to keep near your sink. First, evaluate whether you really need one. If you hardly ever wash dishes by hand, a simple silicone drying mat may work for you; roll it up and store it when it's not in use. If you do need a dish rack but space is tight, there are some that actually mount to the wall above the sink and others that fit over one bowl of a double sink. A fold-up one could hang from a hook on the wall when it's not in use. Be sure to check out all your options—dish rack style has definitely come a long way. There's one to fit every taste, from earthy wooden ones to space-age clear plastic. Drip trays that are tilted in an attempt to drain water into the sink are often more trouble than they are worth. Opt for a simple drip pan without difficult-to-clean grooves. If you have dual sink basins, consider fitting your dish rack into the smaller of the two.

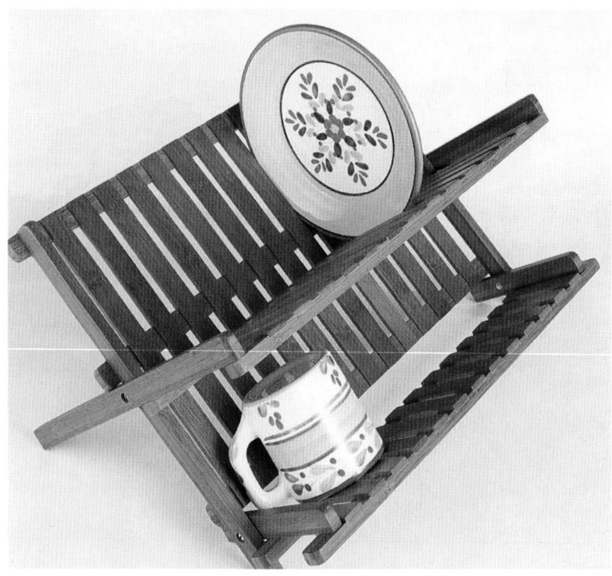

Top Dish towels can be laid to dry over a dish rack at the end of the evening—or left on a rack that mounts on the back of a cabinet door, such as the one shown here.

Middle Pullout dish-towel hangers are quite easy to install. They use only a couple of inches (about 5cm) of space, though they may not be appropriate for a cabinet with shelves.

Bottom The classic wooden dish rack has two advantages: it can be easily folded to clear the countertop for other tasks, and it fits most traditional kitchen decorating schemes.

Essentials for Prepping and Cooking

There's nothing more essential to an efficient kitchen than well-organized tools for meal preparation. You'll use many of these items several times a day, so they need to be close at hand but not get in your way. While many could be stored in a drawer or cabinet, serious cooks will probably want them out in plain sight where they can be grabbed easily.

Remember that the key to efficiency is having everything that you need to start a particular task within reach. In your food-prep area, you will want to store cutting boards, knives, measuring spoons and cups, and a cookbook or tablet holder. In the cooking area, you will want utensils, spices, potholders, and perhaps a spoon rest and trivet.

Of course, cooking and food-prep tasks often overlap, so in an ideal world, your food-prep area is next to your cooktop. If it isn't, decide where things such as cutting boards and spices will best suit your cooking style. You could double up on some items—for example, keep one cutting board near your sink and one near your stove. Splitting up some groups may work too, such as keeping whisks, spatulas, and such in the prep area and stirring spoons in the cooking area. You may even choose to keep serving spoons, forks, and ladles in a crock of their own.

Top Cutting boards don't only protect countertops. They also serve as trays, allowing you to move prepared ingredients to and from the cooktop.

Bottom left Allow for plenty of counter space behind your cooktop whenever possible. Use the space to keep cooking oils and ingredients at the ready.

Bottom right This range hood offers an enormous amount of storage for items you use often during meal preparation.

Prep-Tool Placement

A good set of knives is a cook's best friend, and there are plenty of options for storing them. Avoid the big, bulky square knife blocks unless you've got plenty of space. Consider a long, thin rectangular one instead. Other options include a wall-mounted magnetic knife strip, or a knife block that can hang from an upper cabinet. If you store knives in a drawer, use knife guards or a special drawer insert made for holding knives. Avoid drawer storage if you have small children in the house—or put a child lock on the drawer.

Other meal-prep essentials include measuring cups and spoons, strainers, colanders, graters, presses, and a spot for your cookbook. Installing small hooks and hanging measuring cups and spoons from your backsplash or upper cabinet is a great way to keep them from getting lost. (How many times have you hunted for that elusive quarter teaspoon?) Instead of putting your cookbook or tablet in the middle of your work area, invest in a holder that will keep it out of the way and open to the right page. Cookbook holders are yet another item that can hang under wall cabinets or from rail systems.

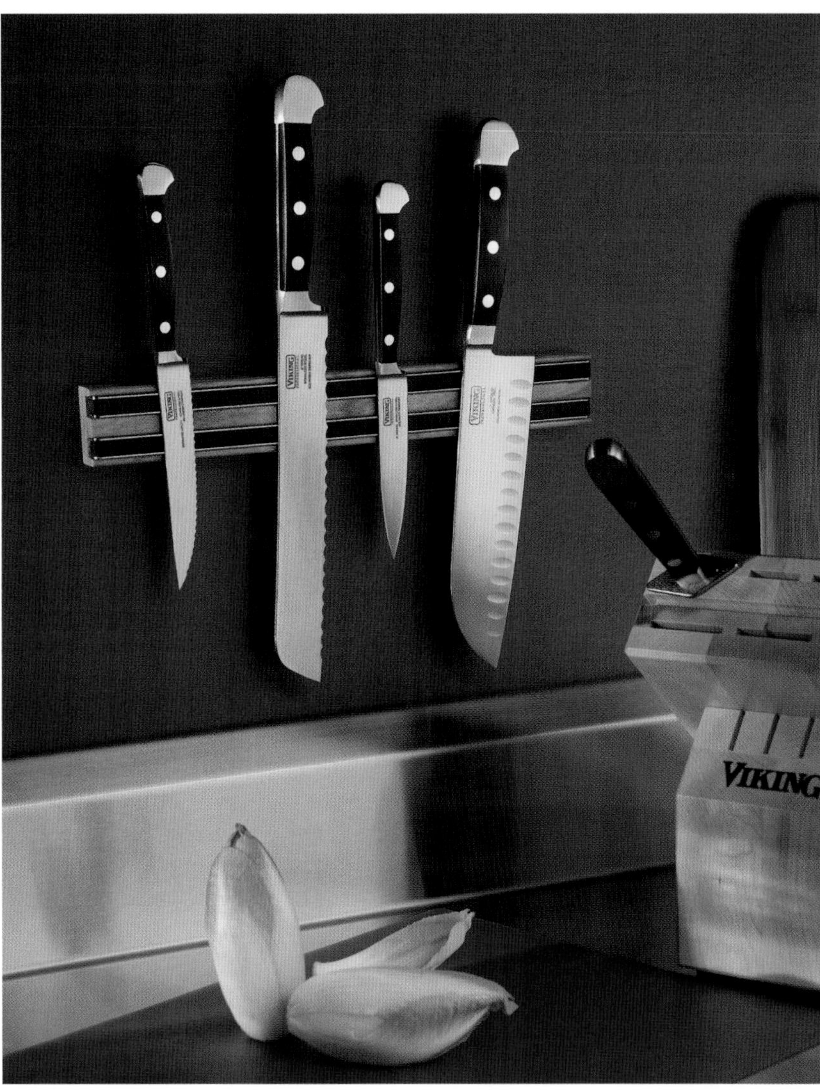

Top Use a wall-mounted magnetic strip, available in various lengths, to keep your favorite knives handy.

Bottom A simple holder for your cookbook or electronic tablet will keep your hands free while referring to a recipe.

Cutting Boards

Cutting boards come in myriad shapes and sizes, and you may want to have more than one. If counter space is limited, opt for a thin plastic or silicone one that will not get in the way and can be stored easily. Some fit across one bowl of your sink (another great example of converting "wasted" space to usable space). Hanging your cutting board keeps it handy.

Top A pullout cutting board expands your counter space, but be sure it's sturdy enough to withstand chopping.

Bottom Tight on counter space? Use the space over your sink when it's not in use. This combination cutting board and colander has nonslip edging.

Cooking with Ease

You'll definitely want to have your most-used cooking utensils within reach of the stove. Hang spatulas, spoons, and tongs from a rail system along the backsplash of your stove, or keep them in a wide-mouthed utensil crock next to the cooktop. Be sure the crock is large enough to easily accommodate the handles of your utensils so you won't have to struggle to get them in or out. The crock should also be heavy enough to prevent it from tipping.

Spoon rests can help contain the mess as you cook, though you may find that cleaning the counter is just as easy as cleaning the spoon rest. A trivet is a good idea if your countertop material can't handle hot pots. You will want to keep the trivet next to the stove, along with a hook for hanging potholders. Keep in mind that anything you store near the stove is going to get grease on it, so you will need to clean frequently. If you have a cooktop instead of a range, an excellent place to store cooking utensils is in a wide drawer just below it.

Opposite Keeping items out around your cooktop or range is great for efficiency but will add to your cleaning chores because of grease and splattering. The best approach is to keep out only what you use every time you cook.

Top When selecting a container to hold utensils, opt for something heavy enough not to topple, even when loaded to the brim. This utensil crock is a flower pot.

Bottom Containers designed specifically for utensils are also available. This slim stainless-steel model comes with a detachable spoon rest and has a shallow front compartment to hold bottle openers and other short tools.

Countertop Spice Strategies

Options for storing spices on or near the counter include baskets hanging from a rail system, magnetic containers on a metal strip, or wall racks. If you must sit spices on the counter, a round carousel in a corner is a good use of dead corner space. Try to pick a spot that is away from direct sunlight and sources of heat and humidity.

When it comes to organizing the spices, keep in mind the following: you should be able to read the labels at a glance. It helps to remove spices from the store containers and put them in uniform jars. Get in the habit of putting containers away with the labels facing out. You may want to experiment with organizing them by name or by color. Remember also that spices don't last forever. Throw out the ones you never use and replace the rest every one to three years, depending on the spice, how it's stored, and how particular you are about the flavor.

Top Narrow shelves, available with most rail systems, are a good way to store the spices you use most frequently.

Bottom Corner shelves are also available with many rail systems. They provide a perfect spot for oil and vinegar.

Top left Carousels are a compact way to store seasonings on the counter. Choose one that spins easily.

Top right A two-tier carousel allows for more storage.

Bottom If you have the space, a countertop drawer is an ideal way to house your spice collection. The spices will be where you need them and easy to see.

Countertop Food Storage

There are a few reasons you might want to store food on the countertop. First, it may make sense to keep staples, such as sugar and coffee, in canisters on the counter because you use them often. Second, you may be short on cabinet space and thus the counter becomes a necessary storage area. Third, you may want to keep produce in plain view so it gets eaten instead of forgotten.

Canisters come in dozens of shapes and sizes. To minimize the amount of counter space they consume, select ones that are stackable or ones that aren't too deep so that you still have plenty of space in front of them to work. Canisters should be made of a clear material or well labeled so that you can tell what is in them at a glance. Use them to store anything you use several times a week, including coffee, tea, sugar, flour, salt, cookies, and pasta. They don't have to be grouped together. Place each one where it makes the most sense—coffee and sugar by the coffeemaker, pasta by the stove, and so on.

Breads, fruits, and vegetables are all items that you may want to store at room temperature. Keep produce near your food-prep area in well-ventilated bowls or baskets, away from sunlight or other heat sources. Bread should be stored in an airtight bag, container, or breadbox. (If you're not going to eat it all right away, store it in the freezer.) Breadboxes can be hung on the wall or under a cabinet. Choose one that has a clear door so you don't forget what's inside. Place your breadbox near the fridge (for easy sandwich preparation) or in the food-prep area, near your cutting board and bread knife.

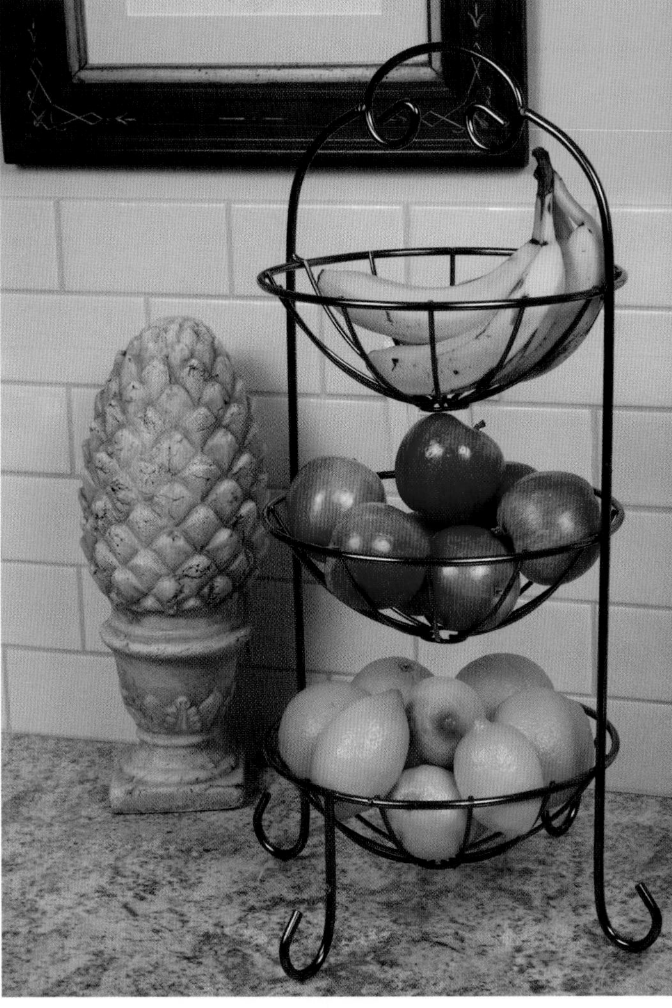

Top A tiered fruit rack promotes ripening, uses space efficiently, adds a splash of color, and is a good way to keep healthy foods where your family will see them.

Opposite bottom Flour and sugar canisters placed in an underused countertop corner allow you to get into baking projects quickly.

SMARTtip

Bowing Out

You can increase your counter space with the addition of a bow window. Along with being an ideal place to grow herbs and display indoor plants, you can also use it for countertop overflow—ripen tomatoes there or display decorative ceramics.

Plates, Glasses, and Mugs

Because kitchens are all about eating and drinking, it's nice to have easy access to plates, glasses, and mugs. The biggest drawback to storing them in the open is that they get dusty. Keep out only the items that you use frequently and store the rest in cabinets. Countertop-area options for plates can include plate racks (set on the counter, mounted to the backsplash, or built in under a wall cabinet) and tiered wire storage shelves (which are meant to go inside cabinets but work fine on the counter, too). Stemware and mugs with handles can be easily hung under your upper cabinets.

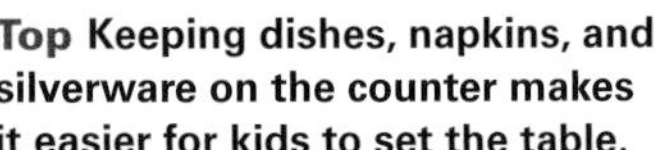

Top Keeping dishes, napkins, and silverware on the counter makes it easier for kids to set the table.

Middle left The apothecary drawers below this dish rack offer handy storage for everything from flatware to spices.

Middle right Under-cabinet stemware racks install in minutes and keep wine glasses accessible. Store just enough for regular use this way and keep the rest in a cabinet so you don't have to rinse them before use.

Bottom left Pegs installed on a board are an underutilized storage solution. Use them to hang mugs, utensils, and measuring cups and spoons.

Bottom right A below-cabinet dish rack is another convenient way to store dishes—and keeps the counter clear for other uses.

SMARTtip

Help Yourself

If you've got kids, keep items within their reach to reduce the number of times a day they ask you to get something for them. Consider placing cups, plates, paper towels, napkins, and the microwave at a kid-friendly level. Also think about the things you want to store out of their reach, such as knives and glasses.

Wine Storage

Wine racks come in every shape and style, so you're sure to find one that fits your storage needs. They range from tall, narrow ones that hang on the wall to fanciful wrought-iron ones that sit on your counter. Others are built in below wall cabinets. Be sure to choose one that holds bottles on their side so that the cork stays moist and prevents air from infiltrating. Place it away from direct sunlight and sources of heat (such as appliances). Most wines you buy at the store are ready to drink—you shouldn't store them for too long, and they are fine sitting in your wine rack until you open them. However, if you are interested in buying fine wines that improve with age, you may want to consider a wine refrigerator. (See page 220.)

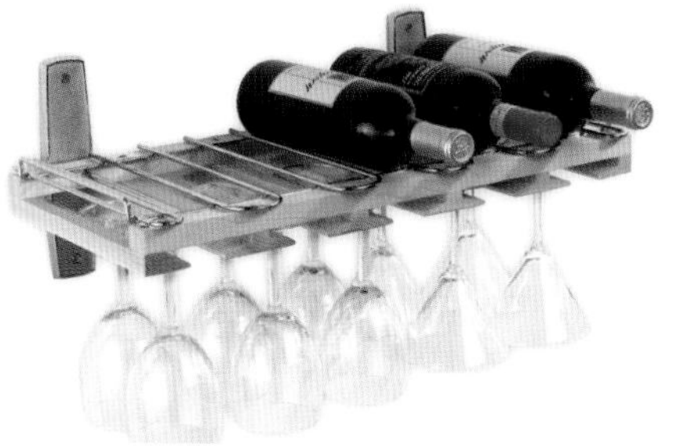

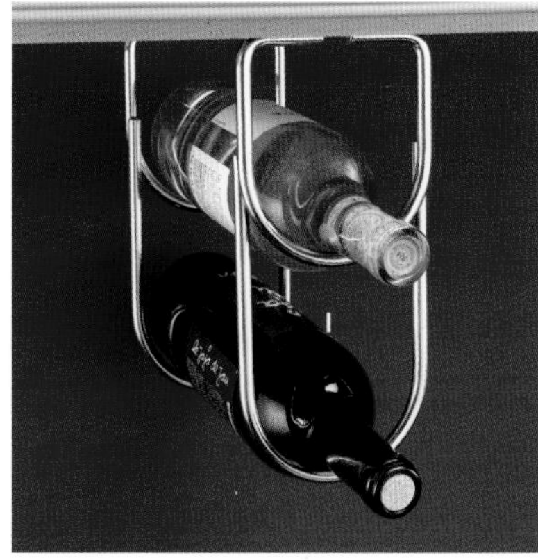

Left A wine rack can be as simple as the two intersecting boards seen here.

Top right This wall- or backsplash-mounted wine rack neatly handles both bottles and glasses.

Bottom right Red or white? This compact rack mounts under any wall cabinet.

Small Appliances

The list of small appliances is endless, ranging from coffeemakers and toasters to food processors and slow cookers. The appliances you use every day deserve a place on your counter. If counter space is tight, look for appliances that can be mounted under a cabinet or in a cabinet wall. Think about how you use them and what you use them with when deciding on location. For instance, you need water to fill your coffeepot, so keeping the coffeepot near the sink may be a good idea. You need bread for the toaster, so having the toaster near your breadbox or freezer would probably make sense.

Appliances you use less often should probably be stored in a cabinet, both to hide the messy cords and to prevent them from getting dusty. An appliance garage is one way to keep things hidden yet convenient. (See page 130.) Below-counter drawers and pop-up shelves are also good ways to store coffeemakers, blenders, and other small appliances.

Opposite This combination kitchen/dining room has plenty of storage space already, so it was no problem to use the bit of wall over the sink area for a permanently installed TV.

Below A Bluetooth speaker is an easy way to bring music into the kitchen.

Cut Clutter with a Built-In Coffee System

Directly wired and plumbed, built-in coffee systems can grind beans, automate measuring, and provide instant hot water. Some models, like this one built into a wall of cabinets, can include a drawer for supplies. Hanging appliances from a wall cabinet keeps the countertop free for other tasks, or, if you have the space, you may choose to set often-used appliances on the countertop.

Music and Television

If you spend a lot of time in the kitchen, you may want to have music or a television to entertain you while you cook. For many of us today, this is a simple matter of playing music through a smartphone, tablet, or Bluetooth-connected speaker. For something more permanent, there are many under-cabinet options. Some TVs drop down and swivel from any angle and then fold away when not in use. If you're going to watch cooking shows, place the TV within view of your food-prep area, or use a tablet that you can move anywhere.

CHAPTER 4

Overhead and Vertical Spaces

Valuable storage space may be untapped only because it's not where you'd expect it to be. Take a good look at the overhead and vertical space in your kitchen, however, and you're likely to find it—sometimes right in front of your nose. Look above your cabinets, across your windows, below your ceiling, behind doors, over islands, and on appliances, cabinets, and walls.

Professional chefs use these spaces to hang pots and utensils, and to store serving platters and plates. You can, too. Cooking becomes more fun and efficient when what you need is in full view and convenient to grab. To get started, look at the kitchen activities list you created at the beginning of this book. Any items connected with high-priority activities are good candidates for storing out in the open. Pots and pans, dishes, mugs, utensils, spices, measuring cups, potholders, paper towels, and dish towels are common choices. Next, seek vertical or overhead space near where you use them. Pots, for example, ideally hang near the sink, which is where you fill them with water as you prepare a meal and clean them after you eat. Knives can go on the wall near where you chop.

When determining which items to hang in the open, consider decorating opportunities, too. Items that you store in the open should be things you find pleasing to see. A word of caution, however: don't go overboard or you'll end up replacing counter clutter with visual clutter. In this chapter, you'll learn dozens of ways to make the most of overhead and vertical spaces.

Left **Overhead storage can take many forms. Here, it's a run of cabinets—with glass doors on two sides—that hang from the ceiling.**

Pot Racks

Pot racks are an eye-catching and space-saving option for storing pots and pans. They come in an array of styles and materials and are appropriate for any kitchen, whether your style is country, contemporary, or something in between. Pot racks are also efficient; they are perfect for cooks who move fast in the kitchen and don't want to waste time digging through cabinets to find the right pot—or waste time putting it away. Pot racks can store a lot more, too. Use them to hang large utensils, sieves, colanders, cheese graters, and tiered mesh vegetable baskets. You can even use them to hang dry flowers or herbs, garlic braids, and woven baskets.

Pot racks will best serve your cooking needs if you hang them within reach of the cooktop or food-prep area. A popular spot for a pot rack is over a kitchen island, assuming you have one. Other good choices

include over food-prep counters, on walls near the range, and over the sink. Racks hung over the sink double as drying racks; hang a wet pan and allow it to drip-dry. If you are truly short on space and don't have a convenient place near the range or sink, hang a pot rack as close by as possible. You may find space on the back of a door or beneath pantry shelves. A short walk is often easier than having to reach into a dark, overstuffed cabinet.

Above Hanging a pot rack over a kitchen island is often your best bet. A steel rod mounted to the rim of this range hood serves nicely as a rack, keeping the pots and pans within easy reach.

Opposite Pot racks, available in dozens of styles, should be mounted so the lowest pan rim is no less than 24 inches (60cm) above counter height. It's better to leave 30 inches (76cm), but this may depend on the height of the user and the width of the island.

SMARTtip

Check the Scale

The scale of your chosen pot rack is important, too. Don't go for something large and elaborate if your kitchen is small. Check out all the styles before making your decision.

Above Pot racks are for more than just pots. You can use them to hang the baskets that you use to gather herbs or vegetables for the evening meal.

Opposite top Wall-mounted pot racks are a good way to use the overhead space near a wall. Note that the brackets must be long enough to prevent large pots from scraping the wall.

Opposite bottom Units with a wire grid allow you to hang cookware anywhere under the rack, as well as around its perimeter.

GARLAND

Rack Types and Materials

Pot racks are generally mounted on the ceiling or a wall. Units come in many shapes, with or without integrated lighting, with single or double bars, with single or multiple tiers, and with grids or chain links. Materials include aluminum, wood, chrome-plated and brass-plated steel, wrought iron, copper, and stainless steel. If you can't find what you want ready-made, find a local metal artisan to design or make a rack to your specifications. Found objects, including wrought-iron gates, work well, too.

To determine which type of rack to use, you'll need to consider the layout of your kitchen, ceiling height, and how much space you can devote to one. You may even want to check the lengths of your longest- and shortest-handled cookware to ensure it won't hang too low or too high. Ceiling-mounted pot racks work best in kitchens with high ceilings or over islands, peninsulas, and sinks—anywhere they won't interfere with traffic or become head hazards. Most ceiling-mounted pot racks will hang 13 to 20 inches (33 to 50cm) from the ceiling. Add the length of your pots or utensils and you'll know whether it's going to interfere with other activities. As a rule of thumb, figure a total length of about 24 to 30 inches (60 to 76cm). Wall-mounted racks are great if you're not tall enough to reach ceiling-mounted racks and if you have wall space near the food-prep area.

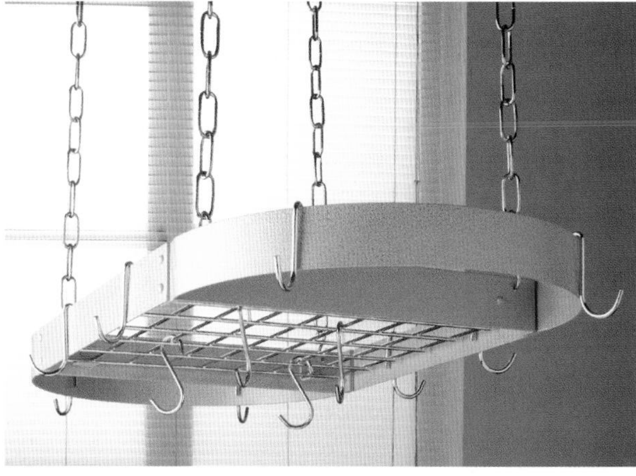

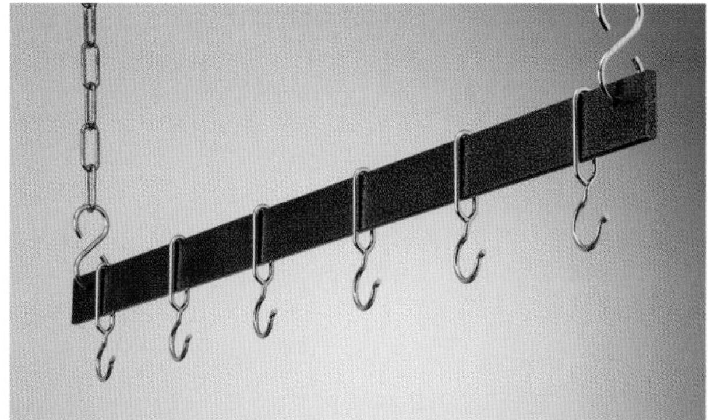

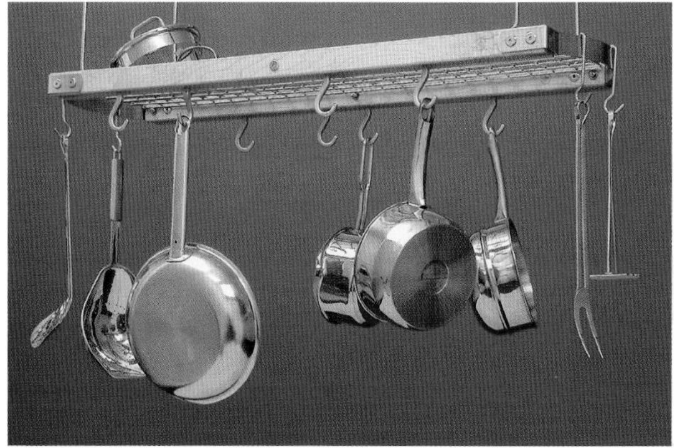

Opposite top This pot hanger is simply a steel bar mounted behind the window valance.

Opposite bottom Pot racks suspended from four points, including the one seen here, tend to be more stable than those suspended from two points as you reach for and replace cookware.

Top left Rack materials range from wood and steel to wrought iron and aluminum.

Middle top left A simple bar with S-hooks attached to two chains works fine as a pot hanger, but expect it to swing each time you use it.

Middle bottom left Several manufacturers offer wall-mounted pot racks that combine hooks with shelves.

Bottom left Pot racks can be decorative as well as functional.

Top right This white-enamel aluminum rack would be at home in many of today's contemporary kitchens.

Bottom right If you can reach it, a pot-rack shelf is a good place to store pot lids.

Hanging Tough

When securing anything to the wall or ceiling, you want to be sure your method of attachment will support the weight of the object. Screwing through the surface into wood framing, such as into a joist or stud, is always the strongest connection. You can find framing by using an electronic stud finder as described on page 161. Sometimes a glancing light against the wall or ceiling will reveal the location of drywall screws into framing. If no framing is located where you need it, lighter objects like small shelves can be secured to walls using one of the types of anchors described on page 160.

Fastening to a joist is mandatory when hanging racks or shelves from the ceiling. Save yourself some trouble when buying a ceiling-hung object by locating the joists you'll be using for the installation beforehand; then try to select a rack that will meet your requirements. You can use blocking between joists to

create a strong support for a heavy storage unit, but you'll have to remove an area of drywall in order to fasten the blocking to the joists, and patch the drywall afterward. You can also secure cleats (boards) to the ceiling surface. Fasten the cleats securely to the joists, then fasten the rack to the cleats. (See the illustrations at right.) Finish the edges with molding.

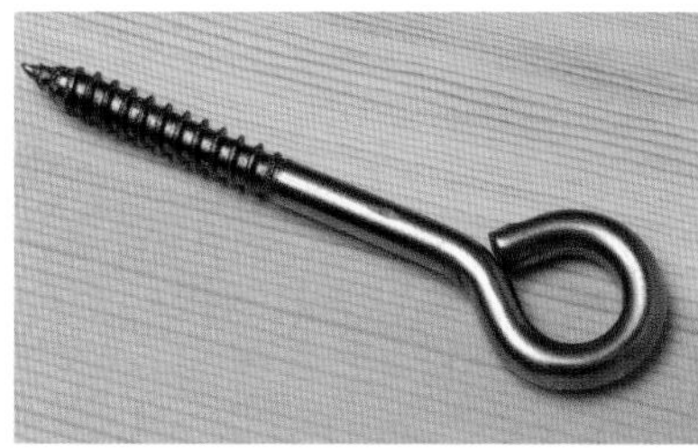

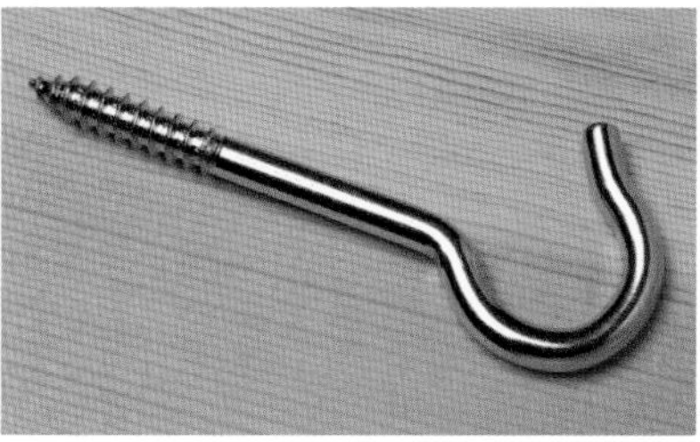

Opposite The ceiling box hides the cleats from which the pot-rack pipes will hang, conceals the downlights, and is trimmed to match the cabinets.

Top Eye bolts (shown here) and hook screws come in many diameters. The larger the diameter, the bigger the load capacity.

Bottom A simple hook screw is adequate for hanging a light-duty pot rack. Be sure to drive it into a joist.

Anchoring Details

If you want to hang your rack where no joist is available, you have two choices. The first is to fasten cleats to the ceiling joists (top). The cleats provide a solid anchor for the rack. Or, you can cut away part of your ceiling to gain access to the joists (bottom). Add blocking as required, and then patch over the opening before installing your rack.

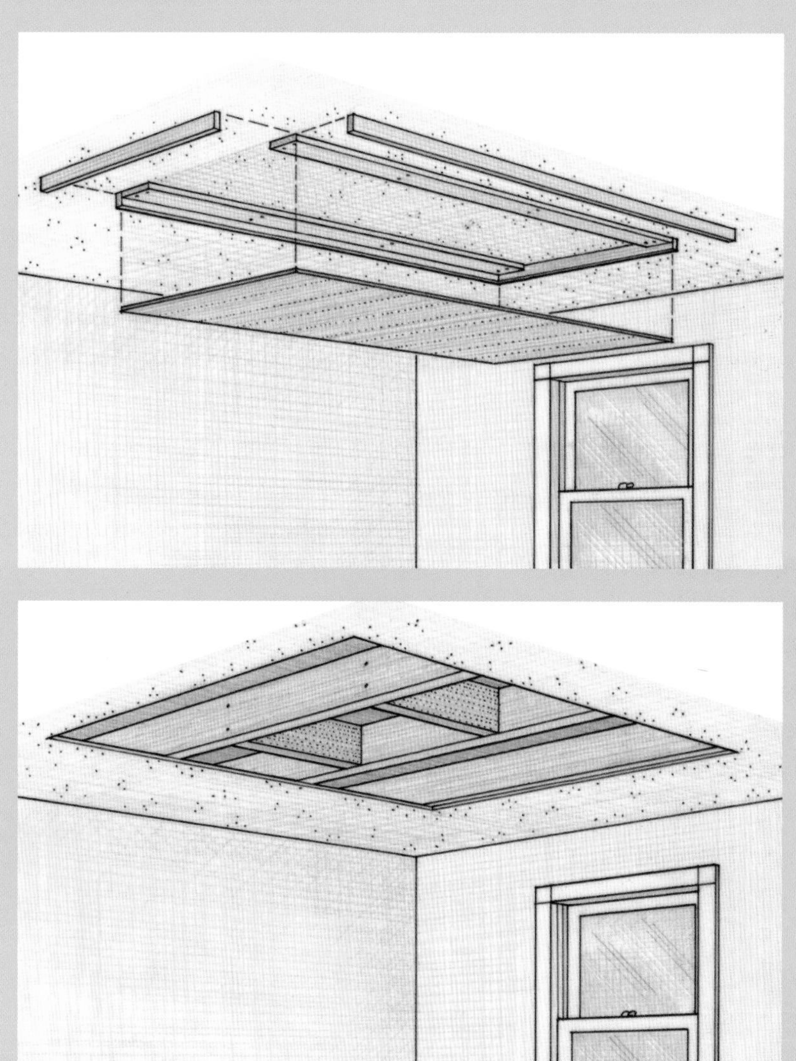

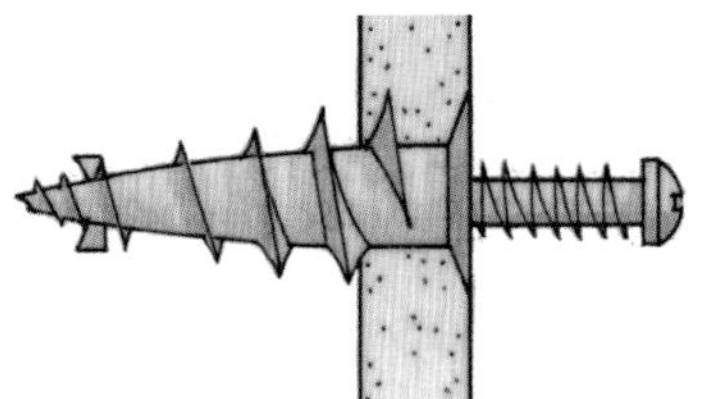

Turn this self-drilling anchor into the wall with a screwdriver, and then use the supplied screw to fasten the object or bracket to the wall.

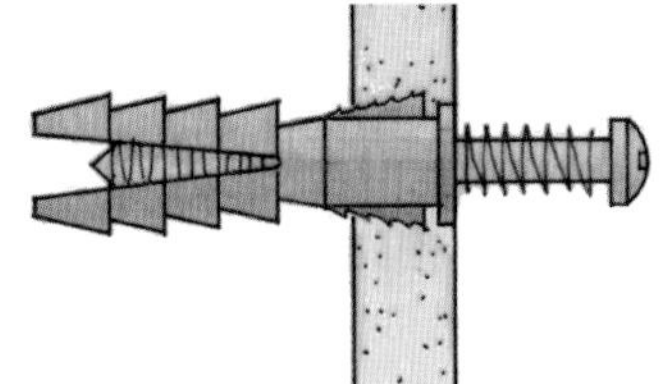

Ribbed anchors work in drywall or plaster. Drill the hole to the specified diameter, tap the anchor flush with the wall, and then fasten the object with the supplied screw.

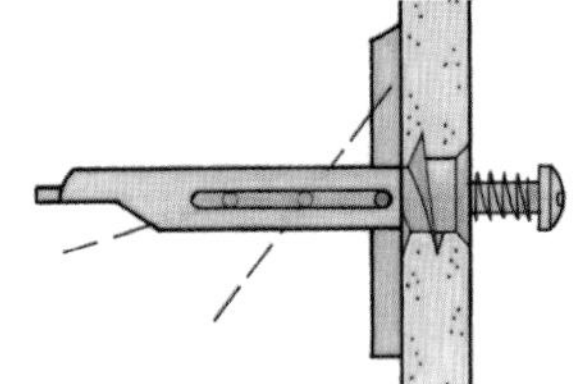

Install this toggle-style drywall anchor with a screwdriver. Secure it and the object to be hung to the wall by inserting and turning the supplied screw to engage the clamp.

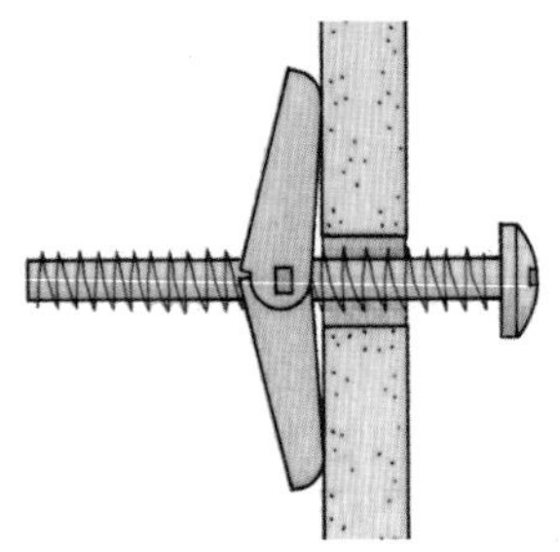

With older-style toggle bolts, drill to the specified diameter, and then insert the screw through the object, insert "wings" through the hole, and tighten.

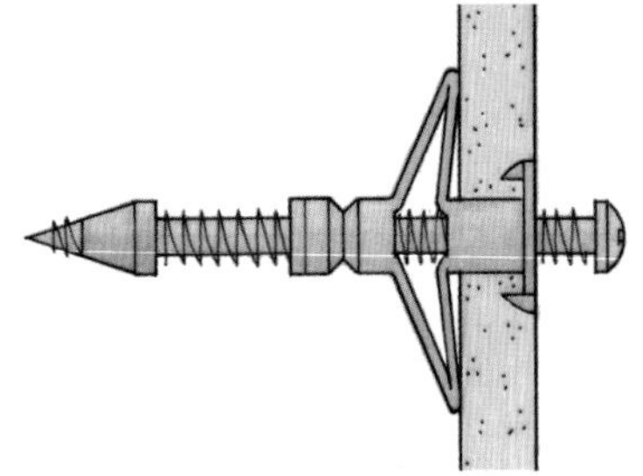

Drive a hollow wall anchor home with a hammer, and then turn the screw to secure. Back out the screw and use it to fasten the object to the wall.

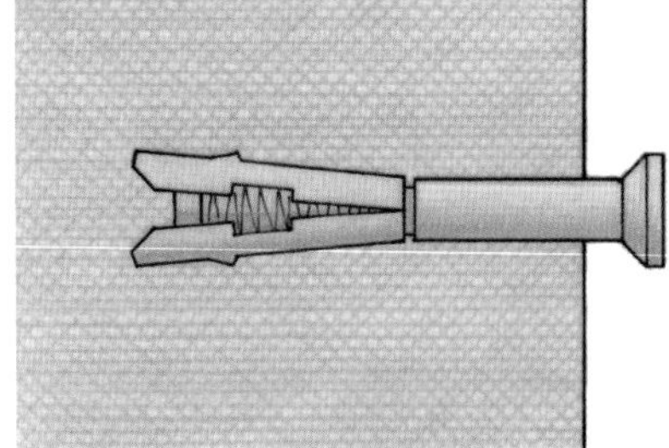

Predrill and insert this masonry anchor. Turn the screw to lock it in place, and then remove the screw cap to reveal a screw upon which you can secure a bracket.

SMARTtip

Searching for Studs and Joists

A good way to locate studs and joists is to use a stud finder, available in most hardware stores for under $20. A battery-powered electronic stud finder measures the wall density as you scan across it. A light will flash as it crosses the stud or other framing member. Magnetic stud finders react to the screws or nails used to fasten the drywall to the framing. Be careful, however, because they also react to some types of pipe and cable. Always try to fasten brackets and screws in the middle of the stud. In most houses, studs are 16 inches (40cm) apart, from center to center, except near corners, where the spacing may be closer.

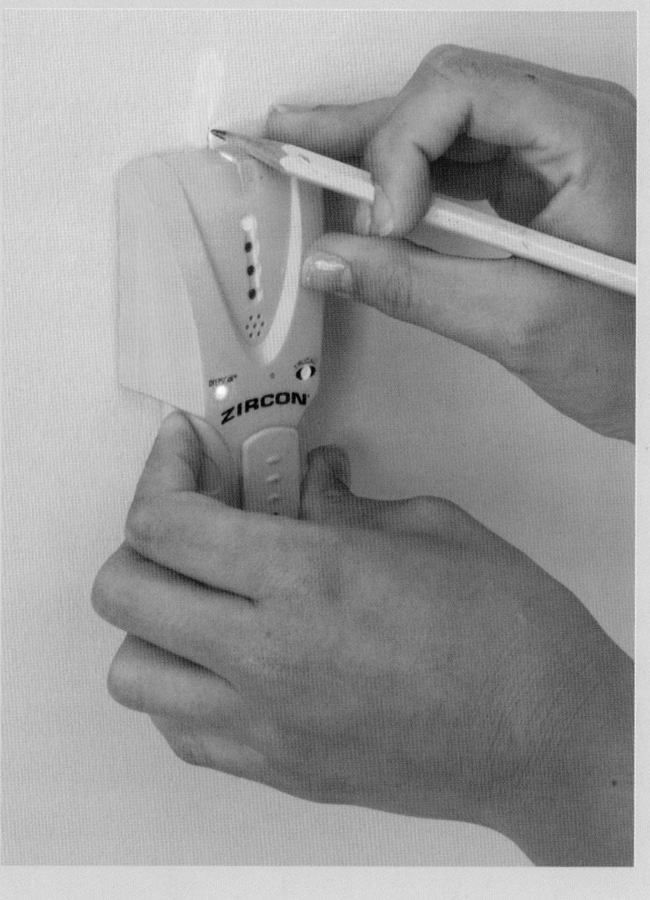

An electronic stud finder can be used to find studs in walls or joists in ceilings. Once you find the first stud or joist, it's a good bet that the center of the next one is 16 inches (40cm) away from the center of the first one.

Left New types of drywall anchors can support more weight than anchors that rely primarily on friction. The system shown here locks onto the back of the wall as you drive home the screw.

Choosing the Hooks

What hooks work best? S-hooks are most common, but you may want to crimp the hook's rack end to prevent it from falling off the rack every time the pot is used. Other, more specialized hooks are also available. (See the illustrations below.) Sliding swivel hooks provide the most flexibility, allowing you to hang the pot or pan in any position. Fixed hooks dictate the spacing and restrict the placement of pots. Movable hooks provide full flexibility for your daily needs.

Top S-hooks are not your only choice when it comes to pot racks. Hooks come in many styles to suit the items being stored and are available for purchase online.

SMARTtip

Going in Circles

Avoid having to walk around your kitchen island to select a pot on the other side of your rack by installing a circular rack that rotates. If this is not an option, hang the pots you use the most in the front of the rack and the pots and pans you employ on special occasions on the opposite side of the rack.

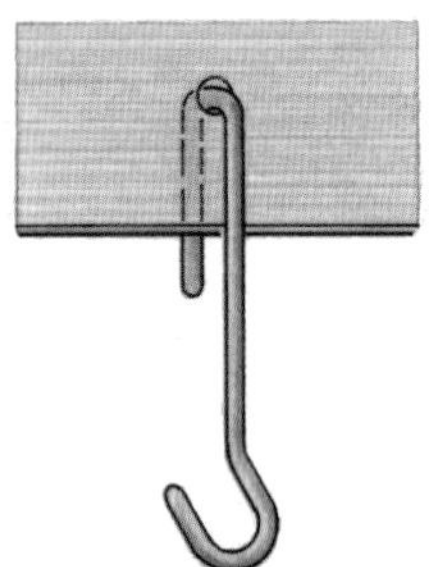

Angled pot hooks have a hook set at a slight angle, allowing pots to nest and saving space.

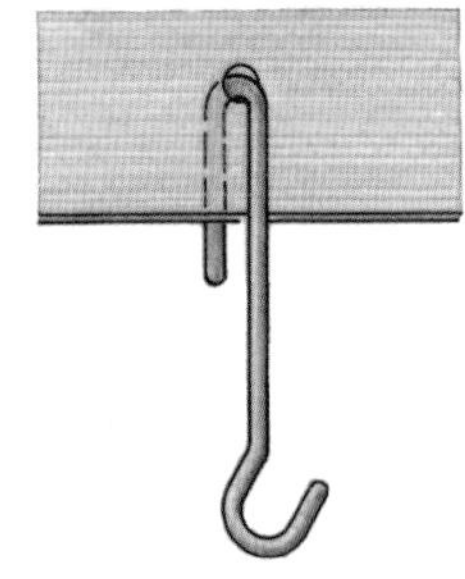

Straight pot hooks have the hook facing you, so cookware is displayed outward.

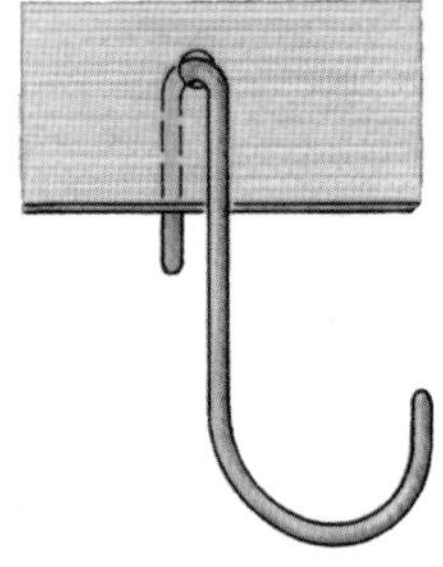

Basket hooks allow you to hang items with thick handles, such as baskets or pitchers.

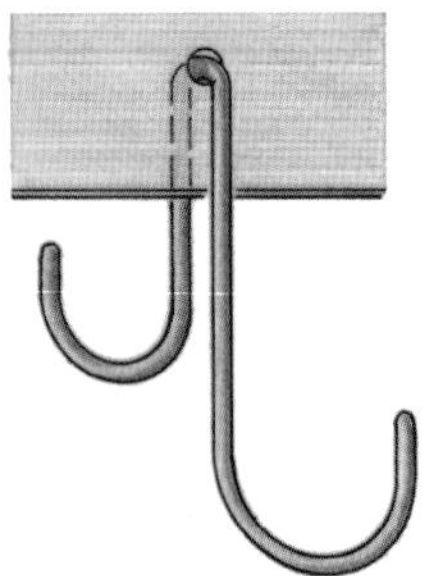

Double-level hooks allow you to hang a pot and its lid together.

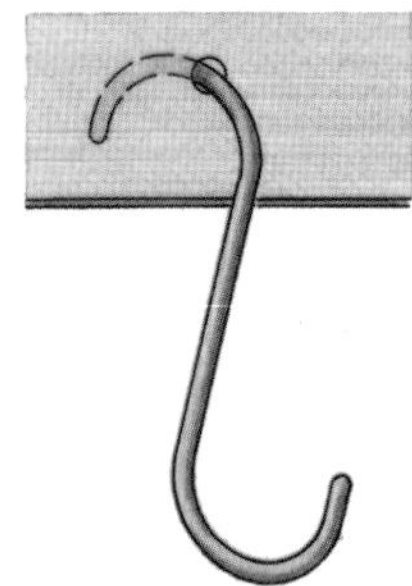

S-hooks, unlike others, can hang from tubing, or use them to connect an eye screw to a chain.

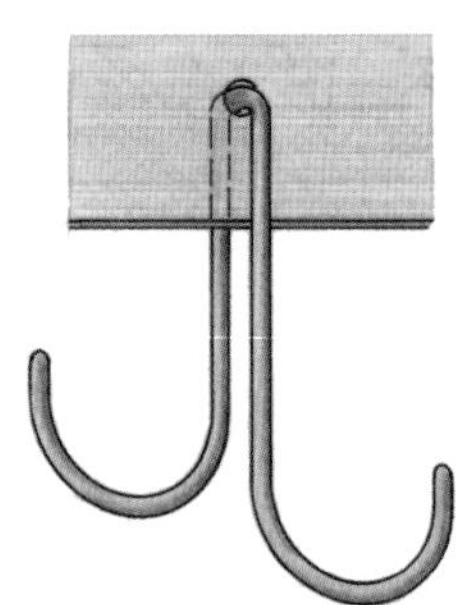

Twin hooks allow you to hang two items from the same hook.

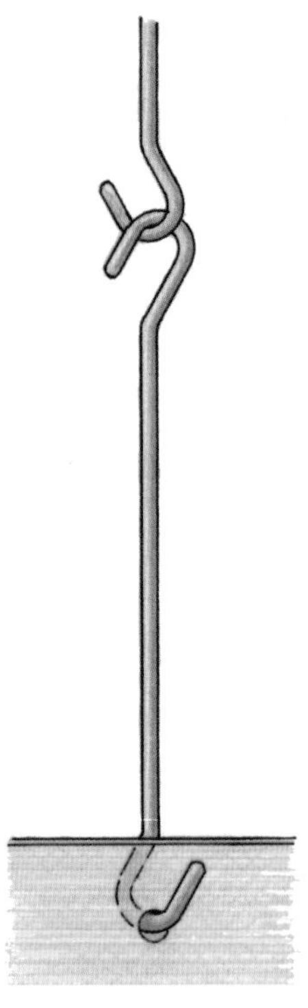

Extension hooks let you lower a rack, making it even easier to reach your pots and pans.

Where to Put the Lids

Now that the pots are hung and beautifully displayed, you may be wondering what to do with all the lids. You've got several options. Lids can hang from a ceiling-mounted pot rack by suspending a chain from the rack and attaching the lids with hooks. Lids can also be stored on top of a grid-style rack. Rail-style pot racks, when mounted on a wall, can also hold lids. Simply slide the lid between the wall and the rail. The lid handle will rest on the rail and hold the lid in place. Both options keep lids and pots in the same place. Vertical lid racks that mount on the side of nearby cabinets or walls are another option. If none of the above work for you, opt for vertical dividers that hold lids upright in a nearby cabinet or deep drawer.

Top **Pot lids hanging on racks on a wall or on the side of a cabinet near the sink will be within easy reach when cooking and close to where they're washed, so they can be put away quickly.**

Bottom **A wall-hung rack allows you to slip lids behind the bar. You may want to apply a protective cover on the wall to keep it from getting scratched.**

Ceiling-Hung Shelves and Cabinets

You don't need a wall for cabinets or shelves—a couple of hefty ceiling joists from which to hang them will do. Ceiling-hung storage also screens unwanted views of the kitchen from the living room and creates a sense of enclosure in an otherwise too open floor plan.

Ceiling-hung storage units are ideally situated over islands and peninsulas. Shelves or cabinets over a peninsula or island used for eating meals are perfect places for dishes and glasses. Install a stemware rack below the cabinet or bottom shelf and your wine glasses will be easy to see and reach. Dish racks can be suspended over the sink to save counter space and for convenience. If the rack is open on the bottom, wet dishes can drip into the sink and air-dry.

You may also hang tiered baskets from the ceiling, as long as they won't interfere with traffic. Fill the baskets with root vegetables and fruit. If near the sink, use the baskets to hold sponges, pan scrapers, and cleaning brushes. You can also hang a knotted rope and attach S-hooks. Drape dishcloths or dry herbs, or hang a mug collection from the rope.

SMARTtip

Watch Your Weight

If your home is old, with undersized joists, be careful about how much weight you hang from the ceiling. If you plan to hang shelves or cabinets and fill them to the brim with heavy items, check with your carpenter to be sure you don't cause the joists and ceiling to sag. Normally, this will only be a problem if your ceiling-hung storage unit is going to be installed in the middle of a long span.

Opposite A cabinet column, often installed at the end of an island, is a great way to claim your kitchen's "air rights." Glass doors, front and back, lighten the cabinet's mass and improve accessibility.

Top Overhead cabinets are another way to use wasted space near the ceiling—and to differentiate one room from the next. Invest in a good step stool so you can access stored items.

Bottom Hanging cabinets from pipes (secured to joists or blocking) makes it look as though the cabinets are floating and keeps an open feeling between adjoining rooms.

Walls, Windows, and Doors

Look for vacancies on walls, windows, doors, and faces and sides of cabinets and appliances. Review the tips for using your backsplash in Chapter 3. Many of them will apply to other vertical surfaces. Rail systems, for example, work just as well on an open wall. Shelves, pegboards, and metal grids are other good ways to use vertical surfaces.

Consider installing a recessed niche in the space behind the wall surface. You may be more familiar with the niche idea in the bathroom—showers and tubs often include niches for shampoos and soaps.

The space inside interior kitchen walls provides a good opportunity for recessed shelves or a niche for a coffeemaker or microwave.

Kitchen windows serve as ready-made wall recesses. Install glass shelves across the window's face and you have a great place for starting seedlings. Just be sure to allow for easy opening and closing without disturbing items on the shelf. Doors offer storage opportunities as well. Their backs are good places for hanging brooms, dustpans, and aprons.

SMARTtip

Taking Sides

The sides and fronts of cabinets and appliances can be used for everything from narrow shelves for spices and small cooking items to message boards and magnetic pen and pad holders. A metal or plastic magnetic holder on the fridge, for example, can provide a place to store vitamins, utensils, plastic wrap, or sandwich bags. A magnetic rack provides a great spot to hang a dish towel or a roll of paper towels. Put up a magnetic file and you've got a place for mail and menus. You can find magnetic kitchen holders at a number of online gadget stores. Install a small rail on the front or side of a cabinet and you can hang oven mitts and light cutting boards.

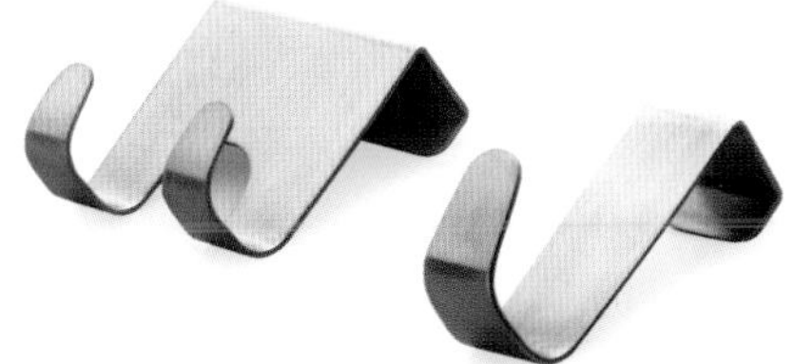

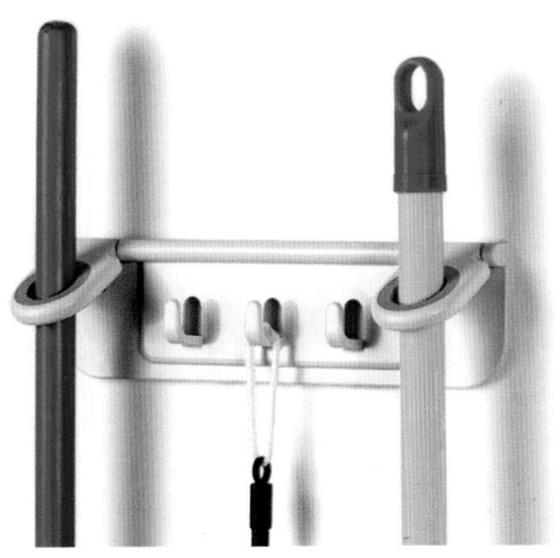

Opposite left Narrow shelves installed in front of a window can be used for storage, though they are best suited for decorative items.

Opposite right Open shelves are a low-cost but effective way to store items you use every day, including dinnerware. Note how cup hooks can be used to capture under-shelf space.

Top Hooks and rods can hang from some base-cabinet doors. They provide a convenient place to hang dish towels.

Middle left Magnetic containers stick to appliances, range hoods, and metal backsplashes. The tops twist to reveal small holes for shaking out contents.

Middle right Other handy magnetic accessories include bins and clips. Store pen and paper in a bin on the fridge door for making grocery lists. Clips can hold lists, school notices, or notes.

Bottom Clever racks mount on walls or behind doors, keeping brooms, mops, and dustpans organized.

Upper Reaches

Why waste the space near the ceiling? It's not easy to reach, but it's fine for seldom-used items. The open space above the cabinets is ideal for your favorite large bowls, pitchers, platters, baskets, soup terrines, and serving trays that come down infrequently but look beautiful on display. Vertical dividers are also a good way to use the space over cabinets. You can store items such as muffin tins and cookie sheets. It's also a good spot for folded paper shopping bags. On walls that don't have any cabinets, consider a Shaker-style row of pegs or a long shelf near the ceiling. Keep in mind, however, that such storage will add to your cleaning chores.

Opposite This kitchen utilizes wide molding above cabinets as well as shelves installed just below the ceiling to store platters, pitchers, and baskets.

Top A narrow shelf is part of the window molding treatment in this Victorian kitchen.

Bottom left This kitchen corner has no cabinets but makes good use of ceiling, walls, and above-window shelving for storage.

Bottom right Use the space above a wall oven for bakeware.

CHAPTER 5

Getting Creative with Leftovers

In earlier chapters, you've seen all of the conventional storage opportunities available to kitchen remodelers and reorganizers—cabinets, countertops, walls, and overhead spaces. Now discover unconventional storage opportunities.

They include leftover spaces—the odd spots here and there that nearly every kitchen has. Did you know that with nearly every remodeling there's often dozens of cubic feet left over between cabinets, beside appliances, and even on the floor? You'll also find kitchen storage that moves. Roll it out when you need it nearby, and park it out of the way when you're done. And what about using furniture you might not expect to find in a kitchen? Many designers are encouraging homeowners to try it. Hutches, bookcases, armoires, dressers—whatever fits and helps you meet a storage need. Perhaps you'll decide to make the sideboard you inherited from your grandmother the focal point of your new kitchen.

Finally, you'll learn about other sorts of leftovers—items that often must be stored in the kitchen but that don't have anything to do with cooking dinner. Look around, and you're likely to find that kitchens are typically crowded with boots and coats, umbrellas, brooms and mops, laundry supplies, cleaning supplies, household tool kits, plants and potting materials, and pet supplies and grooming tools. And how about all of the stuff you use to cook, serve, and dine outdoors? In this chapter, you'll get some ideas about what to do with all your leftovers—with the exception of what you had for dinner last night!

Left Leftover spaces don't have to be large to be useful. The hidden shelves inside this support are the perfect place for seasonings.

Use Every Inch

If you need every inch of storage space you can get, you may want to consider some unusual spots. Most cabinets aren't available in widths smaller than 9 inches (23cm), so "fillers" (panels that match your cabinets) are often used to disguise gaps where cabinets meet a wall or appliance. But extra-narrow pullout drawers are now available in 3- or 6-inch (7 or 15cm) widths and are designed with a panel or pilaster on the drawer face. They are perfect for small spice jars.

Toe kicks at the bottom of each base cabinet are another underutilized area. Pullout drawers can easily be installed in the toe kick, giving you additional storage space for table linens, baking sheets, newspapers, and other items.

In addition, nearly every home has an odd corner or nook that can be employed for storage. The little wedge of space at the end of a run of cabinets may be perfect for a recycling bin or for shelving. If stairs run through your kitchen, use the space below for a wine rack or shoes. The narrow space beside the fridge can store a collapsible step stool. A small, shallow niche in the wall is a prime spot to put the salt and pepper shakers. Make the most of the space under a window seat by installing base cabinets.

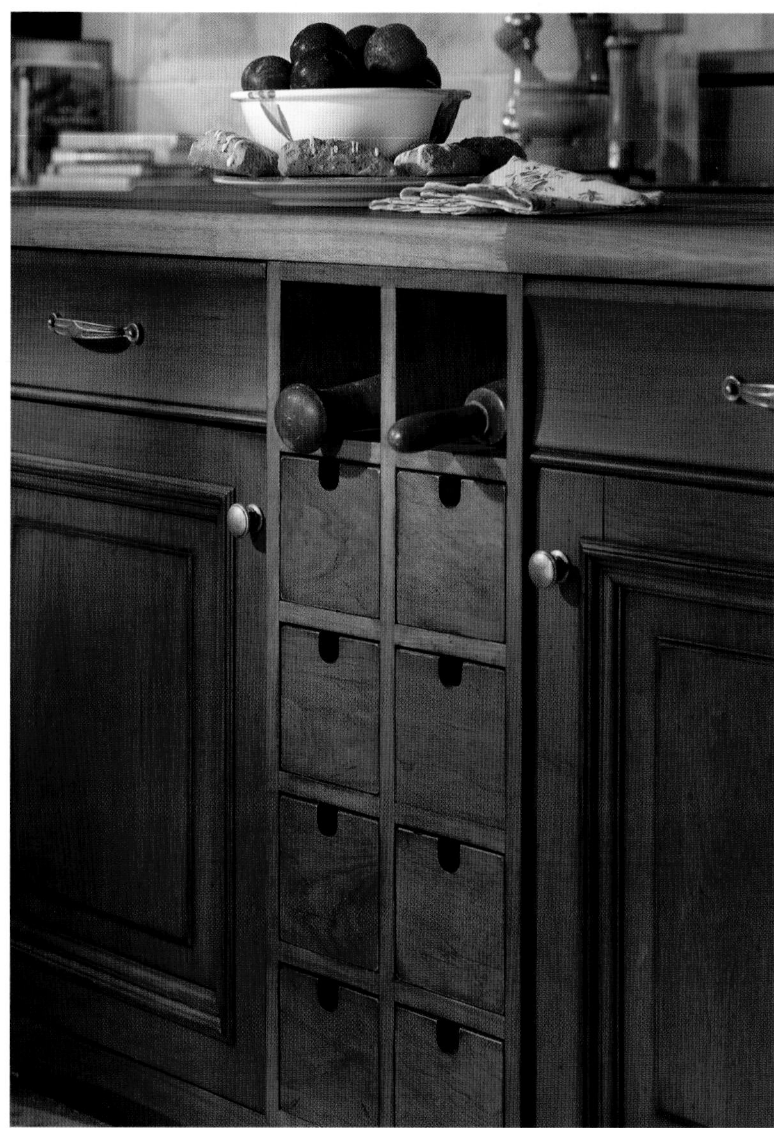

Opposite Pullouts are a great way to use spaces where a full cabinet would not fit. The narrow shelves, open on both sides, make finding items quick and easy.

Top Apothecary drawers and cubbies are another good way to use the leftover space between cabinets.

Bottom Storing large trays is often a problem. Here, two trays fill out a run of cabinets. The trays' sides match the wood used for the cabinetry.

TRADITIONAL
TAGINE
SPICES

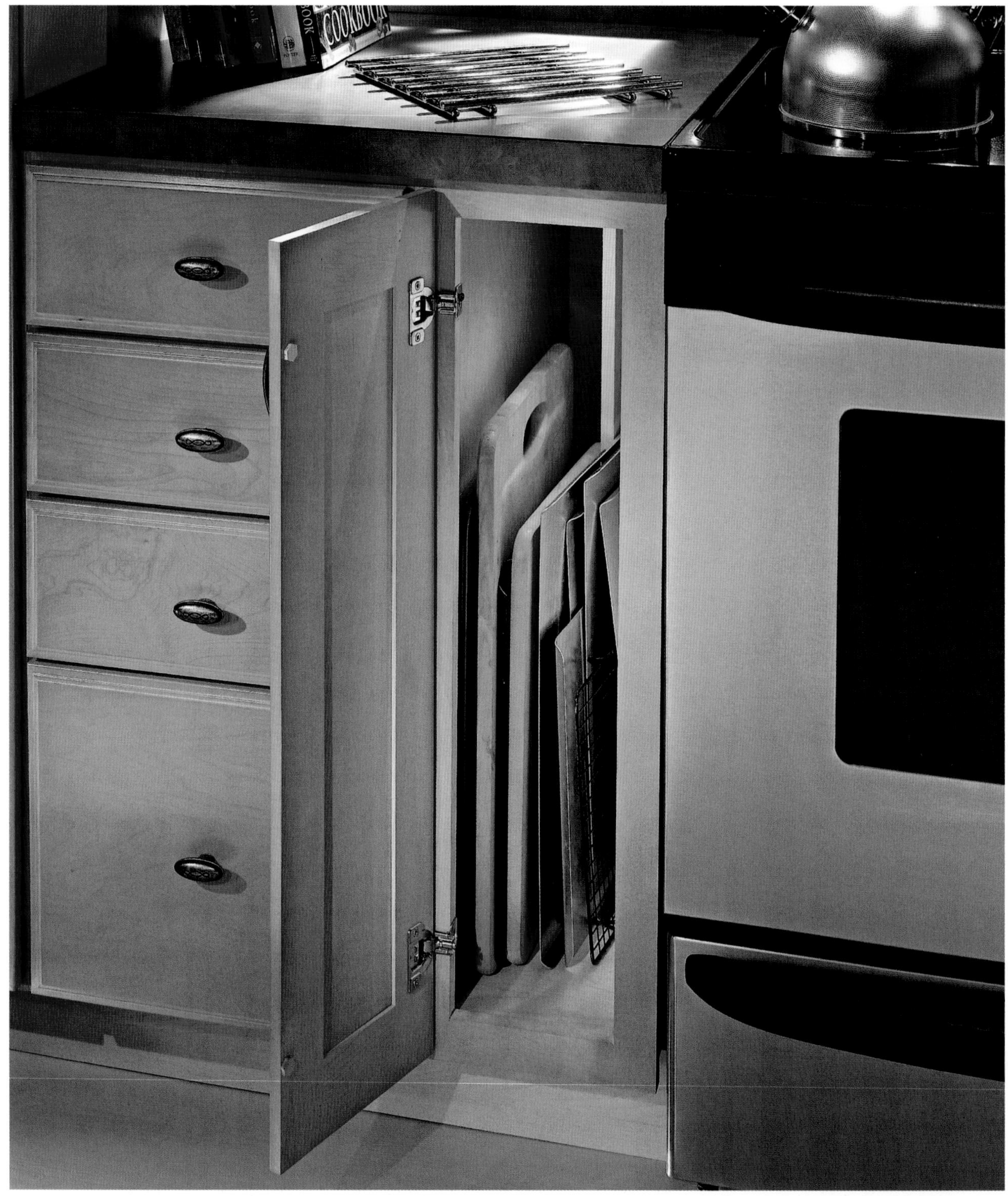

Above "Filler" spaces are also ideal for storing large, flat items, including cutting boards, cookie sheets, and pizza stones.

Top Pullouts with a pegboard panel allow you to store items that are ill suited for shelves. Use one side for utensils and the other for household tools.

Bottom left If your leftover space is next to the fridge, use a tall and narrow pantry pullout. Storing all foods together in one area makes it easier to unload groceries.

Bottom right A toe kick pullout makes use of the normally wasted space below base cabinets. Use it for storing items you don't use every day.

Leftover Spaces

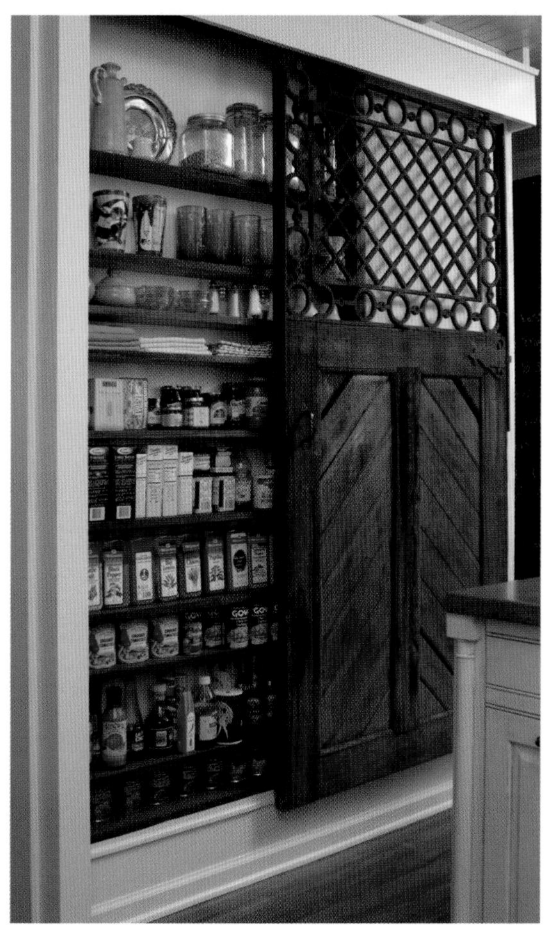

Opposite Window seats are wonderful for taking your morning coffee or for snacking before dinner. Make full use of the space below for seasonal items, such as holiday dishes and mugs.

Top left These triangular shelves fit an odd shape between cabinets and the range. They were fashioned from leftover countertop material. Veneer tape was used to cover the plywood edges.

Bottom left It looks custom-built, but it's not. Cabinet manufacturers have become savvy about using every inch for useful storage.

Top right Shallow shelves 3 inches (7.6cm) recessed in this kitchen wall are enough to house a large collection of spices. The door is made from a salvaged leaded-glass panel.

Bottom right An open staircase was walled off to create this compact pantry. The reclaimed door glides on top-mounted rollers.

Broom Closets

Often custom-built to fill gaps between cabinet runs and the wall or between large appliances and the wall, broom closets are typically too small for everything we pack into them. To make cleaning chores a little less unpleasant, keep your closet well organized. Weed out items that are better off stored elsewhere, and then get as many items as possible off the floor. Use hooks or a wall rack to hang your brooms, mops, and dusters, as well as smaller items like dustpans and fly swatters. Use the space you've opened up on the floor to store a small vacuum cleaner or mop bucket. A heavy-duty hook installed above your vacuum can help keep the hose and extension cord from becoming tangled. Keep frequently used cleaning supplies in a cleaning caddy.

Whether you're remodeling or building new, don't forget to leave space for a broom closet. Designers often put them where there is leftover space, such as in a corner—anywhere outside the kitchen's work triangle. As with any cabinet, opt for adjustable shelves. One possible configuration is a cubby for vacuum filters at the bottom of the closet with a shelf or cubby for the vacuum just above it. Vacuum accessories, brooms, and mops can be hung from the closet walls.

Don't have a broom closet? Try hanging mops and brooms on the wall behind a door, the wall of a basement stairway, or in the space between the refrigerator and the wall. (Slide-out broom racks that work great for narrow spaces are available.) If you have a walk-in pantry or laundry room, devote a section to cleaning supplies.

Above The leftover space between the ovens and the wall is just the right size for a pullout to store a broom and dustpan.

Opposite Often, one of the best spots for tall cleaning tools is beside the fridge. This conveniently placed broom closet does the trick.

SMARTtip

Tool Tips

Don't go all the way to the garage every time you need a screwdriver. Keep frequently used tools in the kitchen. A screwdriver with multiple bits stored in the handle will cover most household needs, along with a small hammer, measuring tape, needle-nose pliers, an adjustable wrench, utility knife, staple gun, duct tape, glue, pencil, and flashlight. Store them in a small toolbox, cleaning caddy, basket, or plastic container, or in a drawer.

Furniture that Stores

Storage in the kitchen needn't be limited to cabinets. Furniture pieces add visual interest to the kitchen, and you can take them with you when you move. Consider hutches, baker's racks, bookcases, and freestanding cabinets. Hutches are nice for storing dishes and table linens. Baker's racks often have built-in holders for wine glasses and wine bottles and are a great way to show off collectibles. They often work well in front of windows where you don't want to block light. Bookcases are perfect for pantry storage and can be dressed up with cloth-lined baskets or stainless-steel containers. Freestanding cabinets, such as traditional jelly cabinets, can hide just about anything behind their closed doors. Don't be afraid to think outside the box. A tall CD tower, for instance, could hold spices instead.

Opposite top One of today's design trends is to make kitchen storage look like furniture. Here, it literally is, with the designer using a dresser to anchor one end of a kitchen island.

Opposite bottom This armoire (at right) no longer stores clothing. It's now full of food and cookware.

Top Furniture-like pieces, including this creation, are now available from several cabinet manufacturers. This piece is perfect for storing everything from table linens to candles.

Bottom left Cabinetry that is not built-in lends itself to country-style kitchens.

Bottom right A piece of kitchen furniture that looks traditional on the outside, this beverage center is well appointed inside, with pullout trays, a cutting board, shelves, and lighting. The doors slide out of the way when the unit is in use.

Movable Storage

All kitchen storage doesn't have to be built-in. A butcher-block cart is a classic example of movable storage—wheel it into the center of the kitchen when you've got work to do and wheel it out of the way when you're done. Carts are a great place to store prep items, including knives, utensils, and spices. And a butcher-block top eliminates the need for a cutting board. A stainless-steel cart with a drawer can provide an outdoor prep area where you can store grilling utensils. (See "Outdoor Cooking Supplies," page 186.)

Bins and baskets are also good movable storage options. A set of stacked baskets can hold fruit or onions or even linens. Bins with wheels can hold newspapers or other recyclables. And don't forget trays. They're great ways to store—and move—the items you use every day. The great thing about movable storage is you can take advantage of spaces where you can't put a permanent cabinet, such as in front of an infrequently used door to the basement or attic.

Above Carts come in many styles, from this contemporary unit with a stainless-steel top to ones with a Victorian sensibility.

Left Kitchen carts can increase storage and improve efficiency. This unit has a butcher-block top, shelves, towel rods, and a locking cutlery drawer. It can double as a serving cart.

Opposite top Choose a cart with high-quality casters. This unit's large rubber wheels roll quietly and smoothly. If you intend to prep food on the cart, be sure that at least two of the casters will lock, so the cart won't roll as you knead dough.

Opposite bottom Push your cart out of the way when it's not needed. In tight quarters, however, you may want to provide a parking space.

SMARTtip

The Landing Zone

The kitchen is often the first place things land when they are brought into the house. Items from other parts of the house tend to find their way there, as well. If you're not careful, they'll all take up residence in your kitchen. Use a basket with a sturdy handle to hold items that need to go to other areas of the house—and redistribute its contents on a regular basis.

Cleaning Supplies

A cleaning caddy (usually a plastic container with several compartments and a handle in the middle) is one of the best ways to store frequently used cleaning supplies. Stock it with a glass cleaner, surface cleaner, scrubbing sponge, clean rags, a toothbrush (for getting into nooks and crannies), and any other products you use often. A simple bucket works fine, too. Store it, along with other cleaning supplies, under the kitchen sink or in a broom closet or pantry. Special under-the-sink shelving units are available that fit around the plumbing so you can maximize your storage space. Use plastic containers to keep sponges, rags, and brushes organized. Keep short products separate from tall products so they don't get hidden.

Above A pullout crate is a great way to corral your cleaning supplies. Lift it off its tray to carry it to where you plan to do some scrubbing.

Right A plastic caddy, available at many houseware and hardware stores, is another good way to keep cleaning supplies from overrunning a sink cabinet—and to confine inevitable leaks and spills.

Opposite top Cabinets designed for pet supplies have a door that tilts forward, enabling you to dish out your pet's meals quickly,

Opposite bottom Consider building a pet-grooming center into a base cabinet. This pullout unit boasts a pegboard panel for organizing grooming tools.

Pet Supplies

Bags of pet food can be large and bulky, and pet bowls are often underfoot. Large, airtight plastic containers help keep your furry friend's food neat and free from pests. Some are available on wheels, while others have spouts for easy pouring. Consider storing the bulk of your pet food elsewhere (such as in the garage or basement), and store a small container of it in your kitchen. If you're always tripping over food bowls, put them away when not in use and keep a water dish out in another room. Cats can be fed on a shelf or windowsill. Keep pet accessories such as brushes, toys, flea collars, and shampoos together in a container so you can find them easily.

SMARTtip

Don't Ditch the "Junk" Drawer

The "junk" drawer might seem like an anomaly in a well-organized kitchen, but it serves a necessary purpose. Every kitchen has small odds and ends—bag clips, batteries, rubber bands, twine, wire ties, and such—that need to be stored somewhere. An ideal solution is a shallow drawer in an out-of-the-way spot in the kitchen. Use drawer dividers or trays with lots of compartments to keep things tidy. (Trays used for makeup or crafts often work well.) Small spice containers with clear lids are great for storing thumbtacks, pushpins, and other small items.

Outdoor Cooking Supplies

If you cook outside a lot, consider moving some of your kitchen storage outdoors. Outdoor kitchens are a hot trend, and many are outfitted with base cabinets and wall cabinets. Cabinets equipped with drawers, shelves, racks, and hooks provide a place for everything you need while flipping burgers. It makes sense to store items where you use them, so keep those long-handled grilling tools (spatula, fork, tongs, knife, basting brush, and grill-cleaning brush) outside. Consider other items you use when cooking alfresco, too, including but not limited to plates, pots, silverware, serving trays, cutting boards, placemats, napkins, and cleaning supplies. If you do, you'll reclaim some valuable indoor kitchen space.

Top This outdoor cabinet, made from plastic resins and fitted with stainless steel hardware, is unaffected by rain.

Bottom Outdoor kitchens are "in" and are a great place to store those extra sets of everyday dishes and flatware that are crowding your indoor kitchen, as well as your barbecue equipment.

Opposite top Outdoor stock cabinets are made in the same sizes as indoor cabinets but come with cutouts for grills and side burners.

Opposite bottom Stainless-steel doors and drawers can be fitted to masonry islands for an outdoor kitchen that will stand up to storms, even without a roof.

By the Back Door

Many kitchens have exits to the outside and must serve double-duty as a mudroom. Here are some tips to keep this area under control:

- **Hooks for hanging jackets** can never be too large or too plentiful. Select ones that have a generous curve and lip on the end to prevent jackets from slipping off.
- Install a **second row of hooks** about 3 feet (1 meter) off the floor to hang backpacks, purses, children's jackets, umbrellas, and dog leashes.
- Hang a **shelf above your hooks** and store gloves, hats, and sports equipment on it in baskets.
- A **wall coat rack** with a shelf and hanger bar underneath is an alternative to hooks, though hooks are more likely to be used because they are quicker and easier.
- **Coat trees** are ideal for tight spaces. Select one that has a broad, sturdy base and large hooks.
- If you have a closet nearby, an **over-the-door organizer** with clear plastic pockets works well to hold gloves, scarves, and winter hats.
- A **bench, hall tree, or wooden trunk** near the door provides a place to sit and usually has storage underneath for hats, soccer balls, and more.
- A **two-tier shoe rack** can give you twice the space for boots and shoes. Put a plastic tray underneath to collect dirt and water.
- Cabinets that look like **school lockers** provide a whimsical way to store items for each family member.
- **Wall cabinets** are available that have hooks for keys as well as cubbies to hold sunglasses and outgoing mail.

Left This clever cabinet, perfect for the back door, includes storage for keys, cell phones, and office supplies.

Middle Close the cabinet door and there are four slots for organizing your mail.

Right Coat hooks and a bench make a perfect combination near a back door kitchen area. Open shelves below the bench store boots and umbrellas.

Laundry in the Kitchen

Laundry areas are often squeezed into a kitchen closet or mudroom off the kitchen. If you're tight on space, there are several storage strategies you can use:

- When **buying a new washer and dryer,** consider ones that stack so that you can run shelving next to them. Or get ones that are front-loading with the controls in the front and install a counter or shelf right above them. A combination washer/dryer is another way to save space.
- If you have a top-loading washer, **mount shallow shelves** right above the washer that won't interfere with the washer lid, and put deeper shelves up higher.
- **A narrow, wheeled cart** can help you gain some storage space between your washer and dryer.
- Have **two hampers or laundry baskets** for each member of the household—one for dirty clothes and one for clean clothes. Keep the clean set near the dryer so that you can sort as you fold.
- Clever **options for ironing boards** include ones that fold out from a drawer and others that fold down from a wall cabinet. Wall hangers are also available that hold a regular ironing board and an iron.
- Use an **over-the-door hanger bar** to hang ironed clothes.

Above Kitchen cabinet makers also outfit cabinets for laundry rooms. This ironing board slides out of a drawer compartment. Pullout hampers are available, too.

SMARTtip

Storing Seasonal Items

Every kitchen includes items that you only use at certain times of year, such as the turkey baster and giant roasting pan you only use at Thanksgiving or the cute bowls with reindeer on them that you only use at Christmas. Gather the items you use at certain times of year, put each group in a separate box, and label them clearly. Store the boxes in the pantry, closet, garage, or basement. Designate a shelf in your kitchen for seasonal items, and rotate them out of their boxes and onto the shelf during the time of year you need them.

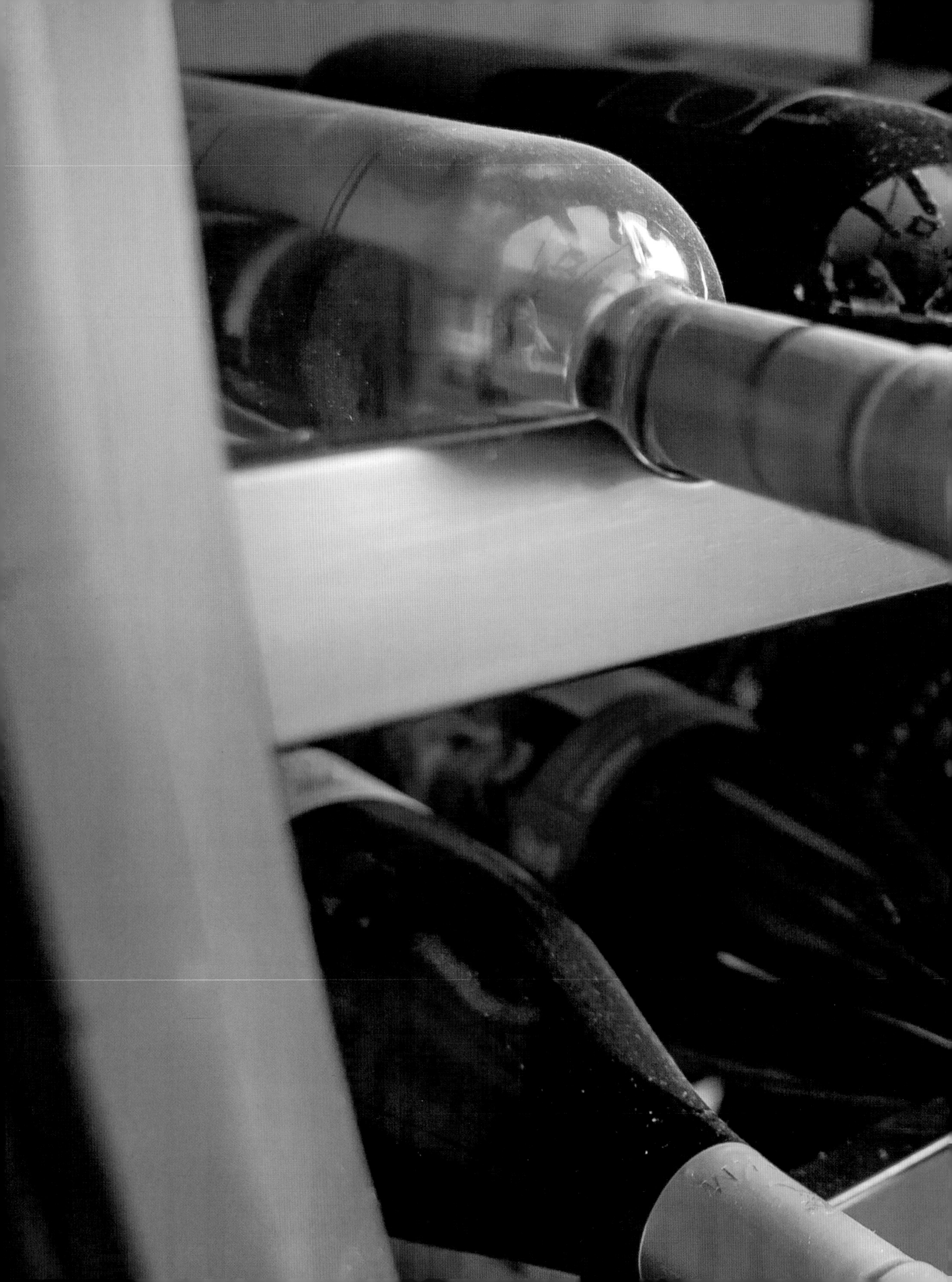

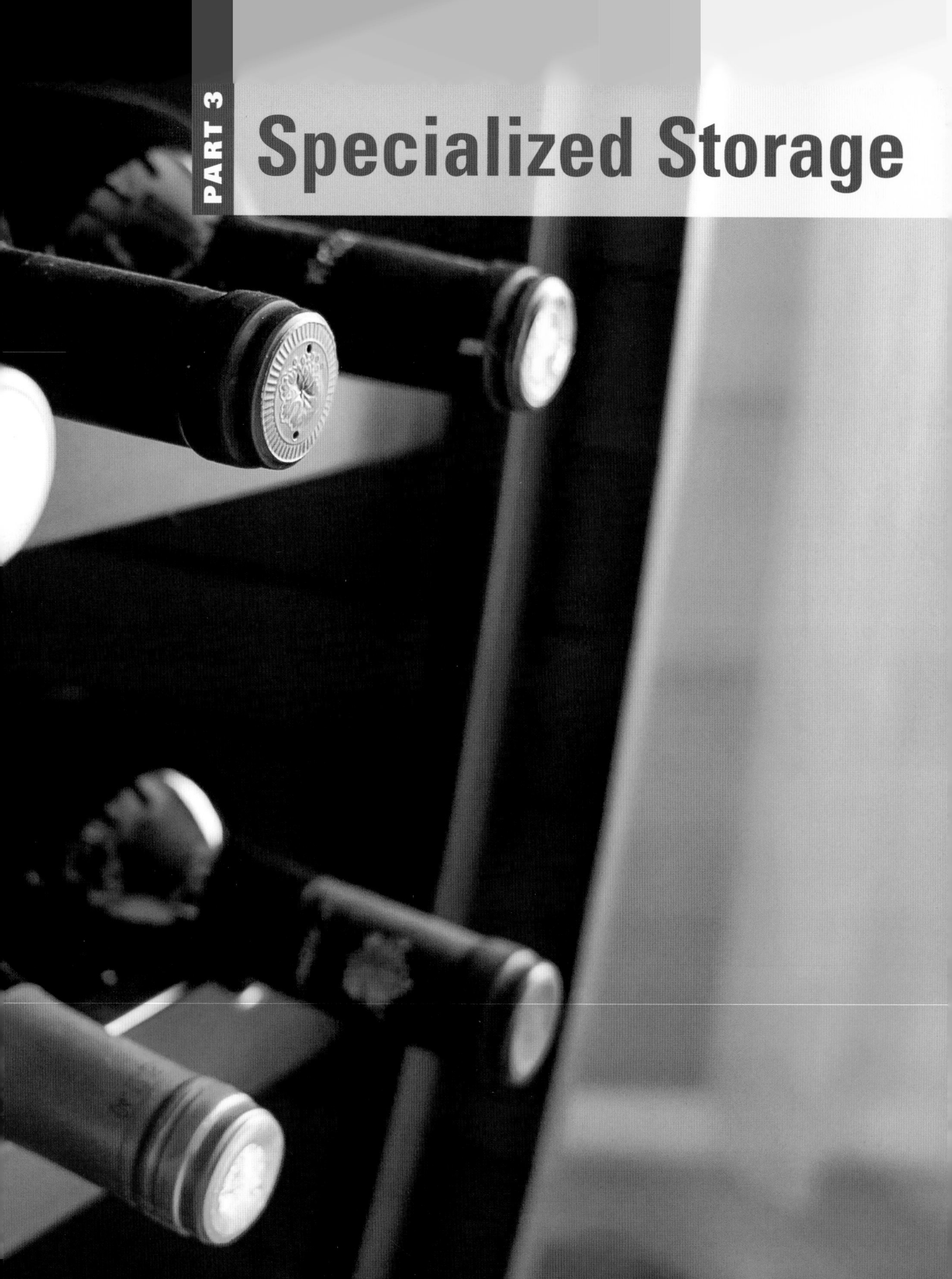

PART 3

Specialized Storage

BLUE SKY
VANILLA
CAPPUCCINO
Tropical COCONUT CREAM Sorbet
Mini Waffles
WHEAT FREE
Gardenburger
WholeFruit SORBET
LEMON
Naturally Fat Free
LEMON
DOUBLE CHOCOLATE
FrozFruit
Tropical COCONUT CREAM
Sorbet
VEGGIE BLENDS
WITH EDAMAME
The WONDER VEGGIE
ORIENTAL BLEND
Amy's MADE WITH ORGANIC VEGETABLES & BASIL
PIZZA
PESTO

CHAPTER 6

Cool and Cold Storage

It's late. You're winding down after a long day, watching the news before going to bed. During a commercial break, you head to the kitchen to get a light snack. You open the refrigerator and you look...and look...and look. You're not really sure what's in there, or where anything is. So you rummage. Before you spot the carrot sticks that you end up eating, you come across a mysterious ball of tin foil that you're too scared to open and not one, not two, but three opened bottles of the same grape jelly. Sound familiar?

The refrigerator is most likely the largest appliance in your kitchen, but having enough room is only part of the storage battle. You need to organize and manage those groceries, too. You'll avoid those dreaded refrigerator searches—with door ajar and energy bills climbing—by knowing what you have, how much you have, and where you have it. It will make meal preparation easier, too.

Of course, not all groceries go in the fridge. Potatoes, onions, garlic, and other staples are best kept in a cool, dry area, such as a walk-in pantry. In this chapter you'll learn where to locate the pantry—and what to put in it.

And let's not forget about the wine! We'll show all you oenophiles the best way to store those vintages that require a little aging.

When it comes to storage and organization, having the right fridge, walk-in pantry, and refrigerated wine cellar makes all the difference—it's an open-and-shut case.

Left **Today's refrigerators offer enough room to store all your food—and provide plenty of bins, shelves, and trays to organize it.**

Refrigerators and Freezers

Where should you put the refrigerator, which is most likely the most massive appliance in your kitchen? You may be limited by electric and water hookups, and for energy-conservation reasons, the refrigerator should be kept away from ranges, dishwashers, sunny windows, and other sources of heat.

With such a large item, you'll want to situate it so it doesn't block traffic flow from one work center to another. And don't put it too far away, either. Keep the refrigerator 4 to 7 feet (1.2 to 2.1 meters) from the sink and 4 to 9 feet (1.2 to 2.7 meters) from the range. People not involved in meal preparation often need access to the refrigerator, so of the three components of the work triangle, the fridge should be located at the outermost corner. Try to keep it away from an actual corner, however, because a lot of space is required to open and close its doors.

It helps to locate the refrigerator near the entrance where you bring in the groceries. Of course, you need to have room to set them down, so make sure you have counter space to one side of the fridge or across from it—on an island, for example. Don't position the island too close to the fridge, however, or you'll create traffic jams when the fridge or freezer is open. Finally, don't overlook door swing. The first parameter is that it opens to the work zones of your kitchen. If possible, it should also swing away from the counter where you empty your grocery bags. This way, it's easier to stock the fridge.

Right The refrigerator should go on the outer edge of the kitchen's work triangle. This allows others to get to it without getting in your way while you prepare a meal.

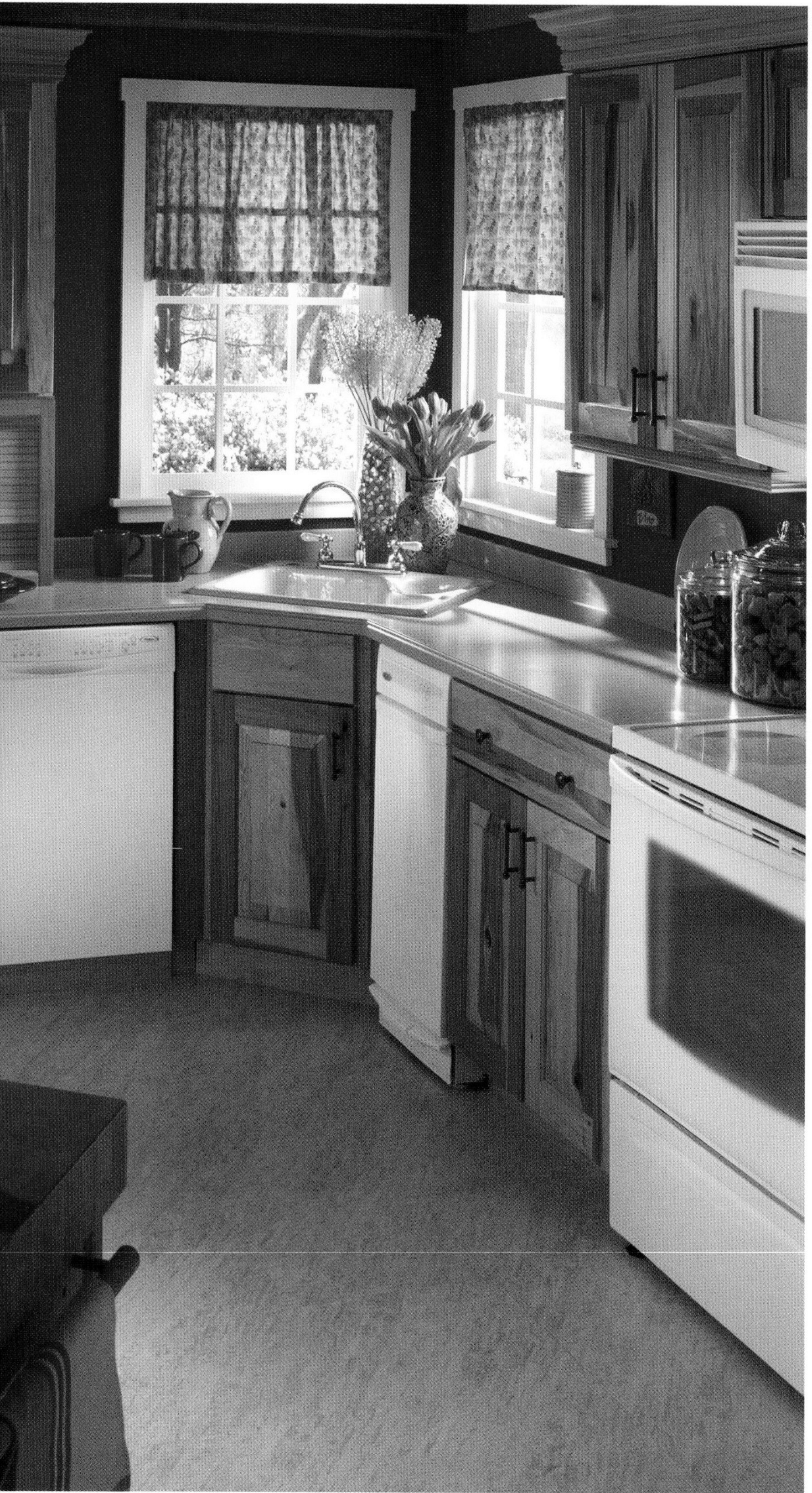

SMARTtip

Up Against a Wall

If your plan is to place a refrigerator so one side is against a wall, you may have a problem. Refrigerators with deep storage bins on the doors need to open more than 90 degrees so you can access shelves or drawers that are inside the box. The wall can't extend past the refrigerator's hinges.

SMARTtip

Give Groceries a Rest

At least 15 inches (38cm) of counter space is needed on one side of your refrigerator. For top-mount and bottom-mount units, try to have the counter space on the side of the refrigerator opposite the hinges, so the open door doesn't get in the way. Ditto for side-by-side models—have the fridge section open away from counter space because you access the fridge more often than the freezer.

Top **Counter space next to the refrigerator is a must. If you don't have much room on either side of the fridge, an island will do the trick, providing plenty of room to set down groceries or a food tray.**

Left **This refrigerator has ample counter space on both sides. Put your grocery bag on the counter opposite the door you'll be opening so that the door doesn't get in the way when you're loading the fridge.**

Fridge and Freezer Styles

The most common setup has the refrigerator and freezer in one unit. Side-by-side models offer the greatest access to both sections and require the least clearance for door swing. They generally offer the most freezer space, too. But items often get pushed to the back of deep, narrow shelves. And if you plan on storing a pizza box or a frozen turkey, the narrow shelves may not allow you to do so. If this is going to be a problem for you, consider a top-mount unit, which has the freezer section at the top, or the bottom-mount variety, which—you guessed it—has the freezer down below. The former is the most common type of refrigerator. The latter is available with French doors. Either style will require you to bend down to access the bottom unit. Your choice may depend on what section you enter most often. (In a typical household, the refrigerator door is opened seven times as often as the freezer door.) If you don't have the room for a full-size unit, a compact refrigerator is a real space saver. Compact fridges—often seen in dorms, offices, and small apartments—have a capacity of about 5 to 6 cubic feet (0.15 cubic meters) and can fit under a counter.

Nobody ever said the refrigerator and freezer had to share real estate. Some people prefer to have separate units, particularly when they want more space for each section. If you shop often and prepare lots of fresh foods, you probably don't need extra freezer space. But if you shop infrequently and eat lots of packaged meals—or if you freeze lots of meats, fruits, veggies, and homemade pastas—you may desire a separate freezer with a larger capacity. Then again, you can join one of the hottest trends in the kitchen industry and invest in refrigerator and freezer drawers. Use them to complement the primary refrigeration unit by storing foods you use frequently in a drawer situated close to where you'll be using them. You can also put drawers on opposite ends of the kitchen, using one as a snack station and the other for guests to grab a drink while you tend to your party-hosting duties. Either way, you'll reduce traffic in the food-prep area.

Opposite A side-by-side refrigerator puts fridge and freezer items at eye level, but it might be difficult to store your child's birthday cake or any other large, flat items.

Right Units with French doors to the fridge above and a roll-out freezer below are popular because they provide easy access to both fridge and freezer.

Smart Fridges

Today's smart refrigerators can help you do more than organize your food—they can help you organize your life. They have touch screens and cameras inside. This means you can check what's in there without opening the door (therefore saving energy), or even while you are at the grocery store, since most smart fridges can be linked to your smartphone. Other features can include individual calendars for the whole family, Wi-Fi for looking up recipes, and even voice interaction functionality that allows you to ask for a recipe and have it read to you while you cook. They can entertain you, too, by streaming music and mirroring what's on TV in another room so you don't have to miss anything if you hit the kitchen for a snack.

Opposite If your kitchen is small—or if it's so large you have room for a secondary fridge—consider getting a compact model that will fit right under the counter. It's perfect for fruits and vegetables.

Top Not all fridges and freezers are combined . A trend is separate units. These built-in models with custom panels were placed next to each other, but they didn't have to be.

Bottom left Want to impress your friends during your next dinner party? Invest in a refrigerator drawer that blends right in with the rest of your base cabinets, and stock it with beverages and snacks.

Bottom right A refrigerator drawer allows you to bring cool and cold storage to wherever it's most desired, but that convenience will cost you—most models sell for more than $1,000.

Refrigerator Configurations

Right A bottom-mount refrigerator with French doors can be opened without interfering with the traffic flow in the kitchen. If the freezer compartment pulls out, look for one that extends fully.

Opposite top left One of the newer refrigerators on the market is the wide-by-side, which combines the best aspects of side-by-side and top- or bottom-mount models. Wide-by-side fridges have shelves wide enough to hold a tray of hors d'oeuvres and a frozen pizza.

Opposite middle left Side-by-side refrigerators typically provide the most freezer space, and they allow you to access the foods you use most frequently without bending.

Opposite top right Bottom-mount refrigerators are a good option for people who want to keep fresh food at eye level. The glass door on this model makes it easy to see what you have on hand without opening the door.

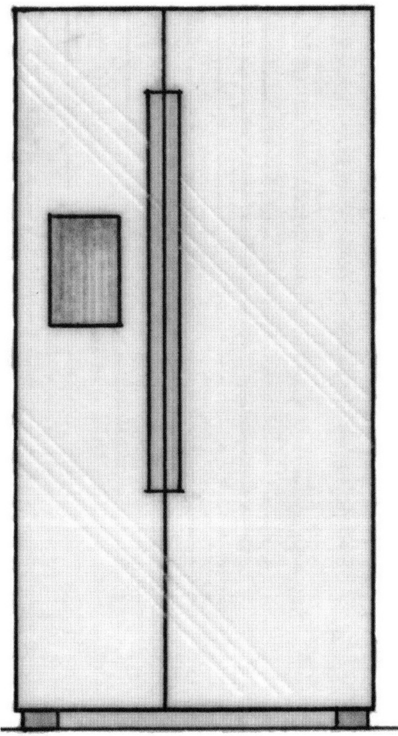

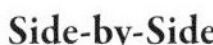

Side-by-Side

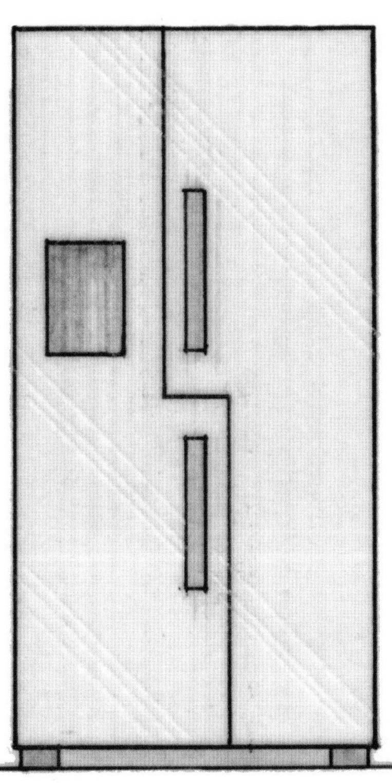

Wide-by-Side

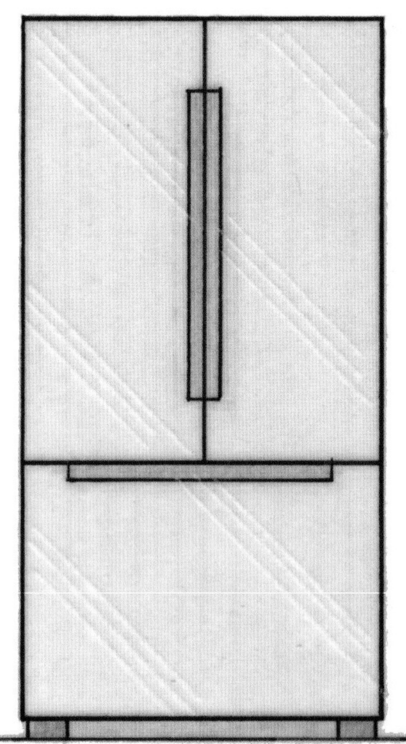

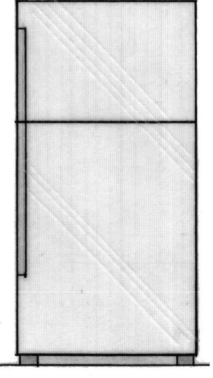

French Door

Top-Mount

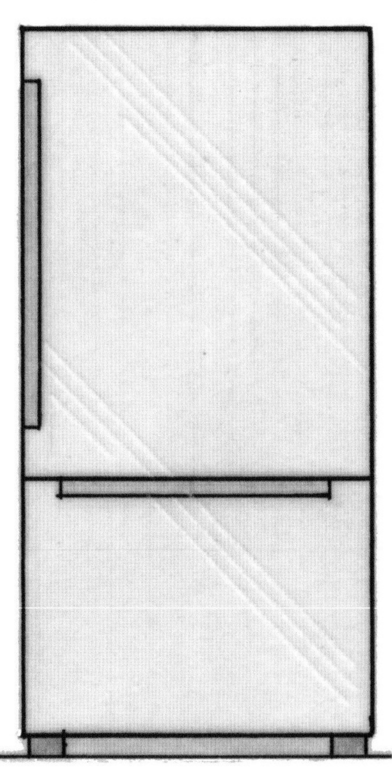

Bottom-Mount

Refrigerator Sizes

When choosing a refrigerator, it's important to get one that's the right size for your lifestyle. If you get one that is too big and don't keep it filled, you'll waste energy. If you get one that is too small, it'll be jam-packed with groceries, many of which won't be accessible. Refrigerators usually have between 18 and 26 cubic feet (0.5 and 0.7 cubic meters) of storage space. An average family of four needs 20 to 22 cubic feet (about 0.6 cubic meters), but if you have a couple of teenagers who are food vacuums, consuming milk and sandwiches like there's no tomorrow, you may want a larger unit.

Don't make cubic feet the only factor when it comes to size. If your refrigerator is going to fit between existing cabinetry or under a wall cabinet, it can't be too wide or too tall. Consider depth, too. Many of today's models are counter-depth, which keeps the fridge from jutting into the room and narrowing traffic paths the way the full-depth models do.

SMARTtip

Time with Trash Day

It's a good idea to go through your fridge about once a week, getting rid of old food. Your best bet is to do this on trash day. That way, you'll keep the foul odors—and the bacteria—out of your garbage can.

Opposite A full-depth refrigerator, which extends a few inches (about 7cm) beyond standard base cabinets, holds more than a counter-depth model but reduces the kitchen's traffic paths.

Left Even when the doors of this counter-depth, side-by-side refrigerator are open, there is plenty of room for another person to walk by unimpeded.

On the Inside

At this point you've probably figured out the fridge style you want and the size that best suits your family's needs. That's a start, but making the most of your space is just as important as having enough room for all those groceries.

Today's fridges make many of the organizational decisions for you. They provide a butter compartment, a meat drawer, a crisper drawer for vegetables, and so on. Newer fridges maintain consistent temperatures throughout, so you can store the butter and other dairy products on the door—despite what you may have heard about door temperatures being the warmest and fluctuating the most. Eggs, however, are an exception. It's best to keep them in their cardboard or foam carton on an upper shelf so kids are less likely to get to them and leave a yolk-filled mess on the floor. The eggs will stay fresher longer in their original carton, and you'll be able to see the expiration date.

The top shelf is a good spot for soda bottles, pitchers of lemonade, and other large containers that you don't want to bend over to reach and lift. Reserve the bottom shelf or the meat drawer—designed to be the coldest spot—for raw meats, poultry, and fish. That way, juices from the raw meats won't leak onto other foods, making a mess—and possibly making you sick. Use the crisper drawers to store your fruits and veggies. These drawers have a higher humidity than the rest of the fridge, enabling them to keep your vegetables from losing moisture and wilting. Be sure, however, to put your fruits and veggies in separate crisper drawers. Fruits give off ethylene gas, which can shorten the life of vegetables. Fruits can absorb odors from veggies, too.

Above When organizing your fridge, do what you'd do in your cabinets: group like items together. Dedicate an entire bottom shelf for all your deli meats and cheeses.

Left Good items to keep on the fridge door are those that come in jars or bottles, such as drinks, jellies, and condiments. They're easier to grab and less likely to get lost here.

Features and Space Savers

Every refrigerator has shelves. Most have shelves that can be adjusted or removed according to your needs. A few newer fridges even have motorized shelves that go up and down with the push of a button. Others have half-width shelves, so you can adjust one side for taller items. A pullout bin is another good way to keep condiments and sauces together and accessible; you don't have to reach over other bottles to get the one you want. An adjustable bin on the door will allow you to fit that two-liter soda bottle with ease.

Let's not forget the freezer. Sometimes this compartment comes without any shelving, which makes it a hassle to try to get something at the bottom of a pile. If you're tired of frozen-food avalanches whenever you try to dislodge one package from the stack, buy an aftermarket wire or stainless-steel shelf. If you're after secure storage and easy access for all those bags of frozen veggies, look for a model with tilt-out door bins. With the right mix of features, your freezer storage will be much more efficient.

If your refrigerator doesn't have all the bells and whistles you'd like it to have, invest in some inexpensive space-saving devices. A two-tier can dispenser holds a dozen 12-ounce cans, which roll forward for easy access. Don't want that gallon of milk to take up so much room? A thin gallon jug—it's less than 3 inches (7.6cm) wide—nestles in along the sidewall. A wine rack hangs from the bottom of a wire shelf. And, of course, there are always the old storage standbys, including lazy Susans for small condiment bottles and clear, stackable containers for deli meats.

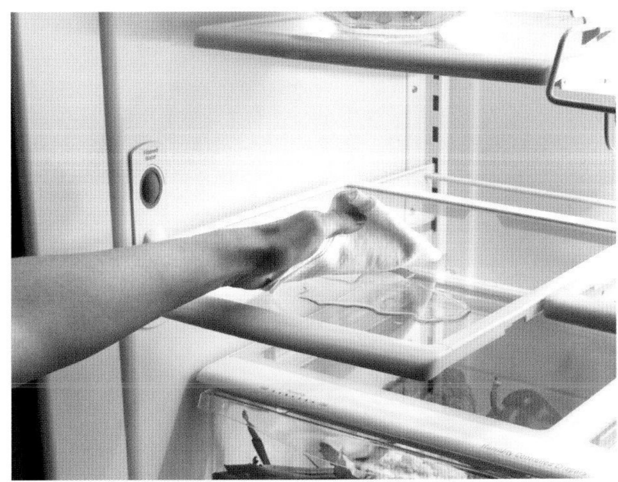

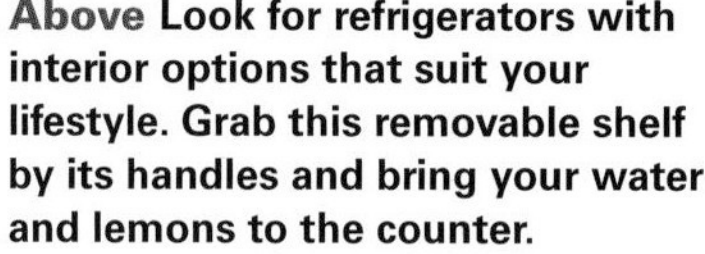

Above Look for refrigerators with interior options that suit your lifestyle. Grab this removable shelf by its handles and bring your water and lemons to the counter.

Opposite Half-width shelves allow you to adjust accordingly. Keep shelves apart for tall soda bottles. Keep them closer together when storing small condiment jars.

Top This refrigerator has a door bin designed to provide easy access to gallon jugs.

Bottom Many of today's refrigerators take the guesswork out of organization. This unit has slots built into the door to hold your favorite canned and bottled beverages.

Thai Recipe Chicken
Five Cheese & Tomato
Green Giant
Earn CASH
PERDUE
Oven Stuffer
Fresh Whole Roaster
Humidity Control
High
Low

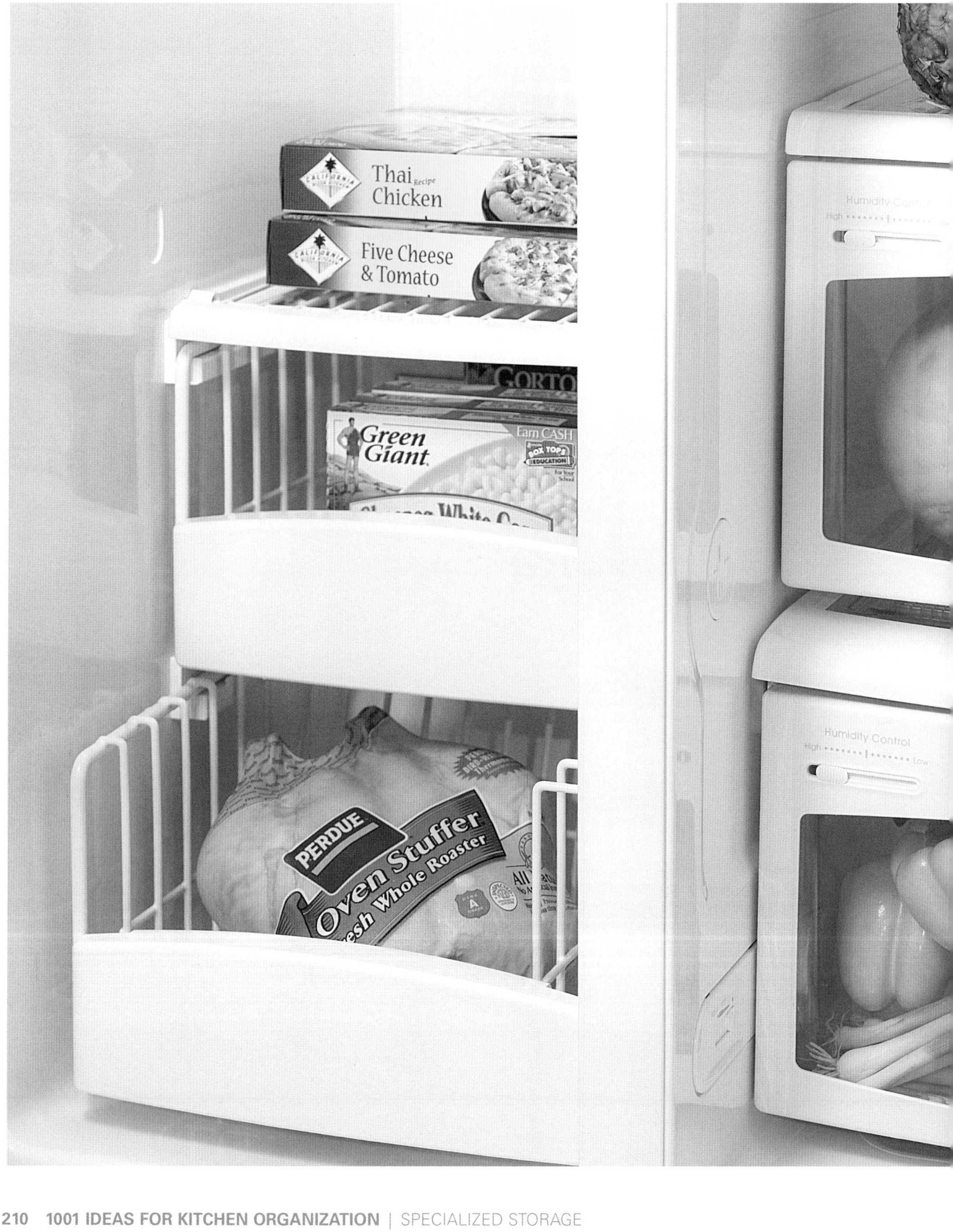

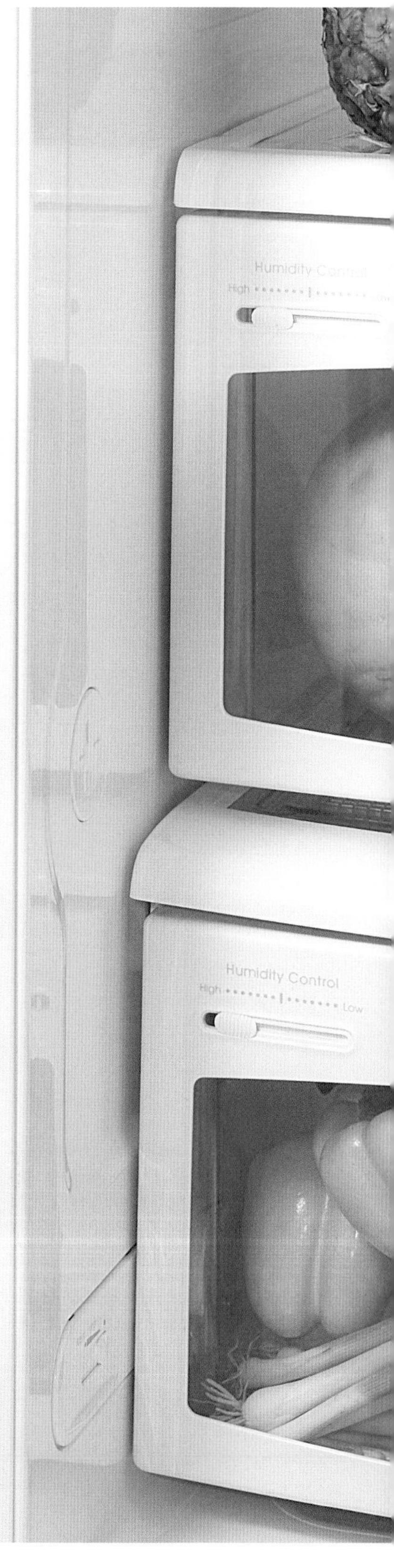

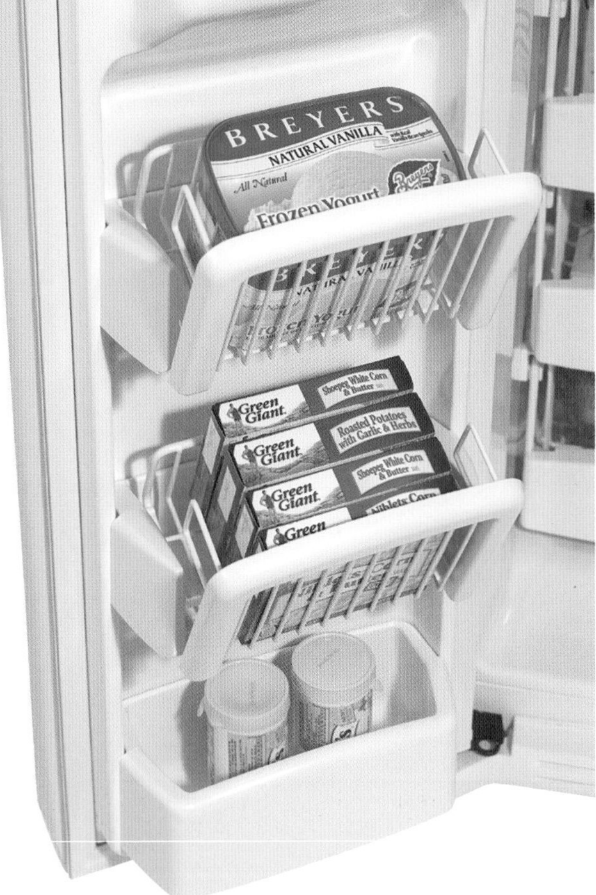

Top left Freezer shelves prevent you from creating high stacks of flat items that inevitably topple over when you try to grab the box from the bottom of the pile.

Top right Need to make room for your big salad? Some new refrigerators come equipped with motorized shelves that move with the push of a button.

Bottom left Tilt-out door bins are a great spot to store a gallon of ice cream or your frozen vegetables, whether they come in boxes or bags.

Bottom right A two-tier can dispenser allows easy access to two six-packs' worth of beer or soda—the cans roll forward when you pull one out.

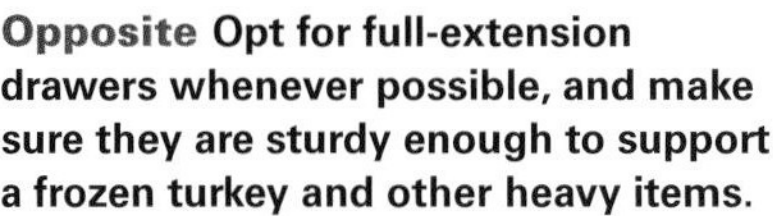

Opposite Opt for full-extension drawers whenever possible, and make sure they are sturdy enough to support a frozen turkey and other heavy items.

Recommended Storage Times for Refrigerator and Freezer

Type of Food	Fridge	Freezer
DAIRY PRODUCTS		
Butter/margarine	2 weeks	9 months
Buttermilk	1–2 weeks	*
Cheese (grated and hard)	6 months	6–12 months
Cheese spreads	3–4 weeks	*
Cottage cheese (creamed)	7 days	*
Cottage cheese (dry curd)	7 days	1 month
Cream (unwhipped)	10 days	*
Cream (whipped)	1 day	2 months
Ice cream	*	2 months
Milk, condensed (opened)	3–5 days	*
Milk, evaporated (opened)	3–5 days	*
Milk, fresh	5–7 days	*
Sour cream	4 weeks	*
Yogurt	7 days (after "sell-by" date)	*
MEAT PRODUCTS		
Beef:		
Corned	5–7 days (in pouch w/juices)	1 month (drained)
Ground	1–2 days	3–4 months
Hard sausage	2–3 weeks	1–2 months
Roast	3–5 days	6–12 months
Steak	3–5 days	6–12 months
Stew meat	1–2 days	3–4 months
Pork:		
Bacon	7 days	1 month
Chops	3–5 days	4–6 months
Ham, canned	6–9 months	*
Ham, half (fully cooked)	3–5 days	1–2 months
Ham, sliced (fully cooked)	3–4 days	1–2 months
Ham, whole (fully cooked)	7 days	1–2 months
Hotdogs (opened)	1 week	1–2 months
Hotdogs (unopened)	2 weeks	1–2 months
Roast	3–5 days	4–6 months
Sausage	1–2 days	1–2 months
Smoked breakfast sausage	7 days	1–2 months
Lamb:		
Chops	3–5 days	6–9 months
Patties	1–2 days	3–4 months
Roast	3–5 days	6–9 months
Veal:		
Roast	3–5 days	4–8 months
Venison:		
Chops	3–5 days	6–12 months
Roast	3–5 days	6–12 months
Steak	3–5 days	6–12 months
Variety Meats:		
Heart, liver, tongue, etc.	1–2 days	3–4 months
Deli and Vacuum-Packed Meat Products:		
Commercial brand vacuum-packed dinners with USDA seal	2 weeks (unopened)	*
Lunch meats (opened)	3–5 days	1–2 months
Lunch meats (unopened)	2 weeks	1–2 months
Pre-stuffed pork and lamb chops or chicken breasts	1 day	*
Cooked, Leftover Meat:		
Gravy and meat broth	1–2 days	2–3 months
Meat and meat dishes	3–4 days	2–3 months
Soups and stews	3–4 days	2–3 months

* Storage here not recommended due to safety or quality issues.

Type of Food	Fridge	Freezer
POULTRY PRODUCTS		
Chicken or turkey, pieces	1–2 days	9–12 months
Chicken or turkey, whole	1–2 days	1 year
Duck, whole	1–2 days	6 months
Game birds	1–2 days	6 months
Giblets	1–2 days	3–4 months
Goose	1–2 days	6 months
Ground turkey	1–2 days	3–4 months
Cooked, Leftover Poultry:		
Cooked dishes	3–4 days	4–6 months
Fried chicken	3–4 days	4 months
Nuggets or patties	1–2 days	1–3 months
Pieces with broth/gravy	1–2 days	6 months
Plain pieces	3–4 days	4 months
EGGS		
Fresh in shell	3 weeks	*
Hard cooked	1 week	*
Liquid pasteurized eggs or substitutes (opened)	3 days	*
Liquid pasteurized eggs or substitutes (unopened)	10 days	1 year
Raw yolks, whites	2–4 days	1 year
FISH		
Keep finfish and shellfish on ice in the refrigerator.		
Fresh Finfish:		
Fatty fish: bluefish, salmon, mackerel, mullet, smelt, tuna, and swordfish	3 days	2–3 months
Lean fish: cod, flounder, haddock, halibut, pollack, ocean perch, and sea trout	3 days	4–6 months

Type of Food	Fridge	Freezer
Fresh Shellfish:		
Crabmeat	2–3 days	4 months
Live crabs and lobster	1–2 days	2–3 months (after killing)
Live mussels and clams	4–5 days	*
Live oysters	7–10 days	*
Scallops	2–3 days	3 months
Shrimp	2–3 days	4–6 months (raw or cooked, not thawed)
Shucked mussels and clams	2–3 days	3–4 months
Shucked oysters	5–7 days	3–4 months
Squid, cleaned	3–4 days	3–4 months
Squid, whole	2–3 days	1–2 months
Smoked Fish:		
Herring	3–4 days	2 months
Salmon	5–8 days	2 months
Whiting	5–8 days	2 months
Cooked Fish:		
Breaded scallops, commercial	*	16 months
Breaded shrimp, commercial	*	1 year
Cooked pieces	3–4 days	3 months
Fish sticks	*	18 months
Surimi	2 weeks	9 months
FRUITS		
Apples	1 month	8–12 months
Apricots	3–5 days	8–12 months
Avocados	3–5 days	8–12 months

Recommended Storage Times for Refrigerator and Freezer (continued)

Type of Food	Fridge	Freezer
Bananas	*	8–12 months
Berries	2–3 days	8–12 months
Cherries	2–3 days	8–12 months
Grapefruit	2 weeks	4–6 months
Grapes	3–5 days	8–12 months
Guavas	1–2 days	8–12 months
Kiwis	3–5 days	4–6 months
Lemons	2 weeks	4–6 months
Limes	2 weeks	4–6 months
Mangoes	*	8–12 months
Melons	1 week	8–12 months
Nectarines	3–5 days	8–12 months
Oranges	2 weeks	4–6 months
Papayas	1–2 days	8–12 months
Peaches	3–5 days	8–12 months
Pears	3–5 days	8–12 months
Pineapples	2–3 days	4–6 months
Plantains	*	8–12 months
Plums	3–5 days	8–12 months
Rhubarb	3–5 days	8–12 months
FRUIT JUICES		
Concentrate	*	2 years
Fresh or reconstituted	5–7 days	8–12 months
VEGETABLES		
Asparagus	2–3 days	8–12 months
Beets	2 weeks	8–12 months
Bok choy	2–3 days	8–12 months
Broccoli	3–5 days	8–12 months
Brussels sprouts	3–5 days	8–12 months
Cabbage	1–2 weeks	8–12 months
Carrots	2 weeks	8–12 months
Cauliflower	1 week	8–12 months
Celery	1 week	8–12 months
Chilies	1 week	8–12 months
Cilantro	2–3 days	*
Corn	Use immediately for best flavor.	8–12 months
Green beans	1 week	8–12 months
Greens: spinach, collards, kale, etc.	3–5 days	8–12 months
Jerusalem artichokes	1 week	*
Jicama	2–3 weeks	8–12 months
Kohlrabi (leaves)	2–3 days	8–12 months
Kohlrabi (stem)	1 week	8–12 months
Lettuce and salad greens	1 week	*
Lima beans	3–5 days	8–12 months
Mushrooms	1–2 days	8–12 months
Okra	1–2 days	8–12 months
Onions, green	3–5 days	*
Parsley	2–3 days	*
Peas	3–5 days	8–12 months
Peppers	1 week	8–12 months
Radishes	2 weeks	*
Squash, hard	*	8–12 months
Tomatillos	1 week	8–12 months
Tomatoes	1 week	8–12 months
Yuca (Cassava)	1–2 days	8–12 months
Zucchini and summer squash	3–5 days	8–12 months

* Storage here not recommended due to safety or quality issues.

Type of Food	Fridge	Freezer
BAKED PRODUCTS		
Breads: Store at room temperature. Storing in the refrigerator promotes staling. Use the date on the label as a guide or use within 3 to 7 days.		
Bread, yeast	*	6–12 months
Muffins	*	2–4 months
Pancakes	*	1–2 months
Quick breads	*	2–4 months
Rolls, yeast	*	2–4 months
Waffles	*	1–2 months
Cakes: Store at room temperature, except for cheesecake. Best used within 3 to 7 days.		
Angel	*	4–6 months
Cheese	3–7 days	4–6 months
Chiffon	*	4–6 months
Fruit	*	1 year
Layer (buttercream icing or plain)	*	6 months
Sponge	*	4–6 months
Cookies:		
Baked	*	4–6 months
Unbaked dough	2–3 days	6 months
Pastries: Store at room temperature. Best used within 1 to 3 days.		
Danishes	*	3 months
Doughnuts	*	3 months
Pies:		
Chiffon	1–2 days	1 month
Fruit	1–2 days	1 year
Mince	1–2 days	4–8 months
Pumpkin	1–2 days	1 month
Unbaked fruit	*	8 months

Type of Food	Fridge	Freezer
BABY FOOD		
Liquid:		
Expressed breast milk	5 days	3–4 months
Formula	2 days	*
Solids (open or freshly made):		
Homemade baby foods	1–2 days	3–4 months
Strained fruits and vegetables	2–3 days	6–8 months
Strained meats and eggs	1 day	1–2 months
Strained meat/vegetable combination	1–2 days	1–2 months
MISCELLANEOUS		
Fresh pasta	1 week	1 month
Mayonnaise	2 months	*
Nuts	6 months	1 year
Sandwiches	1–2 days	1 week
Tofu	1 week	1 month

FOODS THAT DO NOT FREEZE WELL

Because of Flavor Changes:

Artificial salt (salt substitute)
Artificial vanilla flavor
Garlic
Home-fried foods
Onions
Spices (especially clove, sage)

Because of Texture Changes:

Cooked egg whites
Cream sauces
Custards
Gravy thickened with wheat flour
Mayonnaise
Pasta
Potatoes
Soft meringues

Courtesy of Rutgers NJAES Cooperative Extension

Pantries

Not every food you get at the supermarket needs refrigeration. Some items, including onions and potatoes, require cool—not cold—storage. If you've got the room, an unheated walk-in pantry off the kitchen is a great way to store a large volume of such items. You'll save valuable cabinet space at the same time.

A walk-in pantry should be as close to the refrigerator as possible so you can gather ingredients without affecting the food-prep area or cleanup zone. The north side of the house is usually coolest, so if you can put the pantry there, do so. Be sure it's well ventilated and well insulated to keep it from getting too warm during the day. Root vegetables such as potatoes and onions will last longer in a cool, dark, dry pantry than they would in a refrigerator, but you aren't limited to root vegetables, of course. A walk-in pantry is a great place for canned goods, cereal, pasta, drink mixes, flour, cookies, candies, pet food, paper goods, and even appliances that you don't use every day. For additional pantry storage information, see the chart on pages 48–49.

A walk-in pantry is a good way to add cool storage if you have the space, but most people do not. If you don't—or if you aren't planning to incorporate one into a remodeling—a bottom cabinet can act as a pantry, and there are freestanding pantry cabinets. For more information on cabinets, see Chapter 2, "Cabinets and Accessories," page 50.

Left Base cabinets often act as a pantry, providing cool, dark, dry conditions that are ideal for storing certain foods and root vegetables. These pullout bins make it easy to access the contents.

Above A pantry doesn't have to be a walk-in to be useful. This tall pantry with glass doors has plenty of shelf space for cookbooks, bowls, and other kitchen items.

Above This shallow closet with folding doors makes a satisfactory pantry. The homeowner uses it to store everything from pet food and potatoes to cereals and drinks. It even has a spot for a portable kitchen cart that can be rolled to the food-prep area when needed.

Opposite Walk-in pantries are a good way to store food and bulk items, but from a space-usage standpoint they are not ideal. Today's cabinet storage hardware does a better job and keeps stored items closer to where you need them.

Pantry

Refrigerated Wine Cellars

Americans are drinking more wine than ever before. Most of that wine is ready to drink and should be consumed within six months of purchase. Certain types, however, benefit from age. If you've got a number of these in your collection, you'll require a long-term storage solution. If you're an avid collector, it's probably best to have a wine cellar where you can keep several hundred bottles on hand. If your collection isn't so grand, consider a refrigerated wine cellar. You can get everything from a unit designed to fit under a kitchen counter that holds as little as 18 bottles to a floor-to-ceiling model that stores 150.

These wine cellars, also referred to as wine refrigerators, offer exactly what is needed to age fine wines—namely, a cool, dark spot with no vibrations. The ideal storage temperature is about 50 to 55 degrees Fahrenheit (10 to 13 degrees Celsius), with 70 percent humidity or higher. Top-of-the-line models offer multiple temperature zones for storing different types of wine at their optimal temperature. (See "Ideal Wine Storage" on page 221.) Other features to look for include digital keypads, full-extension racks, and a tinted glass door to protect your wines from harmful UV rays.

Fine wines require constant temperatures. Don't put your refrigerated wine cellar near the oven or range, where temperatures fluctuate. Don't put it too close to the refrigerator or dishwasher, either, because the vibrations may adversely affect the taste. And keep it away from items that have a strong odor. Wines may pick up aromas through the cork, so you don't want your bottle of Amarone anywhere near that bag of onions in the base cabinet.

Opposite An island is a popular spot for a refrigerated wine cellar. This model, with its full overlay wood frame, has a triple-temperature zone that allows you to store three different types of wine at optimal serving temperatures.

Top left Full-extension shelves keep bottles firmly in place and make them easy to access. A wine refrigerator keeps temperatures low enough and maintains the high humidity level that is ideal for fine wines.

Top right This stainless-steel wine refrigerator provides a safe, stable home for up to 48 of your favorite bottles. The bottom shelf can be angled so you can easily read the labels behind the tinted glass door.

Bottom You don't need a large space to keep your fine wines at your fingertips. This model is only 15 inches (38cm) wide. It has six removable shelves that hold up to two dozen bottles horizontally, keeping the corks moist.

Ideal Wine Storage

Wine	Temperature
Red	About 60°F (15°C)
White	About 50°F (10°C)
Sparkling	About 45°F (7°C)

CHAPTER 7

Trash and Recyclables

The trash piles up; the trash can gets emptied. The trash piles up; the trash can gets emptied. It's a never-ending cycle. The minute you take out the garbage, the onslaught continues. Junk mail, cereal boxes, diapers, sponges, soda cans, eggshells—the list goes on and on.

According to the Environmental Protection Agency, the average American produces more than 1,600 pounds (7,200kg) of trash a year. As a nation, we produce more than 240 million tons a year. That's one large load of garbage! Yet despite these figures, the trash can—one of the most used items in your kitchen—often gets overlooked. It shouldn't. Having the right kind of waste receptacle—and locating it in the proper place—will make your kitchen more organized and more efficient. Fortunately, there are myriad sizes, shapes, styles, finishes, and configurations on the market. Cabinet companies offer many creative ways to put trash in its place.

Most kitchen trash still gets thrown away, but not all of it. More and more of it is recycled and composted. Recycling cans, bottles, newspapers, and other items should become second nature, like those weekly treks to the curb with trash can in hand. Leftovers don't need to be trashed, either. Many people, especially gardeners, are turning to composting. In this chapter, you'll learn how to best store those kitchen scraps before they find their way to your compost pile.

Call it what you will—trash, garbage, refuse, rubbish, or waste—it all adds up. Quickly. So, how will you handle it? It's time for some serious trash talk.

Left **Everything has its place. Cabinet companies offer clever, convenient solutions that make it easy to dispose of trash and recyclables.**

Trash Can Basics

Before you decide where to put your trash can, you need to determine how many cans you'll need, and how big they should be. An 8-gallon (30-liter) can should suffice for a family of two, but a four-person household will need something that holds at least 11 gallons (40 liters)—that is, if you have only one can in the kitchen. You may be able to make work flow more efficient by outfitting your kitchen with two or more trash stations. If you've got a smaller receptacle in a secondary area, you won't have to traipse across the floor with that dripping package of chicken.

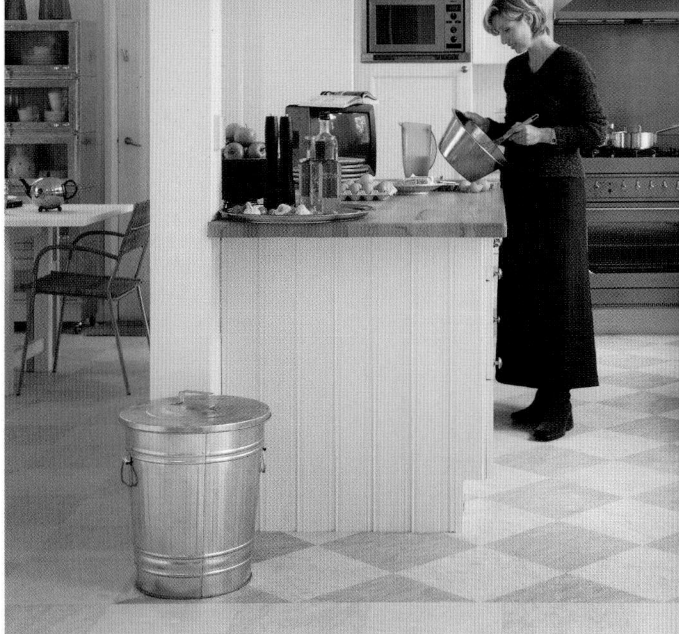

Top Freestanding trash cans may save valuable cabinet space, but at the same time you'll be taking up floor space that may be just as valuable for something else.

Bottom left A can under the sink usually has to be small enough to fit around the plumbing. A better spot for your can is in a base cabinet right next to the sink.

Bottom right If you prefer a freestanding can, your best bet is to keep it in a corner, out of traffic paths—especially those that make up the work triangle.

Opposite top Placing your trash can in a base cabinet offers your kitchen a cleaner, more organized look—and you don't have to worry about knocking it over or kicking it.

Opposite bottom Many homeowners opt to locate their can in an island. The location makes it easy to wipe crumbs directly from the countertop into the can. The cabinet door provides an extra barrier against odors.

SMARTtip

Hang in There

If your trash can is in a cabinet, hang a grocery bag on a cabinet knob while cooking. Use the bag to collect the trash you generate, and then put that bag in the trash when you're finished. You can accomplish the same thing with an empty milk container set on the counter.

Finding a Home

When it comes to where to put your trash can, there is no hard-and-fast rule. Some people have it out in the open. Others choose to conceal it within cabinetry, often under the sink. Those that choose to use a freestanding can out in the open often point to accessibility. A freestanding can is easy to access—no need to grab any cabinet hardware while you've got a wet paper towel in one hand and a handful of crumbs in the other. Plus, it can be as big as you'd like, which is a plus if the thought of taking out the trash on a daily basis makes you cringe. A freestanding receptacle doesn't have to be unsightly, either. Sleek models that coordinate with your kitchen's decor are available. Locating the trash can in the open, however, does have its drawbacks. Many consider it an eyesore—especially if it's a can without a lid. It could be a "nose-sore" as well, because odors are more prevalent. You're also asking for trouble if you have children or pets.

To keep valuable floor space open, many people put their trash cans in a base cabinet. The most common place is under the sink because that's where a lot of trash is generated. The problem is, it's also where people tend to stand. If your hands are full of trash, it's a good bet a member of the family will be at the sink and will have to move before you can access the trash. Another drawback? If you plan to place a can under the sink, it will have to be one that fits around the plumbing.

Your best bet is to put the trash can in a cabinet near—but not under—the sink. It's easy to access while you prepare a meal, but it's still out of sight. And of course, the look of the can is not that important. The biggest drawback to a cabinet location is that it's more difficult to clean up the inevitable spills and drips.

Kinds of Cans

Trash cans come in all shapes, sizes, and materials. You can get a round one, a rectangular one, or even one shaped to fit snugly into a corner. As mentioned earlier, most kitchen cans should be at least 8 gallons (30 liters), and you probably don't need to get anything bigger than 15 gallons (56 liters). Plastic cans are often used for under-the-counter units, but stainless steel is another option. It's particularly popular for freestanding cans because it looks sleek, is durable, won't retain odors, and is easy to clean. Enameled steel is also popular. These cans come in a variety of colors, making enameled steel more versatile from a decorative point of view.

Unless you take out the garbage often, it's best to avoid freestanding models that don't have a lid. Sure, it's easier to toss the trash away or sweep the crumbs from the counter directly into the can, but a lidless can is all too tempting for kids and canines. It may attract insects, too.

A lid is a must if you want to contain odors, prevent spills, and control bugs. The lid doesn't have to be attached. Put a hook nearby, and hang the lid on the hook while you're prepping the meal. When you're finished with cleanup, simply put on the lid. Any lid must fit securely. Many lids are controlled with a foot pedal. This keeps your hands clean, which is sanitary, and keeps your hands free, which is efficient. If you use a foot-pedal model, get one with a lid that remains open until you press it closed. Otherwise, you're forced to keep your foot on the pedal the entire time. Bullet cans with push doors aren't that practical in the kitchen. The openings are usually too small for cereal boxes and other bulky items. If you're looking for a trash can that will fit in with your twenty-first-century kitchen, consider a model with an infrared motion detector that opens without touching it.

Left **A freestanding trash can next to the counter makes cleanup a breeze.**

Middle **With a model that operates via infrared technology, the lid opens when you put your hand near it. There's no need to use your hands or your feet.**

Right **Bullet cans don't make much sense in the kitchen because their openings are not big enough to handle large items.**

Top left A can with a lid will keep curious pets from knocking the trash all over the floor.

Top right Lids with a foot pedal offer quick and easy access. Make sure the pedal is wide enough to use from different angles.

Bottom Stainless-steel cans are popular for freestanding models, but plastic cans are typically used under the counter.

SMARTtip

Starting at the Bottom

Leave several extra bags at the bottom of your trash can. When you empty the full bag, you'll have your next one ready to use. Replenish the stash once a week.

Pullouts for Trash

To maximize efficiency, put your under-the-counter trash can on slides. Extend it when you need it, and then push it back when you're finished. It's particularly helpful to have the can extended while you're preparing a meal. Pullout containers are also available in multiple-can units, which allow you to separate items as necessary. (For more information, see "A Recipe for Recycling," page 234.) Some models swing out. When you open the cabinet door, the lid lifts and the container pivots out with the door. Other kitchen cans are mounted directly on the inside of a cabinet door. Typically, a wire frame holds standard plastic or paper grocery bags over a drip tray, which should be removed and washed at least once a week. This is an inexpensive, simple solution, but your capacity will be limited. This approach is best suited for light use.

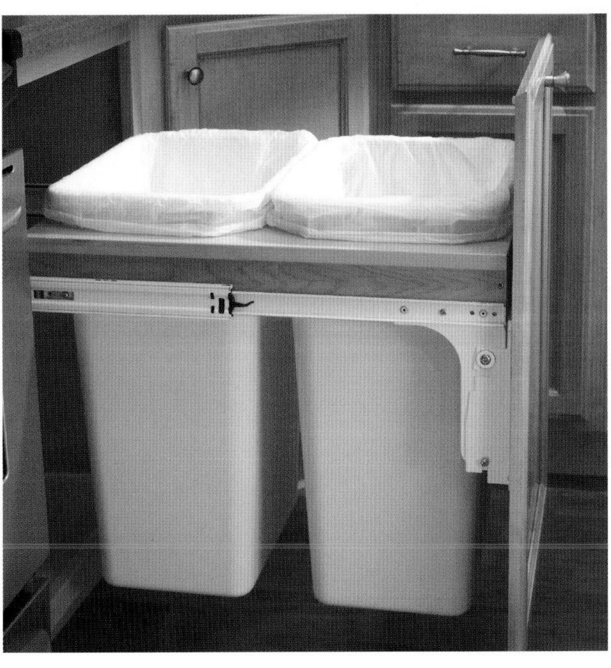

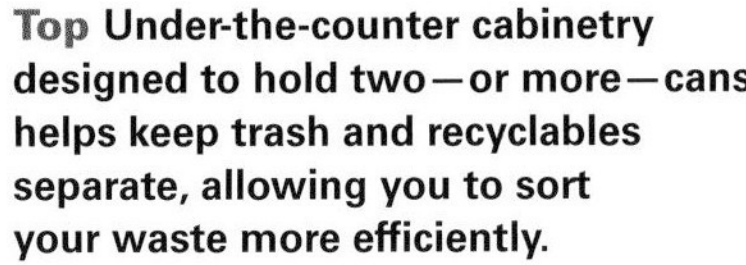

Top Under-the-counter cabinetry designed to hold two—or more—cans helps keep trash and recyclables separate, allowing you to sort your waste more efficiently.

Middle Pullout systems, which can be configured front and back (as shown) or side by side, are popular. Pull them out only when you need them, and keep them out of sight the rest of the time.

Bottom If you have a pair of cans under the counter, you can use one for paper trash and devote the other to messier items, such as food scraps.

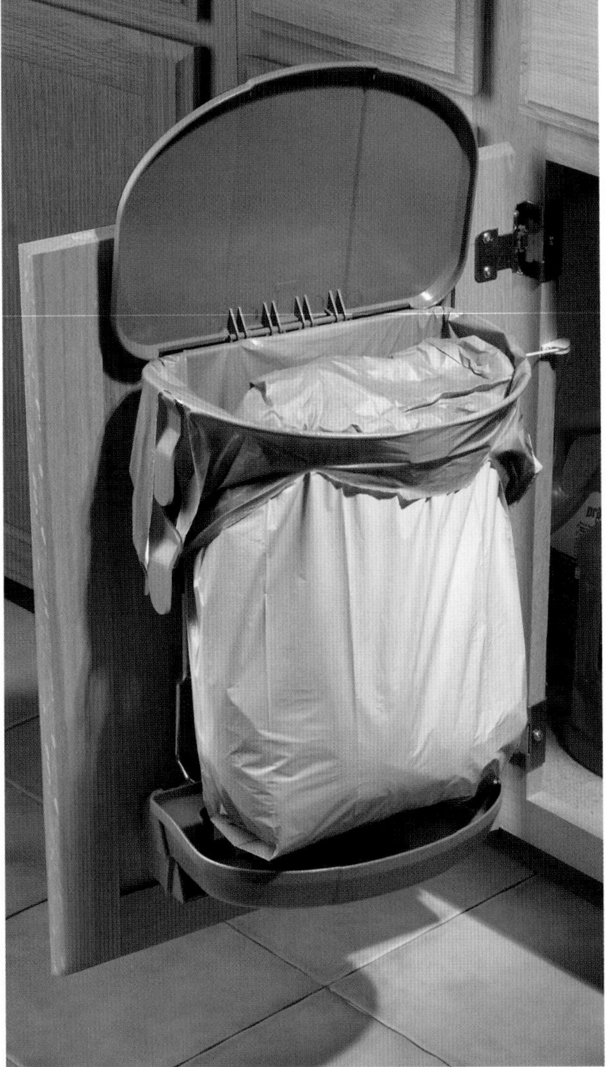

Top left Not all under-the-counter cans are pullouts. With this simple setup, a wire frame mounted on the inside of the door holds a plastic can. The kitchen can is used every day, so invest in a model that is strong, durable, and easy to use.

Top right This on-the-door system holds a plastic bag over a tray that supports the bag and catches drips. If you don't generate a lot of trash, this setup works great, but heavy items could cause the bag to tear.

Bottom left Hardware kits are available that allow you to attach your cabinet door directly to a pullout system. This makes accessing the trash can a one-step operation.

Bottom middle The cabinet door lifts off the brackets with ease, and putting it back on is as simple as aligning the slots with the screws.

Bottom right Thanks to a cord with a hook that connects the top of the lid to the interior of the cabinet, this can's lid opens automatically when the unit is pulled out. An accessory basket in the rear holds extra bags.

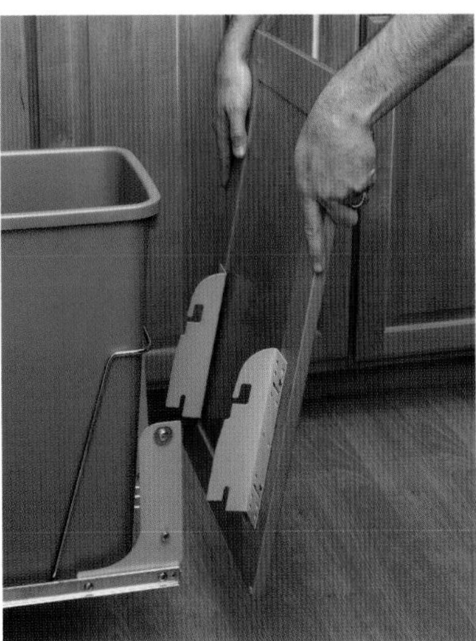

Top left This top-mounted container was installed in a cabinet near where the most trash is generated, making it easily accessible at the most crucial moments.

Top middle Stainless-steel cans are popular because they will last a long time and are easy to clean. They don't retain odors, either, which is why some people use them as compost pails. (See page 240.)

Top right A double-pail system is often used to separate trash from recyclables (as shown), but it can also work well in a household that amasses a lot of garbage.

Middle This round is mounted to the side of the cabinet. When you open the door, the lid lifts, and the can pivots out.

Bottom This narrow can works in a similar fashion to the round can (middle). When the cabinet door is opened, the lid lifts automatically and the can swings out for easy access.

Upgrading to a Pullout

Pullouts make it easier to hit the mark with both trash and recycling containers. To make either of the units shown here (recycling pullout, photos 1 to 3; and trash pullout, photo 4), use drawer-slide hardware and see the installation tips on page 78. Coat the pullout trays with polyurethane varnish to make cleaning spills easier.

1. Make your own twin-pail rollout for recyclables and returnable containers using a pullout tray. If your cabinet has a fixed shelf, you may first need to remove (or notch) it using a jigsaw.

2. Attach a ¼-in. (0.6cm) plywood back to keep containers from tipping backward when you pull out the tray. Use a bar clamp to hold the back in position while driving three pairs of flathead screws.

3. Attach a long handle to the pullout tray's front corner to make operation more convenient. Fashion it from a dowel or an old broom handle. Drill pilot holes for screws using a countersink bit, and then secure it using 1-in. (2.5cm) flathead screws.

4. This full-extension trash pullout was made using 1x6 (25x150mm) boards. Use ½-in. (1.3cm) plywood for the bag box, and cut rabbets in the top so it will sit snugly in the box opening. Attach the assembly to the cabinet door (hinges removed) using four 2-in. (5cm) flathead screws.

Down the Hatch

Another light-use solution (and one that's ideal for composting; see page 240) is to mount a waste container directly into the countertop. The opening is flush with the countertop, which makes it easy to sweep those meal-making scraps directly into the container. When the container, which typically holds about 3 or 4 gallons (10 to 15 liters), is full, empty it into the regular trash can or compost bin, wash it, and put it back into the countertop. Keep the lid on when you're not using it. While this setup is convenient, you might not want to give up valuable counter space for a unit with such small capacity. In that case, you can just move a freestanding trash can to where you are working and return it to its normal home when you are done.

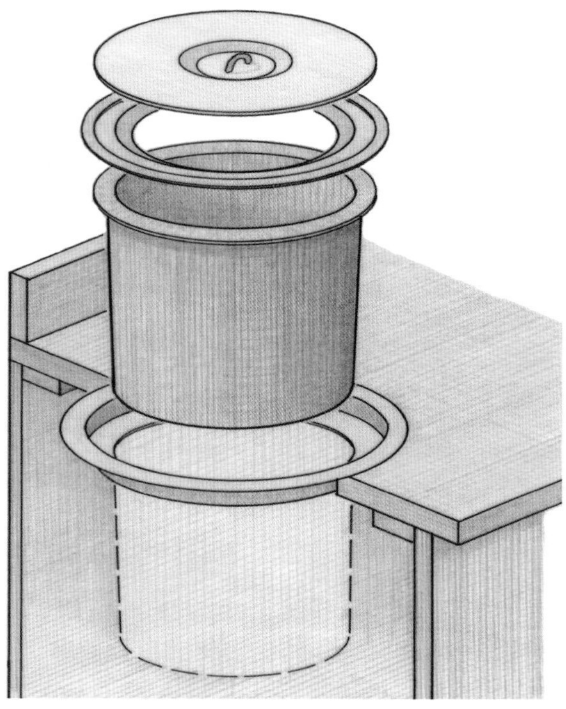

Countertop Waste-Container Assembly

Above (all) If you're looking for the ultimate in convenience, consider installing a waste container directly into the countertop. You'll be able to collect trash in the small pail before transferring it to your regular can, or you can gather food scraps while you prepare a meal, and then bring them out to the compost bin.

Left A stainless-steel mounting ring, installed in the countertop, holds the small pail in place. The rubber seal helps keep odors at bay. The stainless-steel lid closes tightly when the unit is not in use.

It's in the Bag

A good trash can holds a bag securely. The question is, where are you holding your bags before you need them? The simplest setup is to keep the bags in their original box and to store the boxes on a rack on the inside of the cabinet door closest to the can. If you use a freestanding can, bags can be stored in a nearby base-cabinet drawer, pullout tray, or toe kick drawer.

There are also special storage devices that mount on a wall or a cabinet door. Having one is not a bad idea, but if you use grocery bags as trash bags, consider kicking this habit. Using grocery bags doesn't save much money. They don't hold much, either, and they have a tendency to drip.

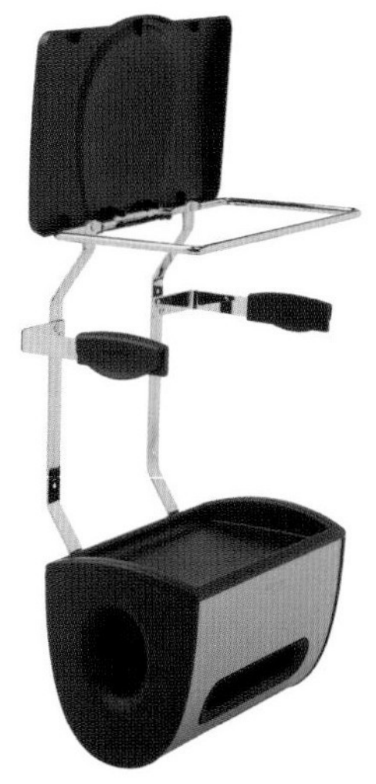

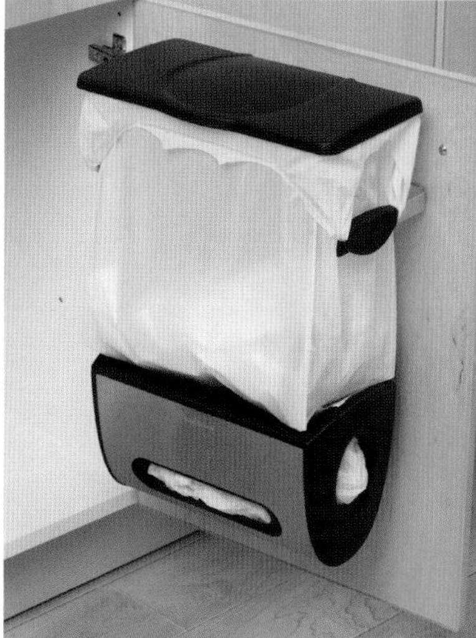

Top left This unit has a frame to hold a plastic bag, a lid to contain odors and prevent spills, and a storage chamber at the bottom that holds bags and doubles as a drip tray.

Top right Bag holders prevent your bags from taking over a cabinet. They attach to the wall or the inside of a cabinet, usually with screws, adhesive pads, or suction cups.

Middle The unit pictured top left can be attached to a wall or to the inside of a base-cabinet door. The bags in the storage area can be pulled out one at a time.

Bottom Cabinet companies provide a place for everything. This pullout trash accessory includes a small compartment in the rear that is perfect for storing your boxes of trash bags.

BYOB

Plastic shopping bags have become a serious environmental problem. They fill up landfills and sometimes find their way into the mouths of marine animals that mistake them for food and choke to death. In fact, many cities now ban disposable shopping bags. To do your part to help the environment and keep plastic bag clutter out of your home, bring your own bags (BYOB) to the supermarket. Keep a few large canvas or cloth bags in your car so they'll be handy whenever you shop. Some supermarkets now credit you a few pennies if you bring your own bags.

A Recipe for Recycling

Your community likely offers some sort of recycling program. These programs vary from city to city. Knowing what the recycling rules are in your area will help you determine the best way to store and organize your cans, bottles, and other recyclables. You can plan space according to how many recyclables you generate between curbside pickups or runs to the local recycling center.

Kitchen recycling centers are available through cabinet companies and storage-product manufacturers. Lots of your recyclables—milk jugs, laundry detergent bottles, and so forth—are heavy or bulky, or both. For this reason, base cabinets are sensible storage areas. Storage systems are available in one-, two-, three-, and four-bin units for easy, convenient sorting. A three-bin unit with bins for glass, plastic, and aluminum, for example, would be especially useful in cities where homeowners must separate their recyclables. People in cities with single-stream recycling, meanwhile, could use the same unit, dedicating one bin to trash, one to containers for which they can collect deposits, and one to recyclables.

These preassembled units help streamline the process. They ease it, too, because they tilt out or slide out of the base cabinet. You don't have to constantly open a door and move one pail to get to another one. The bins come in different shapes, sizes, and colors. If you have the room and the pipes won't get in the way, putting your recycling center under the sink is a good idea. Bottles and cans get rinsed and go straight into the appropriate bin. You could attach a rollout drawer at the bottom for newspapers. However, newspapers pile up quickly and take up a lot of space, so it probably makes more sense to store your old newspapers in an area off the kitchen prior to recycling. Corner-cabinet recycling centers, similar to a lazy Susan, are also available from various cabinet companies.

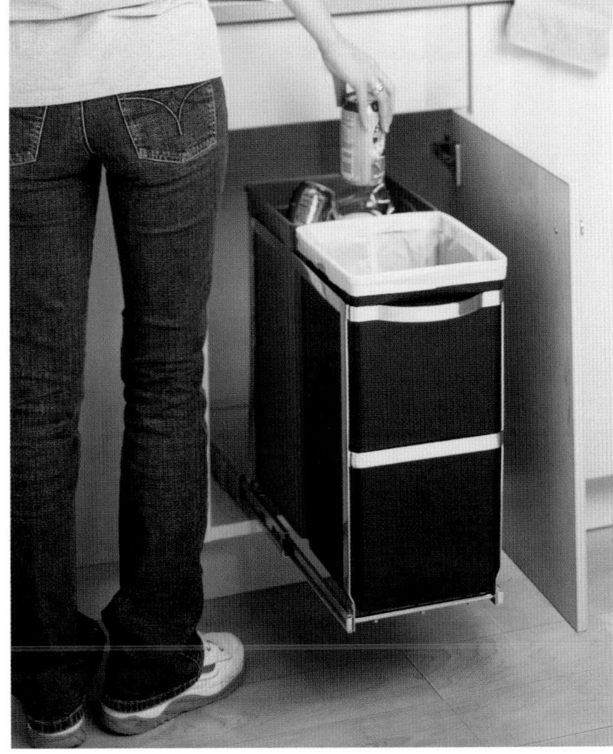

SMARTtip

Divvying Up the Duties

If you have two kids and you use a two-bin unit—one for trash, one for recyclables—that's perfect! One child can be responsible for taking out the trash, and the other can handle the recyclables. No complaints about unbalanced chore duties!

Opposite left Most recycling centers are designed for existing cabinetry and can be purchased through cabinet companies and at home-improvement centers. Corner-cabinet recycling systems, which make good use of often-wasted space, are available. This unit has three bins.

Opposite right Having a bin for bottles and cans right next to the one for regular trash makes end-of-meal cleanup a breeze. The more kitchen space you can devote to recycling, the fewer trips to the garage you'll have to make.

Top left Pullouts with two or three bins make sorting recyclables easy. This three-bin system is perfect for separating plastic, glass, and aluminum. If you need a visual reminder, bins can be purchased in multiple colors.

Top right This household does all of its recycling in a base cabinet, but it's often best to devote a small space in the kitchen for recycling and keep the bulk of the storage somewhere else—usually in the garage.

Bottom Your recycling center doesn't have to be fancy. A simple shelf with wire framing attached to the inside of a base-cabinet door houses a standard paper bag, which is great for collecting junk mail and other recyclable paper.

An Easy Way Out

If your kitchen is adjacent to the garage or porch, you may want to install a through-the-wall system for moving your recyclables out of the kitchen. Most homeowners install two doors—one for recyclables and one for containers with deposits—in a backsplash or wall. The systems save steps and eliminate the need for empty container storage in the kitchen.

Some homeowners have installed chutes from the kitchen to a storage container in the basement to handle recyclables. We hesitate to support this system. The chute can be difficult to clean, and if the drop is too big, glass items are likely to break on impact. Other items may bounce up and out of the container.

Dedicating a base cabinet to a recycling center makes the most sense, if you have the room. If not, your best bet is to keep a smaller container in the kitchen and use it as intermediary storage before bringing items to the bigger bins—often provided by your community—in the garage or a nearby pantry, mudroom, laundry room, or screened-in porch. The small bin will act as a helpful recycling reminder.

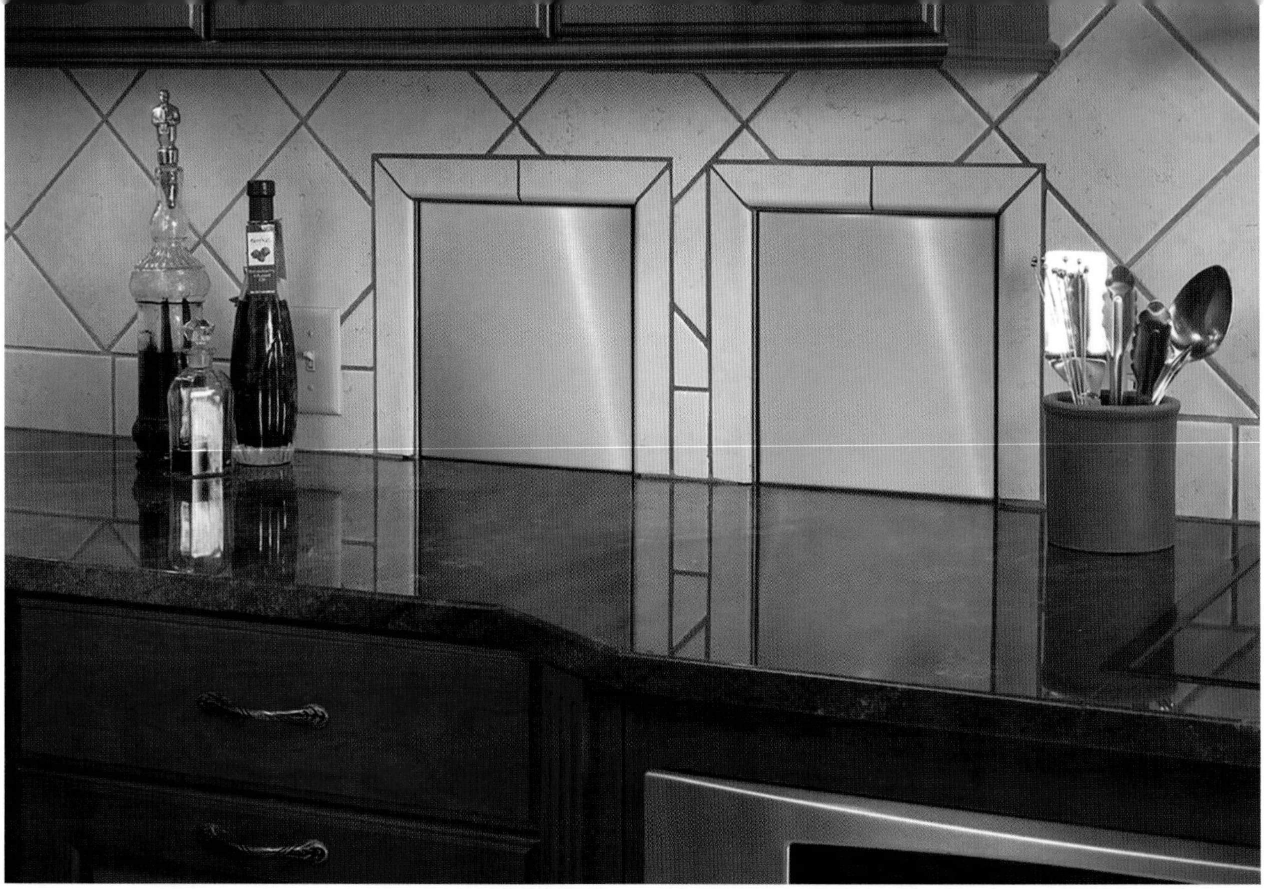

SMARTtip

Rinse and Pinch

Rinse cans and bottles before recycling them to avoid odors and attracting insects. Also, put the lid of a soup or tuna can inside the can and pinch the sides of the can together to keep the lid inside. This prevents you from slicing your hand on the edge of a loose lid.

Opposite Just push the door open and drop your cans, bottles, jars, and other recyclables down the stainless-steel chute.

Top For odor-related reasons, it's best to empty an indoor recycling bin every day or two. Or, install a through-the-wall system and eliminate odor concerns.

Bottom The chute empties into a larger container, usually located in the garage, eliminating the need to keep a trash can in the kitchen.

SMARTtip

Less Volume

Are the recyclable goods in your kitchen piling up too fast? You can reduce the volume with some simple steps. Crushing cans, breaking down boxes, and putting small jars and plastic containers into bigger ones are three easy ways you can reduce recycling bulk in your kitchen.

Above **The spring-loaded, airtight access door is the only part of the through-the-wall system that is visible from the kitchen.**

Left **The separate doors on this tiled backsplash allow the homeowners to use one chute for trash and the other for recyclables.**

Composting

You can recycle more than just glass, metal, plastic, and paper. Another effective waste management technique is composting. By collecting organic kitchen waste, you'll cut down on the amount of trash that finds its way to the curb each week. But what type of container should you use to store those scraps? And where should you keep it?

Your kitchen compost container should be kept near the sink, because that's where you handle many of the items that need to be composted. A small pail located under the sink is the most popular choice. The pail can hang on the inside of the cabinet door if it has a handle. Other people choose to keep the pail on the counter, next to the sink. Compost pails can also be kept on top of the refrigerator—or in it. Keeping your pail in the fridge between dumping reduces odors and pests such as fruit flies.

You must be vigilant about emptying the pail regularly. It's best to do so daily, if possible, to prevent airborne allergens. You'll be emptying the pail every day or two, so you don't need anything too big. Some people use an old ceramic pot. Almost anything with a secure lid will do. The lid keeps odors in and pests out. For some, however, the container has to look nice and fit in with the kitchen's decor. This is especially true for those who keep the pail on the counter. Fortunately, there are containers made specifically for composting that won't be an eyesore. Stainless-steel pails are popular because they resist odors and stains. Your pail will be used to hold all sorts of messy items, so use something that can easily be cleaned. If you're not interested in disinfecting on an almost daily basis, consider compost pail liners. When full, these 100-percent biodegradable bags can be tossed into the compost bin with your compost.

Opposite top The best place to keep your compost container is in a base cabinet near the sink, which is where you handle a lot of the scraps that wind up in the compost bin.

Opposite bottom Your container doesn't have to be specifically made for handling compost. This stainless-steel trash can, which pivots out when the cabinet door opens, would work well, too.

Top These enameled-steel compost pails have secure lids, removable liners that allow for easy transport to the compost bin, and charcoal filters in the lid to cut down odors.

Bottom Line your compost container with a biodegradable bag, and there is no need to carry the pail out to the compost bin—and no need to clean the pail on a daily basis.

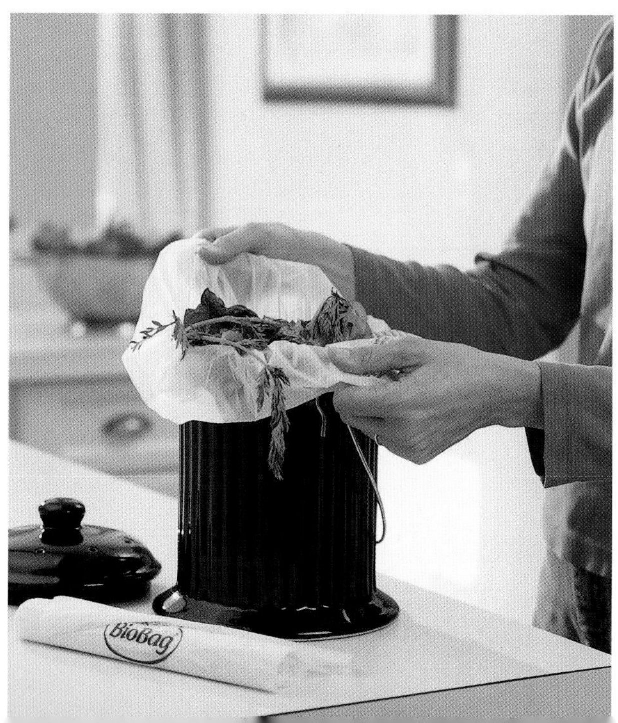

Making the Most of Compost

You prepared breakfast, and you tossed the eggshells into the trash. You ate breakfast, and you threw out the few cut-up pieces of cantaloupe that nobody got around to eating. You sipped your morning coffee, and you trashed the coffee grounds before you headed to the office. Why? Why throw away items that can be given back to the earth?

Instead of tossing these items into the trash can and contributing to already close-to-capacity landfills, consider composting. You can make a difference. And it won't cost you much money—or much time. Composting is simply the biological decomposition of organic materials to produce a rich fertilizer. It's environmentally beneficial and a great way to recycle kitchen waste.

Collect your organic kitchen scraps in a small compost pail until they're ready for the compost bin, often located in a corner of the garden. The bin can be purchased at any major home-improvement center or garden center. It will convert food waste and other organic material into compost. Organic waste is biodegradable. When buried in a landfill, it's of no use to anyone. This doesn't have to happen. You can convert organic waste into a useful product in your own kitchen and backyard.

So tomorrow morning, toss those eggshells, cantaloupe pieces, and coffee grounds into a compost pail. You'll be glad you did. So will the earth.

SMARTtip

Shop Smart

A simple solution to cut down on waste is to become a smarter shopper. When choosing between similar products, for example, select the one with the least unnecessary packaging. Packaging makes up half of what we throw out. Also, keep in mind that single-serving packages can fill up recycling containers quickly. They're especially inefficient from both storage and financial points of view, as well.

Top Ceramic compost pails are popular in country kitchens because they fit in with the decor and can be kept on the counter.

Bottom left A compost pail makes it easy to save your kitchen scraps until you're ready to bring them to the compost bin.

Bottom right Composting gets your natural trash back into your garden and encourages the growth of flowers and vegetables, so why throw those carrot peelings away?

In or Out?

What to Compost

- Animal manure
- Cardboard rolls
- Clean paper
- Coffee filters
- Coffee grounds
- Cotton rags
- Dryer and vacuum-cleaner lint
- Eggshells
- Fireplace ashes
- Fruits and vegetables
- Grass clippings
- Hair and fur
- Hay and straw
- Houseplants
- Leaves
- Nutshells
- Sawdust
- Shredded newspaper
- Tea bags
- Wood chips
- Wool rags
- Yard trimmings

What Not to Compost

- Black walnut-tree leaves or twigs
- Coal or charcoal ash
- Dairy products (butter, egg yolks, sour cream, yogurt, and so forth)
- Diseased or insect-ridden plants
- Fats, grease, lard, or oils
- Meat or fish bones and scraps
- Pet wastes (dog or cat feces, soiled cat litter, and so forth)
- Yard trimmings treated with chemical pesticides

Note: If you are fertilizing fruits or vegetables with your compost, stick to items you know are chemical-free.

Top The kitchen scraps from your compost pail will eventually find their way to the compost bin, typically located in a sunny spot in the backyard.

Middle Compost pails are usually about 10 inches (25cm) high and hold 1 or 2 gallons (3.7 to 7.5 liters). Be sure to empty the pail every day or two.

Bottom Fruit and vegetable scraps can be recycled into compost that can be used to fertilize your lawn and garden.

CHAPTER 8

Kitchen Offices and Message Centers

Kitchen offices have become popular as more and more people multitask meals and work and families center their activities around a kitchen hub. Before devoting the space and budget to a full-fledged kitchen office, however, decide if you really need one. If you have a home office, a kitchen office may be redundant. But if your countertops have become dumping grounds for the daily mail, permission slips, and keys, you can probably benefit from a kitchen office.

A well-planned kitchen office will be a center for family communications and can ease the management of dozens of daily tasks. It serves as a place to consolidate shopping and errand lists, maintain the family calendar, sort mail, and pay bills. Your kitchen office may incorporate a bulletin board where you can leave messages for other family members and hang to-do lists, receipts, keys, dry-cleaner slips, and appointment cards. Or, your message center can be separate from your kitchen office.

The kitchen office also offers a central location for all of your electronics. Read e-mail, surf the Internet, retrieve messages from the answering machine, and charge cell phones. Having everything in the kitchen allows you to take care of business while waiting for the water to boil or toast to pop up.

This chapter offers dozens of suggestions for planning your kitchen office, whether it's part of a complete remodeling or simply a reorganization of the one you have. You willl also find kitchen office and message center solutions for homeowners with limited kitchen space—or no space at all.

Left A kitchen office helps keep nonculinary kitchen matters in order. This one has a permanent desktop computer setup.

Where to Put It

If you're remodeling your kitchen, put the kitchen office outside of the work triangle, where traffic will be lighter. Common choices include the end of a long counter, an unused corner or nook, or at a transition to or from the kitchen, such as along a hallway wall or near a back door.

Short on real estate in the kitchen? Look to utilize space in a nearby closet, pantry, dining area, or mudroom for your kitchen office. A closet, with the door removed, can be fitted with shelves and a desktop for a compact but functional workspace. A wide closet with bifold doors can accommodate file cabinets and will let you close the doors when you tire of staring at your to-do list.

A walk-in pantry provides a private, out-of-the-way spot for the kitchen office. Slide a stool under an existing pantry counter and use it as your desktop. Utilize the shelving for cookbooks, directories, and other office-storage needs. Don't forget to install lighting, a telephone line, and electric outlets as needed. If you have a mudroom, consolidate boots, backpacks, and jackets, and claim a corner for a kitchen office that houses everything from invitations and permission slips to mail and lunch money.

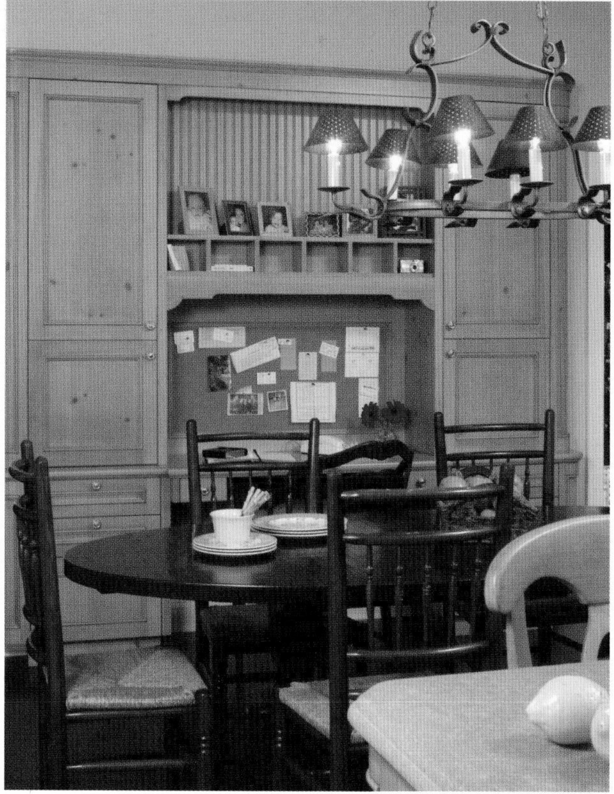

Opposite Incorporate a small desk in a custom island, as the designer did here. It's on the nonbusy side of the island and is also a great place to enjoy a quick snack.

Top Kitchen offices are often placed at the end of a run of cabinets and outside the working geometry of the kitchen, as shown here.

Bottom The dining area of a kitchen is another popular spot for a kitchen office and message board. Be sure to have plenty of drawers and cabinets if you choose this route, however. They will help keep the office from becoming an eyesore.

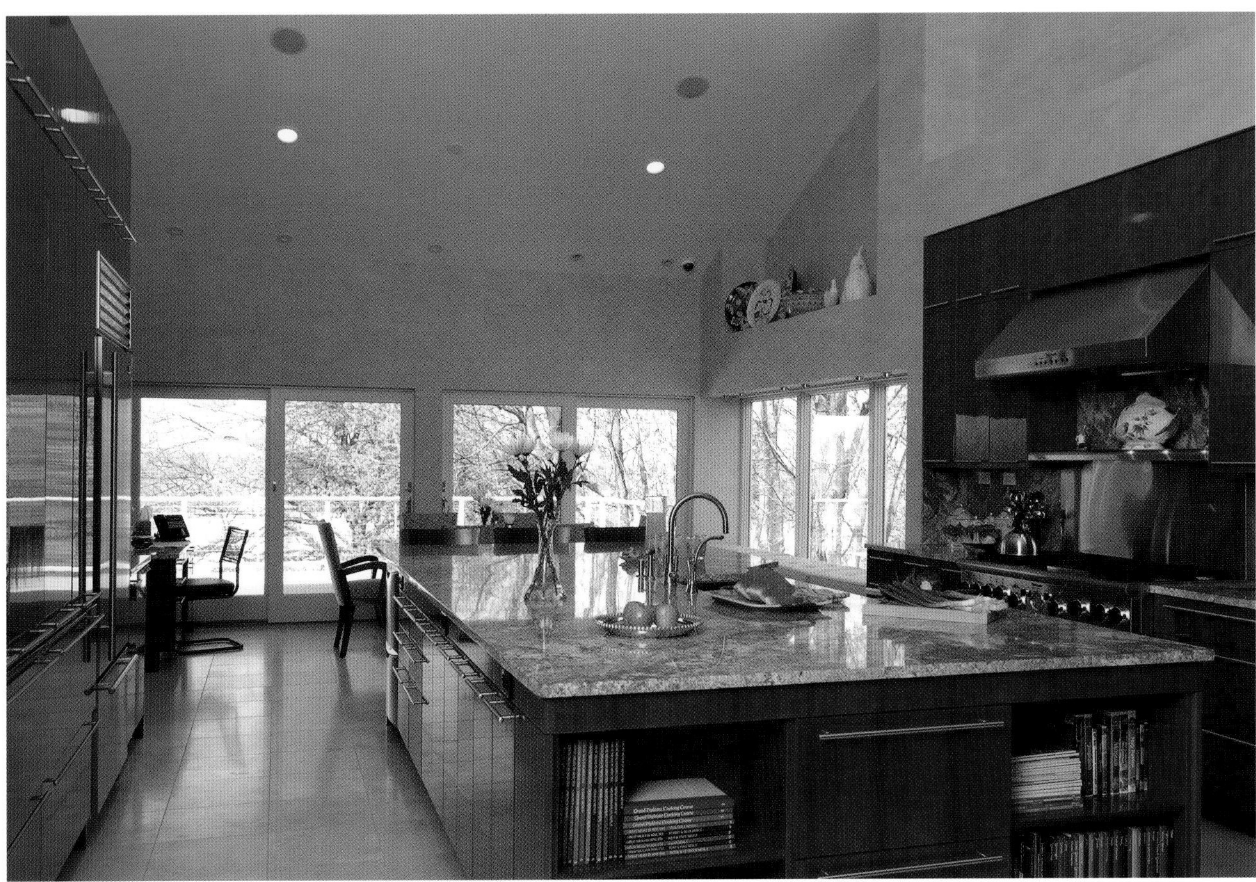

Above Placing your kitchen desk near a window will make it feel less confining. This office is positioned well out of the cook's way.

Opposite Prominently positioned at the entrance, this custom-built office has cabinets on the right side and is open on the left, thereby allowing an unobstructed view of the kitchen.

Office Duties

Before you design a kitchen office or reorganize an existing one, take some time to identify who will use it and how it will be used. Typically, the primary user is the person who manages the household. If the space is to be shared with other family members, you will need to create separate storage spaces to keep confusion to a minimum. Drawers, vertical files, and in-boxes can help keep the kitchen office organized. Label one for each family member, and ask everyone to go through them regularly.

Next, assess how much space you have. For a laptop perch, you can get by with an area that measures as little as 24 x 15 inches (60 x 38cm). For a laptop and a small writing area, you will need a 3 x 2-foot (90 x 60cm) area. If you like to store other items on your desk, the space will need to be bigger. Make a list of everything you'll want to store in the kitchen office. Be specific. See the list on page 251 to get you started.

If you're reorganizing an existing kitchen desk, take a good look at what's causing the clutter. If it's junk mail, keys, and pocketbooks, work on finding places for these items. Multiple in-boxes help sort high-priority mail from catalogs. Use wall hooks to store keys and pocketbooks.

Above A well-organized kitchen office allows you to take interruptions in stride, enabling you to respond effectively to unexpected requests for checks, homework assistance, phone numbers, and available calendar dates.

Office Supplies

Items You Might Find in a Kitchen Office

- Address book
- Address labels
- Bulletin/message board
- Calculator
- Calendar
- Cell phone
- Cell phone charger
- Checkbook
- Clock
- Computer/laptop
- Cookbooks
- Copy paper
- Coupons
- Desk pad
- Envelopes
- Electronic tablet
- Eyeglasses
- Glue
- Highlighters
- Ink/toner cartridges
- Keys
- Letter opener
- Mail (incoming and outgoing)
- Notepads
- Paper clips
- Paper shredder
- Pencil sharpener
- Pencils
- Pens
- Printer
- Pushpins
- Recipes
- Rubber bands
- Ruler
- Scissors
- Stamps
- Stapler
- Staples
- Tape (transparent and mailing)
- Telephone
- Telephone books

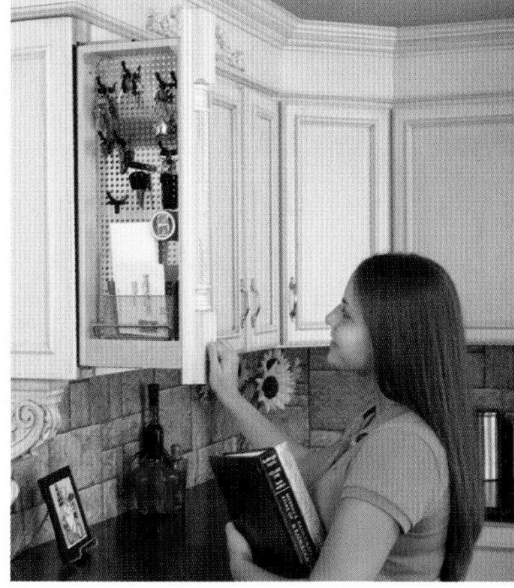

Top Cabinet manufacturers offer stock components that you can combine in various ways to meet your needs. This office utilizes drawers, shelves, and cubbies.

Bottom This pullout provides a home for keys and mail, two items that tend to collect on a kitchen desktop.

Desk Design

Will your desk be freestanding or integrated into the flow of counter space? For a more eclectic kitchen, a freestanding, decorative desk, slid into a corner or alcove, may be just right. Just pick a desk with the appropriate desktop and drawer space you need. Freestanding desks work best in a farm-style kitchen where other kitchen components are stand-alones. A freestanding desk is also a great option for kitchens that open into a family room; the desk acts as a transition piece from one room to the next.

Desks incorporated into the stream of counter and cabinet space are more common. A kitchen desk that's part of a run of base cabinets gives the room a sleek, unified look. Many kitchen-cabinet manufacturers offer desk options with their standard cabinet selections, including file drawers that are as beautiful as they are functional. An integrated desk will either be at the same level as the rest of the counter or a few inches lower. Desks designed at counter height will require a tall chair and are suitable for quick jobs, such as checking e-mail. Desks set a few inches lower are more comfortable for long sitting sessions. You may need to opt for an adjustable chair, however, to suit a nonstandard desktop height. If you don't plan on sitting at the desk for extended periods of time, consider a stool that fits under the counter.

Above The dual-level design of this island allows half to be used as a food-prep area and half to serve as a kitchen office. Compartments built into the back of the higher section help keep the desktop clear.

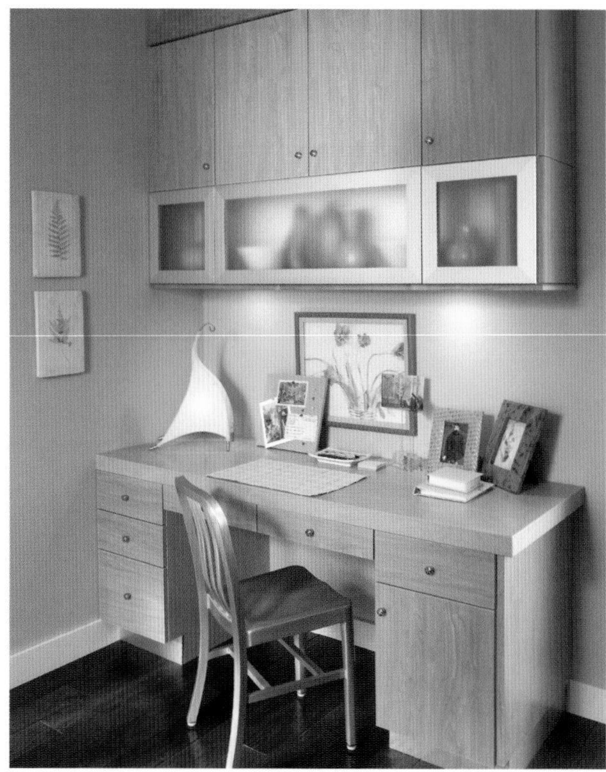

SMARTtip

Seeing Things Clearly

Use open shelving and clear storage jars and containers in your kitchen office and you can see what you have without having to open everything. Also enforce the habit of returning things to their "home." That way, the next time you reach for the stapler, it will be where it belongs. Simple strategies such as these will add peace and minutes to your busy day.

Above A full-size, freestanding desk usually means more elbow room and storage.

Selecting the Fixtures

An office desk and related storage can be purchased ready-made, built from stock cabinetry, or custom-designed. Regardless, select components that will help you stay organized. For example, consider a variety of drawer sizes, including a shallow drawer for stamps, pens, paper clips, and notepads. Two-tier drawers have a sliding upper tray that's perfect for storing small, everyday supplies, and bottom compartments that provide hidden storage for a wallet, a checkbook, or other items that you want to keep out of sight. Keyboard trays will maximize your desktop space. Larger drawers will hold your folders and copy paper. Add shelves, cubbyholes, and drawers to your plan to suit your needs.

Wall and base cabinets, if you have the space, will transform your space into a real, functioning office. Wall cabinets installed above the desk are great places to store cookbooks. A shelf below the wall cabinet can house the telephone and answering machine. Add a pullout for a printer. They offer easy access, making it less of a nuisance to check power connections or change the printer's ink cartridge. Storing all of your chargers and adapters on a pullout tray, equipped with a small hole in the back, will also help keep unsightly cords out of view and clutter off your desk.

SMARTtip

Stay Off the Desk

Whenever possible, use space-saving electronics—a wall-hanging telephone or a monitor that mounts under a cabinet, for example—to keep the desktop clear. Also consider using wireless technology to avoid the spaghetti tangle of telephone cords and computer cables hanging from the desk.

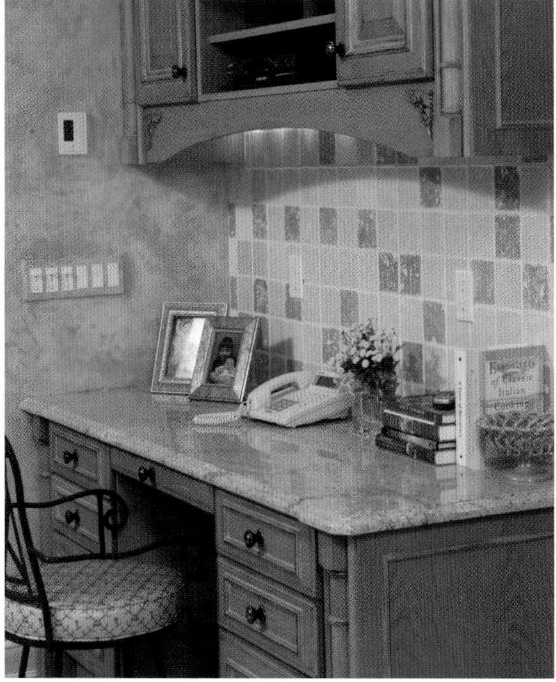

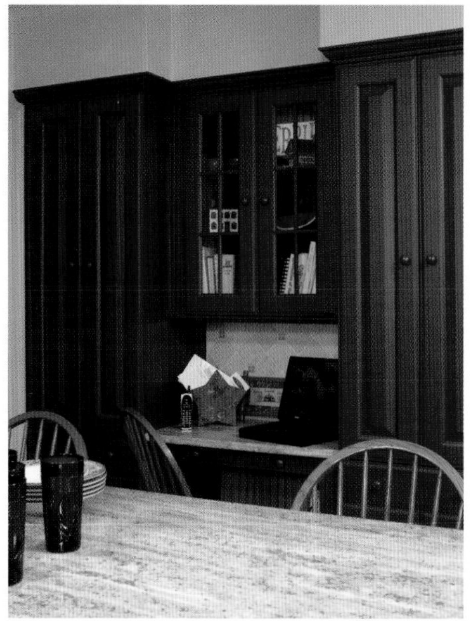

Opposite top Integrated desks set below standard countertop height, such as the one in this kitchen, are more comfortable for sitting at than those at countertop height.

Opposite bottom The similarly situated desk in this kitchen has more open space above the desktop, making it feel less cramped.

Above This freestanding desk was custom-built to match the kitchen's custom cabinetry. Under-cabinet lighting provides good desktop illumination.

Left A shallow drawer and a wall cabinet bridge two tall cabinets to create a small desk area. A chair is borrowed from the snack counter when needed.

SMARTtip

A Mail-Orderly Kitchen

From bills and brochures to catalogs and credit card applications, the mail keeps coming. To keep your mail from piling up and obscuring items on your desk that require attention, follow a few simple guidelines. Sort your mail in the same place every day. Immediately toss unwanted junk mail into the recycling bin. Create a mail station with in-boxes for each member of the family. The in-boxes can be stackable trays, but mail may get buried in them. Cubbyholes, vertical file folders, and baskets tend to work better.

Opposite Desktop cubbies help keep mail and stationery organized, and a classic chalkboard serves as the family message board.

Above A trio of two-tier drawers provides places for pens, paper, folders, and other office supplies—and makes them easy to access.

Top right Pullout racks convert a standard base cabinet into file storage.

Bottom right To get the most out of your kitchen office drawer space, specify full-extension drawer slides.

When Space Is Tight

When your kitchen has no space for an office, get creative. For example, place a secretary desk with a flip-down shelf that doubles as a desktop in a nearby hallway or mudroom. All your kitchen office needs can be tidily stored out of sight, and you'll have the perfect spot to jot down a phone message or add to a grocery list. A freestanding telephone table in a hall just outside the kitchen is another possible solution. Select one with lower shelves for cookbooks and a drawer for storing keys, wallets, notepads, pens, and paper. Hang a framed message board with a couple of mail slots—one for incoming mail, one for outgoing mail—above the telephone table.

If your available space is on a wall or the back of a door, consider building a shallow single- or double-door cabinet (6 to 8 inches [15 to 20cm] deep) that has a cork board on the inside of the door for posting notes, receipts, and business cards. If it's a double-door unit, the other door can include hooks to hang a calendar and keys. Design the cabinet shelves with compartments and open slots for office supplies.

When space for an office just doesn't exist, consider keeping a compartmentalized caddy inside a cabinet or drawer, ideally near the telephone. Fill it with pens, notepads, scissors, tape, stamps, envelopes, and paper clips. When you need to pay a bill, write a list, or help with homework, pull out your office caddy and go to work on the kitchen table or the counter.

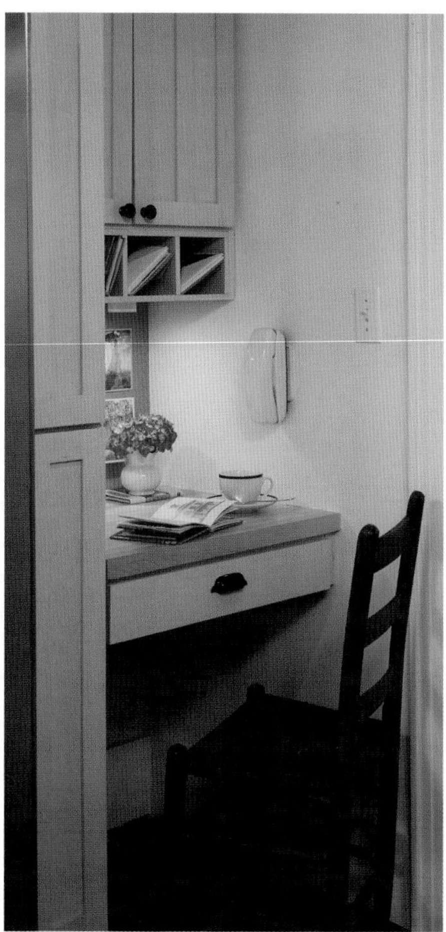

Opposite top If space for a desk is limited and you don't mind standing as you sign school notices and make shopping lists, do away with the kneehole and fill the space with drawers or shelves for your supplies.

Opposite bottom A message center can be integrated into your kitchen desk area to conserve space. This corkboard provides a perfect spot to post notes, to-do lists, photographs, and greeting cards.

Top A small nook is all this homeowner needed to create a mini-office. When space is tight, built-in lighting becomes more important.

Right Sharing space with an appliance is another way to get the kitchen office space you need.

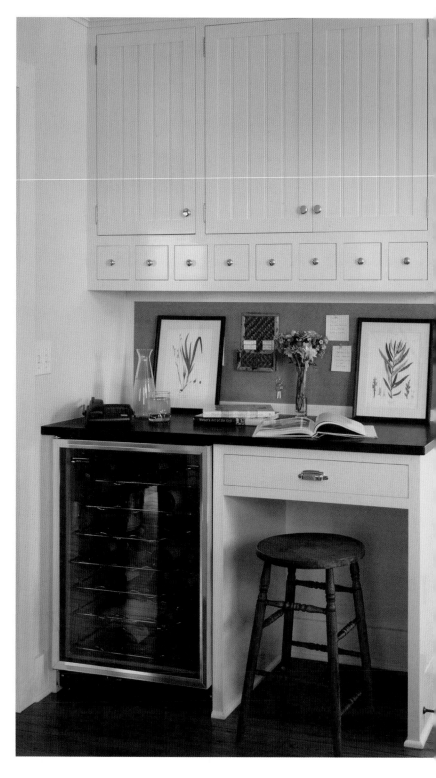

Selecting a Message Board

A message board centralizes family communications, but needs to be maintained. Otherwise, you won't know if "Pick up Billy after practice" is a new message that requires immediate attention or an old one that should have been taken down a week ago. Message boards need to be organized, too. If you clutter it with school photos, soccer schedules, and take-out menus, you'll conceal the messages, defeating the purpose of the board.

To get the most of your kitchen office and message center, choose a message board that meets your family's communication needs—and looks good while doing so. Message boards come in all shapes, sizes, and styles to meet all tastes and needs. Those with a corkboard, blackboard, dry-erase, fabric, or magnetic surface are popular. Some are enclosed behind sliding or hinged glass or acrylic doors. Whichever message board you choose, keep functionality foremost in your mind. If you use a dry-erase board, for example, you won't have to deal with chalky fingers from a blackboard. If you use a magnetic board, you can become even more organized by adding magnetic hooks for your keys, a magnetic shelf for your cell phone, and a magnetic cup holder for pens and notepads.

Opposite left Need a large message board to get your family's attention? Consider chalkboard panels for your fridge and freezer doors.

Opposite right Some dry-erase message boards are also compatible with magnetics. This one mounts neatly behind a cabinet door.

Above Cork has been rediscovered as both an ideal message board and flooring material. The corkboard shown here is in a natural color that complements the rest of the kitchen, but cork is available in various shades and color tints.

SMARTtip

Make Your Own

You can also make your own message board. Some homeowners, for example, choose to cover the entire wall of a mudroom hallway with cork. That way, there's room for messages as well as a large calendar, invitations, tickets, and family photos. Don't like the look of cork? Cover it with fabric.

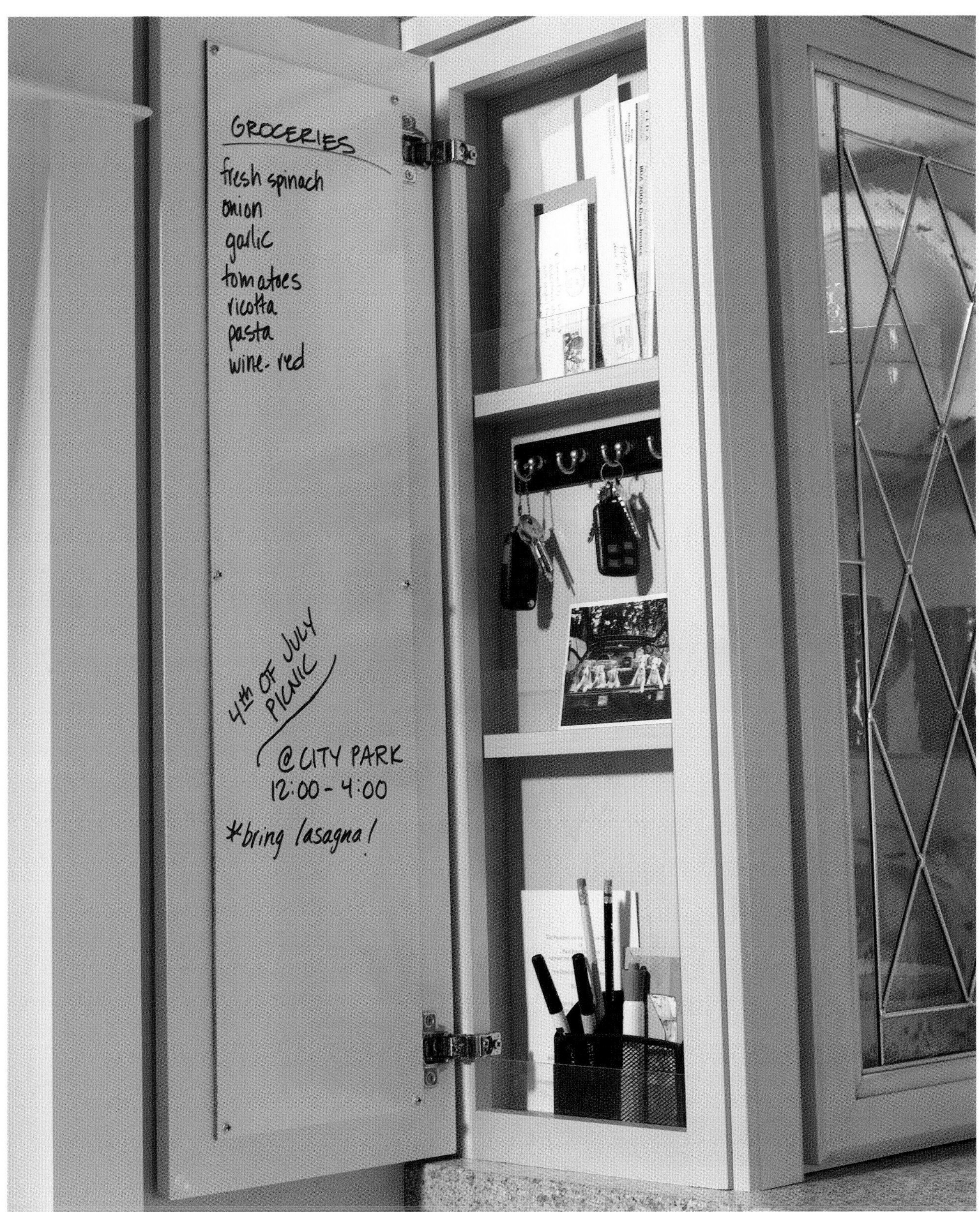
GROCERIES
fresh spinach
onion
garlic
tomatoes
ricotta
pasta
wine-red
4th OF JULY PICNIC
@ CITY PARK
12:00 - 4:00
*bring lasagna!

Message Centers

To maximize efficiency and organization, a message center should be above or near your kitchen desk. If wall space there is limited, or if your messages are more likely to be read in a different location, it's OK to separate the message center and the desk.

Locate your message center where it will be easiest to use. Remember, this is your central communication point. A location in a heavily trafficked area, which will allow plenty of regular viewing, is your best bet. The refrigerator door, the back of an entry door, the inside door of a wall cabinet, the wall on an end run of cabinets, and a mudroom hallway are popular options.

Message centers incorporated into the kitchen desk area help consolidate all your noncooking activities. Put the message board at eye level so it's easy to post and read notes. If the desk is at a window, an under-the-sill bulletin board may serve your needs.

Opposite Offered by several cabinet manufacturers, shallow end units for wall cabinets come equipped with a message board, shelves, and key hooks. Acrylic panels hold mail, folders, photos, and the like in place.

Above Let your fridge do some of the thinking for you. This smart fridge has a built-in information center that provides a five-day weather forecast and stores digital photos. It also includes a calendar and several preloaded recipes.

Right Leftover space beside this fridge accommodates three panels for pinning up messages and your latest family photos.

Resource Guide

The following list of manufacturers and associations is meant to be a general guide to additional industry and product-related sources. It is not intended as a listing of products and manufacturers represented by the photographs in this book.

Aristokraft Cabinetry

A Division of MasterBrand Cabinets, Inc.
1 MasterBrand Cabinets Dr.
P.O. Box 420
Jasper, IN 47546
812-482-2527
www.aristokraft.com

Manufactures kitchen cabinetry in a range of price categories. Offers spice racks, rollout pantries, organizer inserts, and other storage solutions.

Bertch Cabinet Mfg., Inc.

P.O. Box 2280
Waterloo, IA 50704
319-296-2987
www.bertch.com

Manufactures custom, semi-custom, and stock cabinetry with accessories such as vegetables bins, wine racks, and knife blocks.

Blomus

Completely Stainless / Blomus USA
2523 Middle Rd.
Trenton, NC 28585
877-977-8335
www.blomususa.com

German manufacturer and designer of contemporary stainless-steel products, including canisters, paper towel holders, fruit baskets, and wine racks.

CCF Industries

4716 PA Rt. 66
Apollo, PA 15613
800-581-3683
www.ccfdrawers.com

Manufactures high-quality dovetailed drawers, including cutlery drawers, bread drawers, spice drawers, wine drawers, and double-decker drawers.

ClosetMaid

650 SW 27th Ave.
Ocala, FL 34474
800-874-0008
www.closetmaid.com

Manufactures storage and organization products, including pullout shelving, drawer organizers, and plate racks.

Country Casual

7601 Rickenbacker Dr.
Gaithersburg, MD 20879
800-289-8325
www.countrycasual.com

Designs and manufactures outdoor furniture and accessories, including dining tables, benches, chairs, and trash receptacles.

Crystal Cabinet Works

1100 Crystal Dr.
Princeton, MN 55371
763-389-4187
www.crystalcabinets.com

Manufactures semi-custom cabinetry in a wide variety of materials, styles, and

finishes. Specializes in helping homeowners achieve period looks, including Arts and Crafts, Shaker, and Country French.

Dana Creath Designs

1822 Newport Blvd.
Costa Mesa, CA 92627
714-662-0111
www.danacreathdesigns.com
Designs and manufactures forged-iron pot racks and pot racks.

Decora

A Division of MasterBrand Cabinets, Inc.
1 MasterBrand Cabinets Dr.
P.O. Box 420
Jasper, IN 47546
812-482-2527
www.decoracabinets.com
Manufactures a range of specialty cabinets, including base-cabinet pantries with varying combinations of door shelves, pullouts, and stationary shelving.

Diamond Cabinets

A Division of MasterBrand Cabinets, Inc.
1 MasterBrand Cabinets Dr.
P.O. Box 420
Jasper, IN 47546
812-482-2527
www.diamondcabinets.com
Manufactures kitchen cabinets in a variety of styles. Its website features Logix, an innovative line of cabinets that offer many useful storage solutions.

Frigo Design

5860 McKinley Rd.
Brewerton, NY 13029
800-836-8746
www.frigodesign.com
Manufactures frame and panel sets for appliance doors, metal floor and wall tiles, metal backsplashes, and an assortment of kitchen essentials.

Gaggenau

780 Dedham St.
Canton, MA 02021
www.gaggenau.com
Manufactures restaurant-grade appliances for the home, including refrigerators, ovens, and cooktops.

Gardener's Supply Company

128 Intervale Rd.
Burlington, VT 05401
800-876-5520
www.gardeners.com
Designs and sells a wide range of garden supplies, including composters and countertop compost pails.

GE Appliances

3135 Easton Tpke.
Fairfield, CT 06828
800-626-2005
www.geappliances.com
Manufactures a full line of kitchen appliances, including ranges, range hoods, and refrigerators.

Hafele America Co.
3901 Cheyenne Dr.
Archdale, NC 27263
336-434-2322
www.hafele.com
Manufactures backsplash railing systems and cabinet storage systems such as lazy Susans, trash pullouts, and drawer organizers.

IKEA
888-888-4532
www.ikea.com
Showroom and mail-order marketer of a wide range of kitchen cabinetry, appliances, and home furnishings at affordable prices. Offers an array of organizers, including cutlery caddies, drawer organizers, spice racks, baskets, food containers, and kitchen carts.

John Boos & Co.
P.O. Box 609
3601 S. Banker St.
Effingham, IL 62401
888-431-2667
www.johnboos.com
Manufactures pot racks, shelves, and kitchen carts, as well as butcher blocks, cutting boards, and counters.

Kitchen Cabinet Manufacturers Association (KCMA)
1899 Preston White Dr.
Reston, VA 20191
703-264-1690
www.kcma.org
A nonprofit industry trade association founded in 1955. Its website helps you find certified cabinet manufacturers in your area and includes a helpful photo gallery and resource section.

KitchenAid
P.O. Box 218
St. Joseph, MI 49085
www.kitchenaid.com
Manufactures kitchen appliances, including refrigerator drawers, cooktops, ranges, and wine cellars.

Knape & Vogt Manufacturing Company
2700 Oak Industrial Dr. NE
Grand Rapids, MI 49505
800-253-1561
www.knapeandvogt.com
Manufactures functional hardware and storage-related components for cabinetry, pullout pantries, and pull-down shelves.

Kohler
444 Highland Dr.
Kohler, WI 53044
800-456-4537
www.kohler.com
Manufactures sinks, faucets, and accessories for the kitchen, including space-saving faucets and built-in dish-soap dispensers.

KraftMaid Cabinetry
15535 South State Ave.
Middlefield, OH 44062
888-562-7744
www.kraftmaid.com

Manufactures stock and semi-custom cabinetry with an array of storage solutions, including pullouts, spice racks, lazy Susans, and drawer inserts.

LG

1000 Sylvan Ave.
Englewood Cliffs, NJ 07632
800-243-0000
www.lge.com
Manufactures home appliances, audio, video, TV, and computer products. Line includes a refrigerator with a built-in LCD monitor.

Lipper International Inc.

235 Washington St.
Wallingford, CT 06492
800-243-3129
www.lipperinternational.com
Wholesaler of wooden and bamboo accessories for the kitchen, including cookbook holders, spice racks, tiered shelves, cutlery trays, and plate stands.

MadeSmart

1000 University Ave. W. Suite #220
St. Paul, MN 55104
800-688-5865
www.madesmart.com
Offers a matching collection of drawer and cabinet organizers. Products include expandable shelves, bakeware holders, helper shelves, and drawer organizers.

MasterBrand Cabinets, Inc.

1 MasterBrand Cabinets Dr.
P.O. Box 420
Jasper, IN 47546
812-482-2527
www.masterbrand.com
Manufactures all types of cabinetry under 13 different divisions, including Aristokraft, Decora, Diamond, Kemper, Kitchen Craft, and Omega.

Maytag

553 Benson Road
Benton Harbor, MI 49022
800-344-1274
www.maytag.com
Manufactures a full line of kitchen and laundry appliances as well as heating and cooling systems for the home.

Merillat Industries, LLC

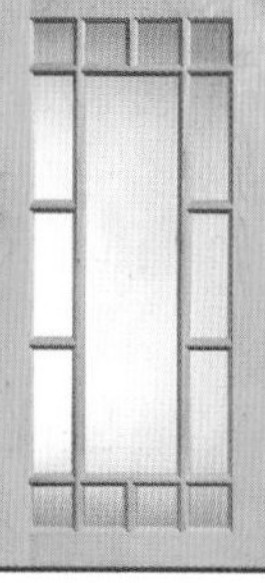

A Division of Masco Corporation
21001 Van Born Rd.
Taylor, MI 48180
866-850-8557
www.merillat.com
Manufactures a large selection of kitchen cabinets in several price categories. Organizational features include a four-bin recycling center, pull-down cookbook rack, and pull-down message center.

Miele, Inc.

9 Independence Way
Princeton, NJ 08540
www.miele.com
Manufactures high-end home appliances, including refrigerators, warming drawers, steam ovens, and built-in coffee systems.

National Association of the Remodeling Industry (NARI)

P.O. Box 4250
Des Plaines, IL 60016
847-298-9225
www.nari.org
Trade association that gives consumer guidance in selecting qualified professionals in the remodeling industry. Its website offers tips on how to avoid remodeling scams.

National Kitchen & Bath Association (NKBA)

687 Willow Grove St.
Hackettstown, NJ 07840
800-843-6522
www.nkba.org
Association that provides industry information for consumers and trade professionals. Its website helps consumers locate design professionals and research design strategies.

Omega Cabinetry

A Division of MasterBrand Cabinets, Inc.
1 MasterBrand Cabinets Dr.
P.O. Box 420
Jasper, IN 47546
812-482-2527
www.omegacab.com
Manufactures custom and semi-custom hardwood cabinetry.

Organized Living

3100 East Kemper Rd.
Cincinnati, OH 45241
www.organizedliving.com
Engineers and manufactures home storage and organization systems for kitchen pantries, entertainment centers, linen closets, and more.

Organize-It

2523 Product Ct.
Rochester Hills, MI 48309
248-299-3550
www.organizeit.com
Sells a wide variety of products for the kitchen, including islands, carts, racks, pullouts, lazy Susans, and helper shelves.

Outdoor Kitchen Cabinets & More

11033 Lakewood Dr.
Lakewood Ranch, FL 34211
941-744-5000
www.outdoorkitchencabinetsandmore.com
Sells all components of an outdoor kitchen, including cabinets, countertops, appliances, and grills.

Racor Home Storage

155 Harlem Ave, N3E
Glenview, IL 60025
800-783-7725
www.racorstoragesolutions.com
Offers a wide range of home storage products, including cabinets for mail and keys.

Rev-A-Shelf

12400 Earl Jones Way
Louisville, KY 40299
800-626-1126
www.rev-a-shelf.com
Manufactures custom storage kits and organizing products for the home, including hard-to-find items such as fold-out ironing boards, appliance lifts, corner-cabinet hardware, and several types of lazy Susans.

Robert Bosch LLC

38000 Hills Tech Drive
Farmington Hills, MI 48331
917-421-7209
www.boschappliances.com
Manufactures a full line of innovative kitchen appliances, including refrigerators with temperature-controlled drawers and exterior control panels, built-in microwaves, and ranges with storage drawers.

Rubbermaid

4110 Premiere Dr.
High Point, NC 27625
888-895-2110
www.rubbermaid.com
Manufactures household storage and organization products, including containers, sink caddies, helper shelves, towel holders, lid racks, and drawer organizers.

Silicone Zone

866-528-7665
www.siliconezoneusa.com
Manufactures a wide range of silicone kitchen tools, including collapsible colanders, measuring cups, bowls, cutting boards, and bakeware.

Simplehuman

19850 Magellan Dr.
Torrance, CA 90502
877-988-7770
www.simplehuman.com
Creates household products designed to efficiently achieve organization and accomplish daily tasks faster. Products include a sensor-activated trash can and a utensil holder with a detachable spoon rest.

StarMark Cabinetry

600 East 48th St. North
Sioux Falls, SD 57104
800-699-0087
www.starmarkcabinetry.com
Manufactures solid wood cabinets in a variety of custom, semi-custom, and stock sizes. Features include pullout filler cabinets and pullout pantry cabinets.

Sub-Zero

4717 Hammersley Rd.
Madison, WI 53711
800-222-7820
www.subzero.com
Manufactures refrigerators, wine refrigerators, refrigerator drawers, and other refrigeration equipment for restaurants and the home.

Thermador

5551 McFadden Ave.
Huntington Beach, CA 92649
800-735-4328
www.thermador.com
Manufactures professional kitchen appliances for the home, including refrigerators with motorized shelves, built-in coffee machines, cooktops, and warming drawers.

U-Line Corporation

P. O. Box 245040
Milwaukee, WI 53224
800-799-2547
www.u-line.com
Manufactures a full line of under-counter refrigeration appliances, including ice makers, wine storage, refrigerators, and refrigerator drawers.

Viking

111 Front St.
Greenwood, MS 38930
662-455-1200
www.vikingrange.com
Manufactures commercial-duty kitchen appliances for the home, including dual-fuel ranges, convection microwaves, and warming drawers.

Wellborn Cabinet, Inc.

38669 Highway 77 S.
Ashland, AL 36251
800-762-4475
www.wellborn.com
Manufactures kitchen cabinetry with many options, including pullout towel bars, slide-out cutting boards, and matching base end panels for islands. Its website features design ideas and a terminology dictionary.

Wer/Ever Products, Inc.

6120 Pelican Creek Circle
Riverview, FL 33578
888-324-3837
www.werever.com
Manufactures outdoor-kitchen cabinets made from solid marine-grade polymer.

Whirlpool

553 Benson Rd.
Benton Harbor, MI 49022
866-698-2538
www.whirlpool.com
Manufactures major home appliances under the names of Whirlpool, Maytag, KitchenAid, Jenn-Air, Amana, and other brand names.

Yorktowne Cabinetry

10501 10th St.
Waconia, MN 55387
800-476-4181
www.yorktownecabinetry.com
Manufactures semi-custom cabinetry, including components for constructing kitchen islands, plate-stacking drawers, and removable pullout trays.

Glossary

Anchor A device, usually made of metal or plastic, inserted into a wall or ceiling to provide support for fasteners when installing shelves, racks, and other storage units.

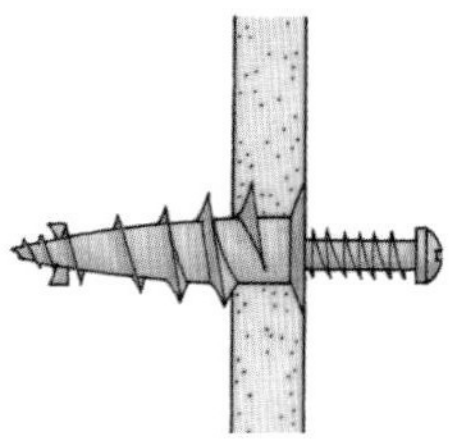

Appliance garage Countertop storage for blenders, toasters, and other small appliances. It usually has a roll-down door known as a tambour.

Backsplash The finish material that covers the wall behind a countertop. The backsplash can be attached to the countertop or separate from it.

Baker's rack An ornamental piece of furniture, often made of wrought iron, that is used to store and display items. Baker's racks were traditionally used in the kitchen to cool pies.

Baking center The area near an oven and a refrigerator that contains a countertop for rolling out dough and storage for baking supplies.

Base cabinet A cabinet, usually 24 inches (60cm) deep, that rests on the floor and supports a countertop.

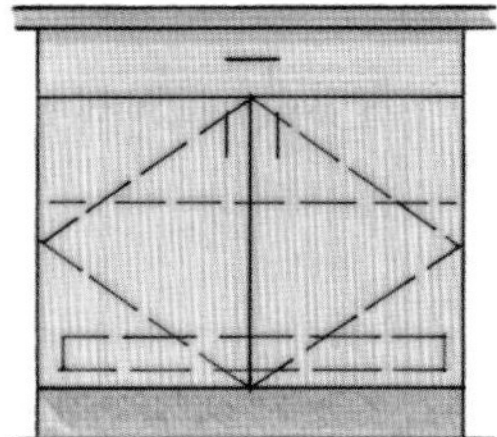

Blind cabinet A cabinet in a corner that's bordered by cabinets on the adjacent walls, one of which partially covers it. The portion that is covered does not have doors and is called the blind side. Access to a blind cabinet is limited.

Blocking The installation of short pieces of lumber between joists or studs for supporting heavy objects.

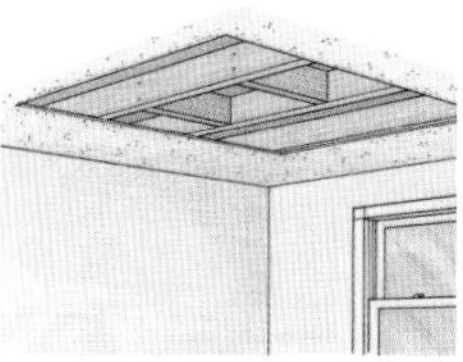

Bottom-mount refrigerator A refrigerator with the freezer space located at the bottom.

Built-in A cabinet, shelf, or other unit that is attached permanently to a wall, cabinet, or other structure.

Butcher block A countertop material composed of strips of hardwood that are laminated together and sealed against moisture.

Cleanup center The area where the sink, dishwasher, trash can, and related accessories are grouped for easy access and efficient use.

Clearance The amount of recommended space between two fixtures.

Cleat A piece of wood or metal that is fastened to a structural member to support or provide an attaching point for another member.

Composition board A building board made into sheets by compressing shredded wood chips with a binder. Also called fiberboard.

Compost A mixture that consists of decayed organic matter and is used for fertilizing and improving soil. Also, to convert (as food scraps) to compost.

Cooking center The area where the cooktop, oven, and food-prep surfaces, appliances, and utensils are grouped.

Cooktop The flat top of a range, or a built-in cooking appliance usually containing four heating units.

Countersink A bit or drill for making a funnel-shaped enlargement at the outer end of a drilled hole. Also, to make a countersink on (a hole), or to set the head of a screw at or below the fastened item's surface.

Countertop The work surface of a counter, island, or peninsula, usually 36 inches (90cm) high. Common countertop materials include plastic laminate, ceramic tile, concrete, stone, and solid surface.

Crisper drawer A closed container in the refrigerator intended to prevent loss of moisture from produce.

Cubic foot A unit for measuring volume. One cubic foot, which is a cube with sides of 1 foot, equals 1,728 cubic inches.

Dado A rectangular channel cut across the grain to make a joint in wood. Also, to provide with a dado.

Dead space Storage space that often goes unused because it's inconvenient or out of reach. The back of a corner cabinet is a prime example of dead space.

Divider A partition between separate spaces or areas. Dividers in drawers or drawer inserts help separate flatware, large utensils, and other kitchen items. Tray dividers, usually found in a base cabinet, vertically store and organize trays, baking sheets, cutting boards, and similar items.

Dovetail A type of joint that resembles a dove's tail and is commonly used to join the sides of a drawer to its front. Also, to join by means of a dovetail, or to cut to a dovetail.

Dowel Wood cylinders that are available in various diameters.

Drawer A sliding box or receptacle opened by pulling out and closed by pushing in.

Drawer insert A device placed in a drawer that helps establish a spot for knives, spice containers, and other items. Also called "drawer organizers."

Drawer slide A device that allows drawers to smoothly pull out. Available in either the standard three-quarter or full-extension models.

Drywall Sheets of gypsum sandwiched between backing paper and a smooth-finish front surface paper. Used as an interior wall and ceiling covering material. Also called "gypsum board" or "wallboard."

Floor plan A two-dimensional scale drawing that shows the top-down view of a room (or rooms), the arrangement of fixtures, and their dimensions.

Footprint The area on a surface covered by something.

Framed cabinet A cabinet with a full frame, built of rails and stiles, attached to a cabinet box face.

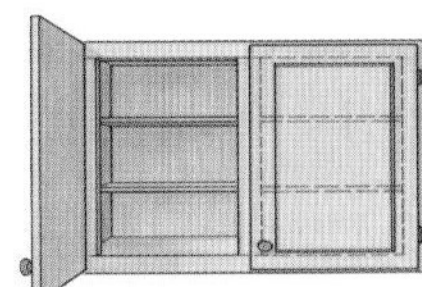

Frameless cabinet A cabinet without a face frame.

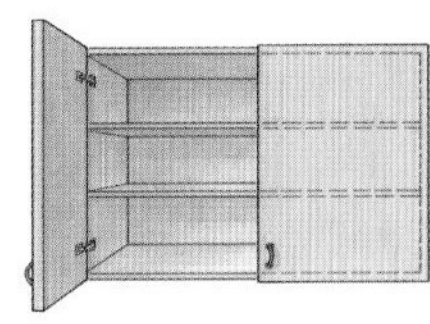

French door refrigerator A refrigerator that pairs side-by-side doors with a bottom-mounted freezer.

Groove A long, narrow channel cut with the grain in woodworking, often for sliding doors.

Hardwood Generally, the wood of large deciduous trees such as maple, oak, and poplar.

Island A unit consisting of base cabinets and countertop that stands independent from walls and has access from all four sides.

Joist Horizontal framing members set parallel to other joists to support a ceiling or floor.

Knockdown Easily assembled or disassembled cabinetry or furniture.

Lazy Susan An axis-mounted shelf, usually installed in a corner cabinet, that rotates 360 degrees, thereby bringing many stored items within easy reach.

Medium-density fiberboard (MDF) An engineered product made from compressed wood fibers and used in the construction of cabinets and shelves.

Melamine A durable plastic often used as a laminate on composite materials.

Mudroom A room, often located near the kitchen, for the shedding of dirty or wet footwear and clothing.

Pantry A small room or large cabinet used for storage, often of packaged or canned goods.

Particleboard A material composed of wood chips and coarse fibers bonded with adhesive into large sheets from ½ to 1⅛ inches (1.3 to 2.9cm) thick. It's commonly used in the fabrication of countertops.

Pegboard A board with small, regularly spaced holes that's used to build organizers on walls and in cabinets and drawers. Specially designed accessories, typically hooks, can be slipped into the holes to create the arrangement you require for stored items.

Peninsula A countertop, with or without a base cabinet, that is connected at one end to a wall or another countertop and extends outward, allowing access on three sides.

Plywood A structural material consisting of sheets of wood glued together, usually with the grains of adjacent layers arranged at right angles to provide strength.

Polymer A plastic-like material, produced with chemical compounds, that's used to create coatings, sheet goods, and many other useful products.

Rabbet A recess cut along the edge or face of a piece of wood so it can receive another piece, or the joint formed by fitting together rabbeted boards. Also, to join the edges in a rabbet joint, or to cut a rabbet in.

Rack A framework or stand on or in which items such as spice containers are placed.

Rail system A horizontal unit installed under wall cabinets, on the wall, or between two vertical supports that is used to hang utensils and other prep items, freeing counter space. The utensils and other items attach to the rail using hooks or other accessories.

Raised panel A board beveled on all four sides that's typically used for building cabinet doors and drawers.

Refrigerated drawer A modular refrigeration unit that is standard cabinet depth and accepts all types of paneling and hardware.

Refrigerated wine cellar A unit designed for long-term (usually six months or more) storage of wine.

Resin Any of various substances obtained from the gum or sap of certain plants and used in varnishes and plastics. Also, a comparable synthetic product.

Root cellar A pit used for storing root vegetables.

Root vegetables Crops, such as potatoes, onions, and turnips, grown for their roots.

Scale The relationship of a structure's size to people, nearby objects, and the surrounding space. Also, the relationship of elements of a structure to the whole.

Shaker A type of plain-paneled cabinetry that has been inspired by the simple, utilitarian furniture made by the Shakers, an eighteenth-century religious sect.

S-hook A hook, shaped like an S, used to hang pots, pans, and lids.

Side-by-side refrigerator A refrigerator with the refrigeration space on the right side and the freezer space on the left.

Silicone An organic silicon compound used especially for water-resistant and heat-resistant lubricants, varnishes, and binders.

Soffit A boxed-in area just below the ceiling and above the wall cabinet.

Stainless steel An alloy of steel with chromium and sometimes another element (such as nickel) that is durable and easy to clean.

Stud A vertical framing member of a wall.

Tiered organizer A space-saving device that stores items on several levels or "steps."

Tilt-out A shallow tray in front of the sink that pivots out for storing sponges, brushes, soap, and so forth.

Toe kick The narrow space below a base cabinet.

Top-mount refrigerator A refrigerator with the freezer space located at the top.

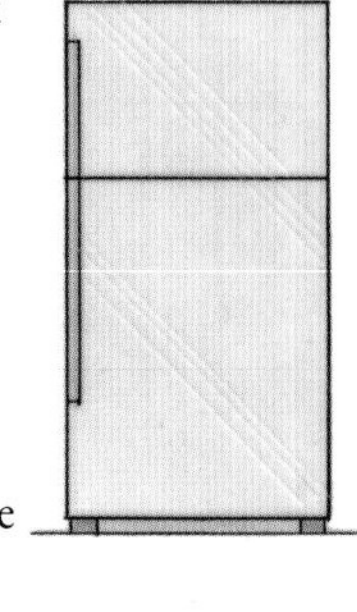

Traffic path The aisle people use in the kitchen, often within the work triangle.

Trivet A stand with short feet for use under a hot dish. Trivets, which are usually metal, are sometimes built directly into a countertop.

Under-cabinet lighting Lights installed on the undersides of cabinets for illuminating the countertop.

Universal design Products and designs that are easy to use by people of all ages, heights, and physical abilities.

Utensil crock A thick earthenware pot or jar, usually located on the counter, used to store utensils.

Wall cabinet A cabinet, usually 12 inches (30cm) deep, that's mounted on the wall a minimum of 15 inches (38cm) above the countertop.

Work triangle The area bounded by the lines that connect the sink, range, and refrigerator. In theory, the sum of the line lengths should not exceed 26 feet (8 meters).

Index

Credits

All illustrations by Vince Babak. Any photo credits accompanied by the word (Shutterstock) are credited to Shutterstock.com and their respective creators named. **Front cover:** courtesy of KraftMaid **back cover:** *left* courtesy of Lipper; *top right* courtesy of Kitchens by Deane; *bottom right* courtesy of Whirlpool **page 1:** courtesy of Bertch Cabinet Mfg. **page 2:** courtesy of IKEA **page 5:** courtesy of IKEA **page 6:** *top* courtesy of U-Line; *middle* courtesy of KitchenAid; *bottom* courtesy of Diamond Cabinets **page 8:** courtesy of KraftMaid **page 10:** *top* courtesy of MasterBrand; *bottom* Robert Perron **page 11:** courtesy of IKEA **page 12:** Robert Perron **page 13:** *left* Artazum (Shutterstock); *right* courtesy of Yorktowne **pages 14–15:** Breadmaker (Shutterstock) **pages 16–17:** courtesy of IKEA **page 18:** courtesy of Rev-A-Shelf **page 19:** *top* Robert Perron; *bottom* courtesy of Rev-A-Shelf **page 20:** *top* courtesy of Thermador; *bottom* courtesy of Bosch **page 21:** *top* courtesy of Thermador; *bottom* courtesy of Miele **page 22:** *left* courtesy of Gaggenau; *right* courtesy of Silicone Zone **page 23:** courtesy of Fagor **page 24:** *top & bottom left* courtesy of KraftMaid; *bottom right* courtesy of Wood-Mode **pages 27–33:** courtesy of KraftMaid **page 34:** courtesy of IKEA **page 35:** *top left* courtesy of Merillat; *top right* courtesy of Crystal Cabinet Works; *middle left* courtesy of Diamond Cabinets; *middle right & bottom left & bottom right* courtesy of Bertch Cabinet Mfg. **pages 38–39:** courtesy of Crystal Cabinet Works **page 40:** *top* courtesy of Rev-A-Shelf; *bottom* Mark Samu **page 41:** *top left & bottom right* Mark Samu; *top right* courtesy of Bertch Cabinet Mfg.; *bottom left* courtesy of IKEA **page 42:** *top left* courtesy of Thermador; *top right & bottom left* courtesy of Wood-Mode; *bottom right* Mark Samu **page 43:** Mark Samu **page 44:** courtesy of IKEA **page 45:** *top* courtesy of MasterBrand; *bottom left* courtesy of IKEA; *bottom right* courtesy of Wood-Mode **page 46:** *top* courtesy of Rev-A-Shelf; *bottom* courtesy of KraftMaid **page 47:** courtesy of Rev-A-Shelf **pages 50–51:** courtesy of IKEA **page 52:** *top & bottom right* courtesy of MasterBrand; *bottom left* courtesy of Improvements Catalog **page 53:** *top* courtesy of MasterBrand; *bottom* courtesy of Wood-Mode **page 54:** *left* courtesy of KraftMaid; *top right & bottom right* courtesy of Rev-A-Shelf **page 55:** courtesy of Rubbermaid **page 56:** *top left* courtesy of Rev-A-Shelf; *top right* courtesy of MasterBrand; *bottom* courtesy of KraftMaid **page 57:** *top left* courtesy of MasterBrand; *top right* courtesy of Wood-Mode; *middle* courtesy of Rev-A-Shelf; *bottom left* courtesy of KraftMaid; *bottom right* Mark Samu **pages 58–59:** Carl Weese for Home & Garden Editorial Services **pages 60–61:** Archi_Viz (Shutterstock) **pages 62–63:** romakoma (Shutterstock) **page 63:** *top & bottom* courtesy of Yorktowne **page 64:** courtesy of KraftMaid **page 65:** *top & bottom* courtesy of Rev-A-Shelf **page 66:** courtesy of Lipper **page 67:** *top* courtesy of KraftMaid; *middle left* courtesy of Yorktowne; *middle right & bottom left & bottom right* courtesy of Rev-A-Shelf **pages 68–69:** Carl Weese for Home & Garden Editorial Services **page 70:** *top & bottom* courtesy of KraftMaid **page 71:** *top left & top right* courtesy of KraftMaid; *bottom right* courtesy of Rev-A-Shelf; *bottom* courtesy of Yorktowne **page 72:** *top left & top right* courtesy of MasterBrand; *bottom* courtesy of Wood-Mode **page 73:** *top left & top right* courtesy of Knape & Vogt; *bottom* courtesy of Merillat **page 74:** *top* courtesy of KraftMaid; *bottom* courtesy of MasterBrand **page 75:** *top left* courtesy of Rev-A-Shelf; *bottom left* courtesy of MasterBrand; *right* courtesy of KraftMaid **page 76:** *top* courtesy of KraftMaid Cabinetry; *bottom* courtesy of Rev-A-Shelf **page 77:** *top & bottom left* courtesy of Rev-A-Shelf; *bottom right* courtesy of MasterBrand **pages 78–79:** Carl Weese for Home & Garden Editorial Services **page 80:** *left* courtesy of Wood-Mode; *top & bottom right* courtesy of Rev-A-Shelf **page 81:** *top left & top right* courtesy of Yorktowne; *bottom* courtesy of MasterBrand **page 82:** *top left* courtesy of MasterBrand; *top right & middle right & bottom right* courtesy of Knape & Vogt **page 83:** *top left & top right* courtesy of Wood-Mode; *bottom left* courtesy of Yorktowne **page 84:** courtesy of Knape & Vogt **page 85:** *top left* courtesy of Yorktowne; *top right* courtesy of Rev-A-Shelf; *bottom left* courtesy of Bertch Cabinet Mfg.; *bottom right* courtesy of Merillat **page 86:** *all but bottom right* courtesy of Rev-A-Shelf; *bottom right* courtesy of Diamond Cabinets **page 87:** courtesy of Rev-A-Shelf **page 88:** *left* courtesy of MasterBrand; *top right & bottom right* courtesy of Rev-A-Shelf **page 89:** *top* courtesy of MasterBrand; *bottom left & bottom right* courtesy of Rev-A-Shelf **page 90:** *top* courtesy of Armstrong; *bottom* courtesy of KraftMaid **page 91:** *top* courtesy of Yorktowne; *bottom* Robert Perron **page 92:** courtesy of Merillat **page 93:** *top* Mark Samu; *bottom* courtesy of Yorktowne **page 94:** courtesy of Merillat **page 95:** *top* courtesy of Wellborn Cabinet, Inc.; *bottom* courtesy of MasterBrand **page 96:** courtesy of KraftMaid **page 97:** *top* courtesy of Yorktowne; *bottom* courtesy of MasterBrand **page 98:** courtesy of Yorktowne **page 99:** *top* courtesy of MasterBrand; *bottom left* Mark Samu; *bottom right* courtesy of Bertch Cabinet Mfg. **page 102:** *top left & top right* courtesy of Crystal Cabinet Works; *bottom* Carl Weese for Home & Garden Editorial Services **page 103:** *left* courtesy of Yorktowne; *right* courtesy of Bertch Cabinet Mfg. **page 104:** *top* courtesy of MasterBrand; *bottom left & bottom right* courtesy of Rev-A-Shelf **page 105:** *top & middle* courtesy of MasterBrand; *bottom left & bottom right* courtesy of Rev-A-Shelf **page 106:** courtesy of MasterBrand **page 107:** *top left* courtesy of Rev-A-Shelf; *top center* courtesy of KraftMaid; *top right* courtesy of Rev-A-Shelf; *middle & all bottom* Carl Weese for Home & Garden Editorial Services **page 108:** *top* courtesy of Rev-A-Shelf; *middle* courtesy of Wood-Mode; *bottom left & bottom right* courtesy of Rev-A-Shelf **page 109:** Mark Samu **page 110:** *top* courtesy of IKEA; *bottom* courtesy of MasterBrand **page 111:** *top left* courtesy of IKEA; *top right* Mark Samu; *bottom* courtesy of Rev-A-Shelf **page 113:** *top* courtesy of KraftMaid; *bottom left* courtesy of MasterBrand; *bottom right* Carl Weese for Home & Garden Editorial Services **page 112:** *top* Mark Samu; *bottom* courtesy of MasterBrand **pages 114–115:** Carl Weese for Home & Garden Editorial Services **page 116:** Mark Samu **page 117:** *top* courtesy of MasterBrand; *bottom* Carl Weese for Home & Garden Editorial Services **pages 118–119:** pics721 (Shutterstock) **pages 120–121:** Daria Minaeva (Shutterstock) **page 122:** courtesy of Merillat **page 123:** *top* courtesy of IKEA; *bottom* reprinted with permission from The Family Handyman magazine, Home Service Publications, Inc., and affiliate of Reader's Digest Assoc., Inc., 7900 International Dr., Ste. 950, Eagan, MN 55121. ®Copyright 2007. All Rights Reserved; design by Mary Jane Pappas **page 124:** *top* courtesy of Miele; *bottom* courtesy of Improvements Catalog **page 125:** *top* courtesy of MasterBrand; *middle* courtesy of Merillat; *bottom* courtesy of KraftMaid **pages 126–127:** Mark Samu **page 128:** *top* courtesy of MasterBrand; *bottom* Mark Samu **page 129:** *top* courtesy of Wellb orn Cabinet, Inc.; *bottom left* courtesy of MasterBrand; *bottom right* courtesy of Yorktowne **page 130:** *top* courtesy of Wood-Mode; *bottom* courtesy of MasterBrand **page 131:** *left* courtesy of Wood-Mode; *right* courtesy of Yorktowne **page 132:** courtesy of Rev-A-Shelf **page 133:** *top & bottom* courtesy of Simplehuman; *middle* courtesy of Lipper **page 134:** *top left* courtesy of Simplehuman; *bottom left* courtesy of Knape & Vogt; *right* Mark Samu **page 135:** *top*

courtesy of Kohler; *bottom* reprinted with permission from The Family Handyman magazine, Home Service Publications, Inc., and affiliate of Reader's Digest Assoc., Inc., 7900 International Dr., Ste. 950, Eagan, MN 55121. ®Copyright 2007. All Rights Reserved; design by Mary Jane Pappas **page 136:** *top & middle* courtesy of Rev-A-Shelf; *bottom* courtesy of Lipper **page 137:** *top* courtesy of Samsung/Staron; *bottom left* courtesy of Fagor; *bottom right* courtesy of Miele **page 138:** *top* courtesy of Viking; *bottom* asiandelight (Shutterstock) **page 139:** *top* courtesy of Wood-Mode; *bottom* Carl Weese for Home & Garden Editorial Services **page 140:** Mark Samu **page 141:** *top* Carl Weese for Home & Garden Editorial Services; *bottom* courtesy of Simplehuman **page 142:** *top* courtesy of Hafele; *bottom* courtesy of Knape & Vogt **page 143:** *top left* Carl Weese for Home & Garden Editorial Services; *top right* courtesy of Lipper; *bottom* Mark Samu **page 144:** Carl Weese for Home & Garden Editorial Services **page 145:** *top* Mark Samu; *bottom* Carl Weese for Home & Garden Editorial Services **page 146:** *top right* Mark Samu; *middle left* courtesy of Yorktowne; *middle right* courtesy of Rev-A-Shelf; *bottom left* courtesy of Wellborn Cabinet, Inc.; *bottom right* courtesy of MasterBrand **page 147:** *left* courtesy of KraftMaid; *top right* courtesy of Adams; *bottom right* courtesy of Rev-A-Shelf **page 148:** *left* courtesy of Miele; *right* Andrey_Popov (Shutterstock) **page 149:** *main* alexandre zveiger (Shutterstock); *inset TV* Dudarev Mikhail (Shutterstock); *inset TV text* MicroOne (Shutterstock) **pages 150–151:** courtesy of Kitchens by Deane; design by Nancy Elizabeth Hill **page 152:** courtesy of Crystal Cabinet Works **page 153:** Robert Perron **page 154:** Mark Samu **page 155:** *top* Mark Samu; *bottom* courtesy of Merillat **page 156:** *top* Carl Weese for Home & Garden Editorial Services; *bottom* courtesy of Organize-It **page 157:** *top left & bottom right* courtesy of John Boos & Co.; *top right & second left* courtesy of Rogar Intl. Corp.; *third left* courtesy of Organize-It; *bottom left* courtesy of Dana Creath **page 158:** Mark Samu **page 159:** *top left & bottom left* Carl Weese for Home & Garden Editorial Services **pages 160–161:** Carl Weese for Home & Garden Editorial Services **page 162:** courtesy of Organize-It **page 163:** *top* courtesy of IKEA; *bottom* courtesy of Organize-It **page 164:** *top* Mark Samu; *bottom* Robert Perron **page 165:** Mark Samu **page 166:** *left* courtesy of IKEA; *right* Mark Samu **page 167:** *top & second from top* courtesy of Organize-It; *middle left & right* Carl Weese for Home & Garden Editorial Services; *bottom* courtesy of Organize-It **page 168:** Robert Perron **page 169:** *top* Mark Samu; *bottom left* Robert Perron; *bottom right* Zoe Pappas **pages 170–171:** courtesy of Merillat **page 172:** *top* courtesy of Wood-Mode; *bottom* Mark Samu **page 173:** courtesy of Merillat **page 174:** courtesy of MasterBrand **page 175:** *top* courtesy of Diamond Cabinets; *bottom left & bottom right* courtesy of MasterBrand **page 176:** courtesy of MasterBrand **page 177:** *top left* Carl Weese for Home & Garden Editorial Services; *top right & bottom right* Mark Samu; *bottom left* courtesy of Merillat **page 178:** Mark Samu **page 179:** courtesy of MasterBrand **page 180:** Mark Samu **page 181:** *top* courtesy of Merillat; *bottom left* courtesy of Wood-Mode; *bottom right* courtesy of Bertch Cabinet Mfg. **page 182:** *left* courtesy of John Boos & Co.; *right* courtesy of KraftMaid **page 183:** *top & bottom* courtesy of IKEA **page 184:** *left* courtesy of Rev-A-Shelf; *right* Carl Weese for Home & Garden Editorial Services **page 185:** *top* courtesy of KraftMaid; *middle* courtesy of Rev-A-Shelf; *bottom* courtesy of Lipper **page 186:** *top* courtesy of Country Casual; *bottom* courtesy of Wer/Ever **page 187:** *top* courtesy of Outdoor Kitchen Cabinets & More; *bottom* courtesy of KitchenAid **page 188:** *left & middle* courtesy of Improvements Catalog; *right* courtesy of MasterBrand **page 189:** courtesy of Merillat **pages 190–191:** M.Photografer (Shutterstock) **pages 192–193:** courtesy of Maytag **page 194:** courtesy of Whirlpool **page 196:** courtesy of LG **page 197:** courtesy of Maytag **page 198:** courtesy of Whirlpool **page 199:** courtesy of Whirlpool **page 200:** *top* courtesy of U-Line; *bottom* Makstorm (Shutterstock) **page 201:** *top & bottom right* courtesy of Sub-Zero; *bottom left* courtesy of U-Line **page 202:** courtesy of Maytag **page 203:** *top left* courtesy of Maytag; *bottom left* courtesy of Viking; *right* courtesy of Sub-Zero **page 204:** *left & right* courtesy of Whirlpool **page 206:** courtesy of Whirlpool **page 207:** courtesy of Maytag **page 208:** *top* courtesy of LG; *bottom* courtesy of Whirlpool **page 209:** *top & bottom* courtesy of Maytag **page 210:** courtesy of LG **page 211:** *top left & bottom left* courtesy of LG; *top right* courtesy of Thermador; *bottom right* Carl Weese for Home & Garden Editorial Services **page 216:** courtesy of Yorktowne **page 217:** courtesy of Kitchens by Deane **page 218:** courtesy of Schulte Corp. **page 219:** Mark Samu **page 220:** courtesy of U-Line **page 221:** *top left* courtesy of KitchenAid; *top right* courtesy of U-Line; *bottom left* courtesy of Viking **pages 222–223:** Aleksandra Suzi (Shutterstock) **page 224:** *top* courtesy of Forbo; *bottom left* courtesy of Merillat; *bottom right* courtesy of Simplehuman **page 225:** *top* courtesy of MasterBrand; *bottom* courtesy of Rev-A-Shelf **page 226:** courtesy of Simplehuman **page 227:** *top left & top right* courtesy of Simplehuman; *bottom* courtesy of Rev-A-Shelf **page 228:** *top & middle* courtesy of Rev-A-Shelf; *bottom* courtesy of KraftMaid **page 229:** *top left* courtesy of Knape & Vogt; *top right* courtesy of Improvements Catalog; *all bottom* courtesy of Rev-A-Shelf **page 230:** *top left & top middle & middle & bottom* courtesy of Rev-A-Shelf; *top right* courtesy of Wood-Mode **page 231:** Carl Weese for Home & Garden Editorial Services **page 232:** courtesy of Rev-A-Shelf **page 233:** *top left & middle* courtesy of Simplehuman; *top right* courtesy of Knape & Vogt; *bottom* courtesy of Rev-A-Shelf **page 234:** *left* courtesy of MasterBrand; *right* courtesy of Simplehuman **page 235:** *top left* courtesy of Rev-A-Shelf; *top right* courtesy of Merillat; *bottom* courtesy of Knape & Vogt **pages 236–239:** courtesy of Enviro-Trash Concepts **page 240:** *top* courtesy of IKEA; *bottom* courtesy of Rev-A-Shelf **page 241:** courtesy of Gardener's Supply Company **page 242:** *top & bottom left* courtesy of Gardener's Supply Company; *bottom right* courtesy of Improvements Catalog **page 243:** courtesy of Gardener's Supply Company **pages 244–245:** Artazum (Shutterstock) **page 246:** Robert Perron **page 247:** *top* courtesy of Merillat; *bottom* Mark Samu **page 248:** Mark Samu **page 249:** courtesy of Crystal Cabinet Works **page 250:** Artazum (Shutterstock) **page 251:** courtesy of ClosetMaid **page 252:** Robert Perron **page 253:** courtesy of KraftMaid **page 254:** *top* courtesy of Merillat; *bottom* courtesy of Wellborn Cabinet, Inc. **page 255:** Mark Samu **page 256:** courtesy of MasterBrand **page 257:** *left* courtesy of KraftMaid; *top right* courtesy of Knape & Vogt; *bottom right* courtesy of Rev-A-Shelf **pages 258–259:** Mark Samu **page 260:** *left* courtesy of Frigo Design; *right* courtesy of Knape & Vogt **page 261:** *main* Mark Samu; *inset TV* Tomislav Pinter (Shutterstock) **page 262:** courtesy of MasterBrand **page 263:** *left* courtesy of LG; *right* courtesy of MasterBrand **pages 264–270:** courtesy of the manufacturer alongside which the photo appears **page 271:** Breadmaker (Shutterstock) **page 277:** courtesy of Yorktowne **pages 278–279:** courtesy of KraftMaid **page 280:** Fotoluminate LLC (Shutterstock)